the limits of love

the limits of love

THE LIVES OF **D. H. LAWRENCE** AND **FRIEDA VON RICHTHOFEN**

MICHAEL SQUIRES

Louisiana State University Press   *Baton Rouge*

Published with the assistance of the V. Ray Cardozier Fund

Published by Louisiana State University Press
lsupress.org

Copyright © 2023 by Michael Squires
All rights reserved. Except in the case of brief quotations used in articles or reviews, no part of this publication may be reproduced or transmitted in any format or by any means without written permission of Louisiana State University Press.

Manufactured in the United States of America
First printing

Designer: Barbara Neely Bourgoyne
Typeface: Adobe Text Pro
Printer and binder: Sheridan Books

Permission to publish new letters and other material has been granted by Paper Lion Ltd. and the Estates of D. H. Lawrence and Frieda Lawrence Ravagli.

The Limits of Love originated, in part, from *D. H. Lawrence and Frieda: A Portrait of Love and Loyalty* (London: André Deutsch, 2008), copyright © 2008 by Michael Squires.

Jacket illustration: *The Villa Mirenda*, c. 1927, by D. H. Lawrence. Reproduced courtesy of the Harry Ransom Center, University of Texas at Austin.

Library of Congress Cataloging-in-Publication Data
Names: Squires, Michael, 1941– author.
Title: The limits of love : the lives of D. H. Lawrence and Frieda von Richthofen / Michael Squires.
Description: Baton Rouge : Louisiana State University Press, [2023] | Includes bibliographical references and index.
Identifiers: LCCN 2023016996 (print) | LCCN 2023016997 (ebook) | ISBN 978-0-8071-8046-4 (cloth) | ISBN 978-0-8071-8098-3 (pdf) | ISBN 978-0-8071-8097-6 (epub)
Subjects: LCSH: Lawrence, D. H. (David Herbert), 1885–1930—Marriage. | Lawrence, Frieda, 1879–1956—Marriage. | LCGFT: Biographies.
Classification: LCC PR6023.A93 Z923858 2024 (print) | LCC PR6023.A93 (ebook) | DDC 823/.912 [B]—dc23/eng/20230629
LC record available at https://lccn.loc.gov/2023016996
LC ebook record available at https://lccn.loc.gov/2023016997

Contents

LIST OF ILLUSTRATIONS *vii*
WORKS BY D. H. LAWRENCE *ix*

Introduction *1*
1 The End of Loneliness *10*
2 England and Germany *19*
3 Italian Paradise *33*
4 A Heart That's Been Smashed *41*
5 A Map of Passion *50*
6 Cornered in Cornwall *59*
7 A Fresh Start in Italy *66*
8 Intoxicated and Alone *73*
9 Crossing the Seas *82*
10 Fevers and Fortune *91*
11 Mountains in America *98*
12 The Mysteries of Mexico *105*
13 Her Ship Goes East *112*
14 Frieda's Rustic Ranch *121*
15 Menace and Malaria *129*

16 The Route to Spotorno *136*

17 Rage and Compassion *142*

18 Revealing the Secret *151*

19 The Third Version in Florence *162*

20 Where Should We Live? *171*

21 The Heroic Fight *181*

22 The Lost Will *190*

23 Taos, Ravagli, and the Manuscripts *199*

24 The Challenge of Texas *210*

25 Last Years *219*

26 At the Close *226*

ACKNOWLEDGMENTS *231*

NOTES *233*

INDEX *259*

Illustrations

D. H. Lawrence's family, in Eastwood, c. 1893 *21*
D. H. Lawrence, in Croydon, 1908 *25*
Dr. Otto Gross, c. 1912 *30*
Katherine Mansfield, 1914 *35*
John Middleton Murry, 1912 *35*
Lady Ottoline Morrell, c. 1899 *43*
William Henry Hocking, c. 1917 *56*
D. H. Lawrence, passport photo, 1919 *67*
Frieda Lawrence, passport photo, 1919 *67*
The Brewsters and Dorothy Brett, c. 1926 *84*
Mabel Dodge Luhan, c. 1920 *88*
Dorothy Brett, 1931 *116*
The landscape of the Villa Mirenda *148*
The Villa Mirenda, near Florence *149*
Giuseppe "Pino" Orioli, 1935 *157*
Matthew, Maria, and Aldous Huxley, c. 1932 *158*
D. H. Lawrence, c. 1929 *177*
Rhys Davies, c. 1940 *179*

D. H. Lawrence, page 7, manuscript of "My Skirmish with Jolly Roger" (1929), later expanded into *A Propos of "Lady Chatterley's Lover"* 182

The D. H. Lawrence Chapel, in progress, 1934–35 204

The D. H. Lawrence Chapel, completed, 1998 205

Angelo Ravagli, ceramic tile of D. H. Lawrence's phoenix, c. 1940 212

Angelo Ravagli, Frieda Lawrence, and Johnie Griffin, c. 1946 216

Works by D. H. Lawrence

Except for drafts of novels, the dates given are dates of first publication.

1911   *The White Peacock* (novel)
1912   *The Trespasser* (novel)
1913   *Sons and Lovers* (novel)
1913   *Love Poems and Others*
1914   *The Prussian Officer and Other Stories*
1915   *The Rainbow* (novel)
1916   *Twilight in Italy* (travel)
1916   *Amores* (poetry)
1916   *The First "Women in Love"* (novel, first draft published 1998)
1917   *Look! We Have Come Through!* (poetry)
1920   *Women in Love* (novel)
1920   *The Lost Girl* (novel)
1922   *Aaron's Rod* (novel)
1922   *England, My England and Other Stories*
1923   *Sea and Sardinia* (travel)
1923   *Studies in Classic American Literature* (essays)
1923   *Kangaroo* (novel)

1923	*The Captain's Doll, The Ladybird* (novellas)
1923	*Birds, Beasts and Flowers* (poetry)
1923	*Quetzalcoatl: The Early Version of "The Plumed Serpent"* (novel, first published 1995)
1925	*Reflections on the Death of a Porcupine and Other Essays*
1925	*St. Mawr, The Princess* (novellas)
1926	*The Plumed Serpent* (novel)
1926	*David* (play)
1926	*The First Lady Chatterley* (novel, first published 1944)
1927	*The Second Lady Chatterley* (novel, first published 1972)
1927	*Mornings in Mexico* (travel)
1928	*Lady Chatterley's Lover* (novel, abridged edition in 1932)
1928	*The Woman Who Rode Away and Other Stories*
1928	*The Collected Poems of D. H. Lawrence*
1929	*The Paintings of D. H. Lawrence*
1930	*The Virgin and the Gipsy* (novella, written in 1926)
1931	*Apocalypse* (philosophy)
1932	*Sketches of Etruscan Places* (travel)
1932	*The Letters of D. H. Lawrence*
1933	*The Plays of D. II. Lawrence*
1979–2000	*The Letters of D. H. Lawrence,* 8 volumes (complete)
1984	*Mr. Noon* (fiction)

the limits of love

Introduction

A CONTEXT

Frieda von Richthofen relished humor. About D. H. Lawrence, soon to be her husband, she wrote to a friend, "You know us – turtle-doves as always, who only coo softly, especially the male dove!" Between Lawrence and Frieda the cooing was only occasional, rarely soft, and often disagreeable, but it was central to their marriage. Their union, blending sun and shadow, did not include children, fixed homes, incomes, furniture—or even borders. Their union was built on the cracked rock of marriage. This book examines what marriage means for two people of opposed temperaments and backgrounds, whose identifies were in flux, who encouraged dissent, and whose lives were tested by frequent exits and returns. Still, although the Lawrences demanded much from such a marriage, especially from the mysteries of love, they also risked keen disenchantment.

Every relationship imposes limits, spoken or implied, on its partners. When limits are crossed, expectations change, and married partners set new boundaries or sometimes end their marriage. A separate response is emotional withdrawal, which leaves partners connected but insecurely. Major withdrawals deeply affected Lawrence and Frieda. Each presented a grave fracture but also exposed their unusual dependency on each other. Lawrence was too proud and private to demand total honesty, and Frieda was too carefree and confused to specify what constituted adultery. The result was a truce. It brokered a love that honored all the outward forms of marriage—steady concern and deep friendship—but tested the limits of inner forms of marriage. These limits disclosed diffidence, irritation, and calculated coldness. The evidence was rarely recorded, but the proof comes in the letters they wrote, modulating from rapture in 1912 ("the woman of a lifetime") to chilly exchanges (on postcards in 1922) to anger in 1926 ("not a penny if Frieda marries again") to Lawrence's refusal to make a will, in 1930, when he was dying.

Between these points of reference are the dozens of compelling novels and stories that Lawrence wrote between 1908 and 1928. They are so much a part of both Lawrence and Frieda that a biography of both, with new material, is especially important. It shows the couple as complementary, admirably sympathetic, but often dissonant.

When we think of great writers, we often think of their spouses. Who reads F. Scott Fitzgerald without asking about Zelda? Or Virginia Woolf without Leonard? Or James Joyce without Nora? The interplay of partners is often elusive. Do spouses enable, sustain, direct, or alter the genius of their partners? The husbands of George Eliot and Katherine Mansfield later sanitized the lives of their spouses. Charles Dickens wrote differently after he fell in love with Ellen Ternan in 1857. Even Shakespeare's wife, Ann Hathaway, about whom we know almost nothing, inevitably shaped his conception of women.

D. H. Lawrence and Frieda von Richthofen offer a rather different case. That is because, unlike Shakespeare and Hathaway (who spent little time together), they shared so much of their lives with each other. Until 1923 the Lawrences were seldom apart. They mediated each other's moods, wishes, obstinacies, sadnesses, and joy. Both expected completion. "Dear God," Lawrence had earlier exulted, "I am [before the wedding] marrying you, now, don't you see. [. . .] It's a marriage, not a meeting." For years their expectations satisfied them. As a team, they weathered one crisis after another—poverty, eviction, suppression, rejection, betrayal.

But serious marital fractures, when they appeared in 1916–17, then again in 1923, developed into emotional disruptions that no amount of living together could disguise. When in 1925 Frieda met an Italian soldier named Angelo Ravagli (who would become her partner after Lawrence's death), the emotional disruptions intensified. Ravagli was all that Lawrence was not—muscular, vigorous, and seductive. Although Frieda sought to be reawakened with passion, she was equally determined to support Lawrence in his last years. She wanted to complete the circle of love, begun much earlier, when, as Lawrence reported in 1913, "Frieda and I are struggling on." And struggle they did.

The Limits of Love follows the struggle in the itinerant life the Lawrences chose. They moved dozens of times from one residence to another—adapting to borrowed cottages in England, a guesthouse in Ceylon, hotel rooms in France, a rat-infested cottage in Australia, primitive cabins in Cornwall and Taos, but also to fine villas in Taormina and Florence. Every time they moved, they discarded the idea of home as a physical place of security and permanence.

What remained to sustain them? In fact, a great deal. They treasured their lasting friendship, common interests, joy of travel, stimulating friends (of high status and low), and, for Lawrence, a growing literary reputation as one of the finest writers of his era, excelling in many genres. But his great talent and fame also strained their marriage and gradually exposed its limits.

For both Lawrence and Frieda, painful experiences had dogged them. In 1910 Lawrence's beloved mother, the anchor of his early life, died; afterward, Frieda wrote, he was "never to quite be whole again." In 1912 Frieda, then married to Professor Ernest Weekley in Nottingham, sacrificed the joy of raising her three young children when she left England and joined Lawrence. She, too, was never quite whole again. Emotionally uprooted, both had endured indelible sadness. But having survived these losses, they freed themselves to assume other kinds of risk as they moved, more and more, away from the safety of convention. In 1914 Lawrence recognized that he had already "trampled in forbidden places." Encouraged by Frieda, who scoffed at nineteenth-century values and their irrelevance, Lawrence wrote ever more openly about the human body and especially about sex as a physical and a spiritual experience. One masterpiece after another—stories, novels, essays, poems—flowed from his pen. Many tested limits; all were remarkable.

Positioned on the fringes of society, the Lawrences were not an ordinary couple. They were neither as cautious as the Woolfs, as sordid as the Joyces, or as outrageous as the Fitzgeralds. But they challenged traditional norms with ease. Having no servants, Lawrence did most of the housework (he was quick and clean) and had the greater talent, but Frieda (though not well educated) was intellectually secure and socially adept. As they coordinated their efforts, neither partner became dominant. If Lawrence wanted to be heard, he spoke up. So did Frieda. "I know you don't mind me saying exactly what I think," she once told Lady Ottoline Morrell. Like Jane Austen's Elizabeth Bennet, she was unafraid of a titled lady. A Florentine neighbor recalled that Frieda boldly defended herself. She disliked feminine reserve and, earlier, in February 1897, had described herself as dancing "wildly" at a German ball. After Lawrence's illness in Mexico, in 1925, she valiantly helped him recover. But later, as he became increasingly sick, she minded that his illness required her daily sacrifice. She had reached a limit. In 1928, on a remote island in France, it was their friend Brigit Patmore who brought Lawrence hot water, breakfast in bed, and a greeting: "Hello, darling." Eventually, he chose to enter a sanatorium for help.

Despite their divergent needs, their sense of themselves was highly individual. Self-possessed and self-centered, Frieda was more confident than Lawrence in securing her female identity and in developing her special talent for friendship. Lawrence often struggled with issues of male identity, trying in his novels to imagine forms of power he did not possess. Mabel Dodge Luhan, a close friend, thought he disliked "manly men"; their strength frightened him. His work shows his struggle to locate characters who fused strength with sensitivity. Weak men—from Siegmund in *The Trespasser* (1912) to Mellors in *Lady Chatterley's Lover* (1928)—characterize many of his fictional figures. After his death Frieda revealed her power to shape his creative work, writing, "It may be my fault, he had no man friend – When [in Australia] he had those ideas of making a revolution with men, I thought . . . he can do more by his *vision,* that is inside him, than making an outer show with men." He listened. And he acquiesced. In visionary novels of startling originality, he integrated Frieda's security with his own insecurities. This fine tension shapes novels as different as *The Rainbow* of 1915 and the Australian novel

Kangaroo of 1923. They earned Frieda's admiration for their fidelity to her vision of love.

But her power over Lawrence and his work carried a danger that biographers rarely acknowledge. Women like Cosima Wagner and Maria Huxley would not let anyone disturb their husbands while they worked. Frieda may have gone further. In 1931 she made a surprising admission to her friend John Middleton Murry: "I held his genius as a *human being*, I *meant* to hold it and would not let *anybody* have a look in." Those words imply rigid control but probably mean only protection. And they do not apply to Lawrence's later work. The sort of guardianship that Frieda describes might have crippled a man of less capacity, but it is unlikely that Lawrence wanted anyone but his wife (and not always her) to "look in" to his inner creative sources.

Lawrence was far more industrious than most writers of his generation. James Joyce published three major works, Lawrence many more. Like Virginia Woolf, Lawrence spent no time repeating his successes but moved rapidly to develop his individual talent. To the end, he kept crossing lines, knocking on closed doors, barging into private spaces, pushing against barriers that curbed his speculations about human nature and sexuality. After *The Rainbow* was legally suppressed, he was never the same; his fury surged in his next major work, *Women in Love*, became veiled in *The Woman Who Rode Away*, then became savagely coded in *Lady Chatterley's Lover*. His insights into egoism, class strife, sexual dominance in males and females, and the breakdown of civilization—all display his intellectual stamina. Again and again, his characters struggle to shore up their personal integrity. In *Women in Love* Rupert Birkin aims to honor his complex sexual feelings and warring impulses while living in a society that aimed to mold him into a schoolmaster ascending into an inspector of teachers. In 1936 Frieda imagined just what would have happened to Lawrence had she not saved him: "God help us! He would have been a mild little local Thomas Hardy, who never said boo to a goose." Unchallenged, he would have slipped into obscurity.

Far from becoming a local colorist, little or mild, Lawrence demonstrated exceptional vitality in writing against social norms. But at some point around 1923, he recognized that he had outgrown the need for Frieda's assistance in shaping his work; on his own, he continued to explore vulnerable selves oppressed by conventional values. As he and Frieda drifted apart, he wrote *The Plumed Serpent* in 1925, which subtly repudiates a female character like Frieda. He was breaking free. Soon thereafter, he embarked on his last novel, *Lady Chatterley's Lover,* published in 1928, in which a loud, florid, loose wife named Bertha incites disgust. Moreover, Frieda rarely mentions Lawrence's huge effort as he wrote the novel's three versions. By then, Lawrence was able to define (and defend) his own path forward. It is an irony that as his health declined, his courage grew stronger, to the point of creating, in *The Man Who Died,* a risen Christ who returns to inhabit a world of ordinary humans with sexual needs. Isis, the hotly desirable woman, is Frieda's opposite—wistful, tender, and submissive.

Yet, after all, it was Frieda who inspired Lawrence to grasp fresh perceptions about intuition, respect, and the virtues of fidelity tested against the close confines of a marriage. She helped him confront human truths that he might not have found on his own. She shaped his understanding of passion as an enabling form of freedom. In 1949 she argued that, for Lawrence, sex was not an idea but an experience: "That experience was the impetus for all his work. That experience he had with me; had he married another woman he would have written quite differently." His subsequent experiments in *writing the body* are original and definitive. He slowly discovered, Frieda said, "new centres of human [consciousness] that he and only he made accessible."

In short, this book presents the Lawrences as a fascinating couple, living—with undeniable difficulty—halfway between tradition and innovation. They were rebels, but they were also domesticated. That is the paradox of their shared lives: acknowledging the limits of love, they fought for freedom but settled for compromise.

MY SOURCES

To portray these two lives with greater clarity and precision than before, I have drawn on hundreds of unpublished letters that Frieda Lawrence wrote, made available to me by my wife, Lynn K. Talbot, who is preparing them for publication. Many new letters, such as those to John Middleton Murry, have appeared only in the last few years. Frieda's letters give her a voice not heard before, a voice of benevolence, good sense, and moral authority. What sets her apart from other spouses is that she seldom subscribed wholeheartedly to anything Lawrence said or wrote. She demanded dialogue yet always respected his immense talent. To see Lawrence and Frieda together is to see them as we see other famous literary couples but, now, in fuller awareness of their individuality, their modernity, and their attempt, despite their setbacks, to find what lay at the center of human happiness.

This new biography does not aim to be a comprehensive account of two lives, week by week or work by work. That has been done by others: The three-volume Cambridge University Press biography, for example, provides thousands of pages. *The Limits of Love* has a different aim. It assesses—appreciatively but skeptically—how the Lawrences' impassioned love for each other, joyful for many months, became colder and coarser as the years passed. Equally important, the book asks how, when their friends had mostly separated or divorced, they managed, after multiple crises, to stay together—and later how Frieda, after Lawrence's death in 1930, managed also to stay with her partner till she died.

This new biography also incorporates important parts of earlier books on which I worked: *Love and Loyalty, D. H. Lawrence's Manuscripts,* and *Living at the Edge.** These three books provided a scaffold from which I reinterpreted both biographical details and Lawrence's major works. The hundreds of Frieda Lawrence letters that I cite in *The Limits of Love* (many for the first time) clarify and illuminate Lawrence's best work; they also freshly illustrate the quality and character of marital love. Frieda was an empowering figure. Everyone agrees that she was an imposing oppositional force in Lawrence's life, but the question remains: Where does opposition end—and obstruction or indifference begin? The question is a haunting one, not easily answered.

The crises that affected the Lawrences—whether emotional, financial, sexual, or philosophical—often baffled them, disappointed them,

---

* These earlier books are *D. H. Lawrence and Frieda: A Portrait of Love and Loyalty* (London: André Deutsch, 2008); *D. H. Lawrence's Manuscripts: The Correspondence of Frieda Lawrence, Jake Zeitlin and Others* (London: Macmillan, 1991); and (with Lynn K. Talbot) *Living at the Edge: A Biography of D. H. Lawrence and Frieda von Richthofen* (Madison: University of Wisconsin Press, 2002).

angered them, and ultimately changed them. Each crisis allowed new limits to be set. Soon after they met, Frieda quickly asserted her sexual freedom, and when she told Lawrence she needed sex, he acquiesced: "If you want [Udo von] Henning, or anybody, have him [. . .] as a dose of morphia." She did—as a deed of assertion, not as an act of marital infidelity. She would not marry Lawrence till 1914, when they found supreme happiness simply in being together.

In 1916 Lawrence also determined to assert himself as Frieda had, more than once in 1912, and to test her acquiescence. By nature she was tolerant. Lawrence was attracted now to a man—a farmer in Cornwall, age thirty-three, unmarried, living with his mother in a house near the Lawrences' cottage. With this man, named William Henry Hocking, Lawrence explored degrees of intimacy that cannot, even today, be known. When Frieda objected, Lawrence retreated, having mostly denied this aspect of himself. In retreat he poured himself into his creative work.

And there matters stood. The couple reasserted their love—fiercely contested but fiercely preserved. When they left England in 1919, they began world travels that occupied them in a continual whirl of activity and excitement. But in 1923 their tolerance for each other ended. Lawrence fiercely balked at returning to England. And so they separated. Frieda sailed home alone. In London she saw again a widower, John Middleton Murry, a lonely friend from earlier days. Uneasy glances from others did not deter their simmering relationship.

For his part Lawrence had left Frieda at the dock in New York, then set off on his own journey to test the friendship of two unmarried men (he called them the Danes) with whom he and Frieda had wintered near Taos, New Mexico. Lawrence wanted the three of them to go south to Mexico, perhaps manage a little banana farm, and become men bonded in virile solidarity. However, the Danes were disinclined to go. Disappointed but stoical, Lawrence finally went to London to join Frieda. Both expected a tender reunion and a continuing marital journey. Instead, Lawrence found a displeasing triangle. Murry was a Judas, pretending affection to both Lawrences. Now a mutual distrust became a steady current under the bridge of their marriage. The undercurrent ran more swiftly in 1925, when malaria caused Lawrence's health to collapse. When he finally improved, he was able to travel to Europe with his wife. But hating England, he badly miscalculated where he should go.

But that is to anticipate the full story of the limits of love. We return to 1912, when, in Nottingham, England, in March of that year, a fine married woman met a fine unmarried man.

CHAPTER 1

The End of Loneliness

When D. H. Lawrence met Frieda, in 1912, both were ripe for change, but neither could have anticipated their sudden attraction. Lawrence was charming but unsophisticated—a British lad with a good education, no money, and a provincial outlook. He was also imaginative and full of creative energy. Standing five feet nine inches tall, he had light hair, a narrow chest, and quick movements. Near London, he spent long days teaching a class of ten-year-old boys and, in the evenings, writing poems and stories; a year earlier, in 1911, he had distinguished himself by publishing a novel, *The White Peacock,* about love broken and betrayed.

Frieda von Richthofen Weekley was strikingly different. She was a mature and confident woman, direct and vigorous. She had a statuesque frame, green eyes, and an ebullient temperament—but had grown bored by her life with a stolid University of Nottingham professor named Ernest Weekley. Often idle, she read books, played the piano, sewed frocks, and took long walks. Her lively, inquiring mind met little challenge. A nanny cared for her three children—daughters seven and nine, and a son eleven—who loved the security and sense of fun their mother provided. She was their center.

Lawrence and Frieda, deep within, were restless and lonely. The force that had brought them together was a need for completion, though anyone who met them would have thought them unsuited for more than friendship. In those days class barriers functioned as gates, keeping people off each other's turf. Lawrence was working-class, often proud of it—yet shared his mother's snobbery. Though not rich, Frieda's father, a German baron named Friedrich von Richthofen, had given her the solid assurance of an aristocrat. Casting aside their class differences, Lawrence and Frieda met several times in the spring—her husband had introduced them—and made excursions into the Midlands countryside. Once, when Lawrence made Frieda's young daughters some paper boats and floated them down a stream, she gazed at him and—in a flash of revelation— knew she had fallen in love. In some curious way he completed her. She couldn't say why—she was neither probing nor analytical. But in her heart she knew. His vitality erased her loneliness, his clever understanding curbed her rashness, and his frail physique invited her protection.

For his part, Lawrence was powerfully attracted to this dynamic, intelligent woman, age thirty-two. Her strong body, straight nose, and bold, throaty laughter intrigued him. To his friend and mentor Edward Garnett, he wrote in April: "[S]he's splendid, she is really [. . .] perfectly unconventional, but really good—in the best sense. I'll bet you've never met anybody like her, by a long chalk. [. . .] Oh but she is the woman of a lifetime." Still cautious, Lawrence told no one in his conventional family about Frieda. Both his sisters, to whom he was close, would have disapproved. Frieda was married!

Lydia Lawrence, his beloved mother, had died sixteen months earlier in Eastwood, the English Midlands town where she had lived since 1875 with a husband she'd come to despise. The wound her death had inflicted on her favorite son had not healed. By 1912 Lawrence, having been so ill that he'd given up his job as a schoolmaster, had grown restless and peevish. He wanted an adventure. He, too, was bored—even with his pretty fiancée, Louisa Burrows, also a schoolteacher. He wanted a release from obligations, and he wanted to break with England and its narrow piety. So, of course, did Frieda. They had both become "perfectly unconventional." But they needed an excuse to leave.

Smitten with this clever man, Frieda soon proposed a plan—to go with Lawrence to the (then German) city of Metz, where she had been brought up. They would celebrate the jubilee of her father's fiftieth year in state service and perhaps, in time, discover the full scale of their attraction. In her autobiography she acknowledges the tide of recrimination rising around them: "We [. . .] crossed the grey channel sitting on some ropes, full of hope and agony. There was nothing but the grey sea, and the dark sky, and the throbbing of the ship, and ourselves." Dark skies, children left behind, families unaware—the signs were ominous. Clinging to "nothing but . . . ourselves" might be a challenge if their contrary temperaments emerged. That would happen within weeks. Indeed, Frieda's temerity left space for a gushing tenderness; Lawrence's timidity left space for a scruffy ferocity. Though Frieda may have been stronger, both of them shared overlapping qualities of character. Their independence mixed their warm affection for each other with cold fear of the future.

Complications quickly arose in Metz. Because the von Richthofen house was full of guests, Lawrence and Frieda stayed at the Hotel Deutscher Hof, secretly meeting her two sisters, the intellectual Else and the chic Johanna. But when Frieda's parents discovered that she had entangled herself with a penniless author, they scolded their wayward daughter and insisted she return to her children and her fine home in Nottingham. Her mother had already made the same bargain. Anna von Richthofen had long endured a loveless marriage and had tolerated her husband's adultery. Frieda refused the bargain. More than anything, she wanted love.

Though Lawrence won over both Else and Johanna with his sweet sensitivity and irresistible charm, he worried about the domestic upset he had caused. Distressed, he left Metz on 11 May to visit his cousin Hannah in Waldbröl, Germany, and from there wrote Frieda a moving letter declaring his love: "Dear God, I am marrying you, now, don't you see. It's a far greater thing than ever I knew. [. . .] I shall love you all my life. That also is a new idea to me. [. . .] Because, I'm not coming to you now for rest, but to start living. It's a marriage, not a meeting. What an inevitable thing it seems. [. . .] I know we are right." As this "new idea" arose, perfectly conceived, he spoke with heartfelt confidence and conviction. Freed by Frieda's love to become more fully himself, he soon felt a sweeping sense of relief. His confession, rare in any relationship, was an anchor in the tumult. Though often tested, his deep loyalty to Frieda rarely wavered. When the couple finally met again in May, near Munich, their passion flowered. Wandering up the Isar Valley, they spent a week in idyllic bliss—hiking the hills, sitting beside lakes, gathering golden bachelor's buttons—then borrowed a chalet in the village of Icking. "The world is wonderful and beautiful and good beyond one's wildest imagination," Lawrence rhapsodized to an Eastwood friend. "Never, never, never could one conceive what love is, beforehand, never." Hating the smell of scandal, Lawrence determined he would always live abroad. Above all, he valued the freedom to make his own choices. He did not have the burden of children.

For Frieda the break was much harder. Torn between her growing love for Lawrence and her obligation to her three children, she went wild with grief. As Lawrence explained to Garnett in July, "She lies on the floor in misery – and then is fearfully angry with me because I won't say 'stay for my sake.' I say 'decide what you want most, to live with me and share my rotten chances, or go back to security, and your children – decide for *yourself* – Choose for yourself.' [. . .] The letters today [from England] have nearly sent us both crazy." The children were equally miserable. They, too, were torn.

In England the moral outrage was fierce. The letters that arrived from Frieda's husband, Ernest, and others, full of fury, were lashes from those who, she thought, had been her jailers. Her choice was cruel. Ultimately, she ignored the advice that others pressed on her. Her husband's admonitions to recall her birth and to ditch the coal miner's son ("that filthy hound") made her desperate for Lawrence's love and assurance. Yet his own commitment sometimes appeared tentative or ambiguous. Locked in opposition, they fought bravely: "we nearly murder each other," Lawrence admitted. But for Frieda the cost of her departure remained high. "I have days when I really bleed for the children," she told Else, yet she also realized that "one cannot *live* for them." To do so would destroy her inner self and the confidence she had spent a decade building.

Above all, Lawrence and Frieda needed a way to broker their radical differences. To rise to higher ground, they hurled themselves into the work of shaping together the final draft of Lawrence's daring new novel, *Sons and Lovers*. A favorite of readers and one of the finest novels in English, it is Lawrence's early masterpiece, published in 1913. It portrays with unsparing fidelity the "grind" of working-class life and examines a family deeply divided between a husband, Walter Morel, and his wife, Gertrude. The Morels—he, impulsive and common; she, lightly educated and deeply disappointed—entrap a frail son named Paul in the grip of their antagonism. Morel drinks, she objects; he yells, she retorts; he inspires fear, she offers protection. Their children watch this marital dance with dismay or anger:

> Walter Morel was, at this time, exceedingly irritable. His work seemed to exhaust him. When he came home, he did not speak civilly to anybody. If the fire were rather low, he bullied about that; he grumbled about his dinner; if the children made a chatter, he shouted at them [. . .] and made them hate him.
>
> "You have no need to shout their heads off," Mrs Morel would say. "We are none of us hard of hearing."
>
> "I'll put my foot through 'em," he bawled. [. . .]
>
> "Goodness me, man," said Mrs Morel at last. "There isn't a bit of peace while you're in the house."

Friction like this profoundly affects Paul, who—attached, like Lawrence, too closely to his mother—turns to art to cope with his psychological damage. Later he finds himself hobbled by his Oedipal conflicts and therefore frustrated in his attraction to women, divided as he is by male and female impulses. He can love only women who are wholly unlike his possessive mother. This leads to heartbreak for his girlfriend, Miriam Leivers. After a long courtship, he discovers that her reticence and purity seem like violations, confusing him sexually. Her touch "caused him almost torture," he says. Sexual thoughts induce shame. Her purity prevents even their first kiss; he feels humiliated. "He hated her, for she seemed, in some way, to make him despise himself."

He seeks an alternative. He finds her in an older married woman named Clara Dawes, who espouses women's rights and who is both appealing and sexually experienced. To show Paul's growing freedom, Lawrence composes an exhilarating scene of seduction that captures their aroused response as a mirror of the deep creative power in the universe: "All the while, the peewits were screaming in the field. When he came to [after his orgasm], he [. . .] lifted his head and looked into her eyes. They were dark and shining and strange, life wild at the source. [. . .] They had met, and included in their meeting the thrust of the manifold grass stems, the cry of the peewit, the wheel of the stars." This passage establishes the religious basis of Lawrence's belief in the restorative power of sex. It "overwhelms" Clara and Paul and gives them "peace" and "verification." It links them to an immense power beyond themselves.

Still, the emotional healing doesn't last. The affair with Clara assuages but does not cure Paul's conflicted, tangled complex of feeling. The novel's final page conveys Paul's plea for mercy: "'Mother,' he whimpered," then turned his face toward the humming, glowing town, away from her memory. He hopes to be free of her. That is enough. By facing these puzzling contradictions head-on, the novel brilliantly portrays Paul's difficult evolution toward understanding his emotional life. Historically, the novel ushers in a new era of realism. Avoiding the sentimentality admired by Victorian writers, it looks candidly at a young man in crisis who attempts, on his own, to save himself from despair.

In March 1912, when Frieda met Lawrence, he was a highly promising novelist already shaping a career. She saw his enormous creative gifts at once. In order to continue their joint work on *Sons and Lovers,* the couple proposed to search out a place of their own, away from the narrow strictures of Germany or England. They needed time and peace. With barely any money, Lawrence and Frieda would trek over the Alps, through Austria, and into Italy. Going south partly by train but mostly on foot, they would steal some bliss out of their joint misery. On 5 August they shouldered their packs and left the chalet in Icking, walked (often in rain) to Mayrhofen in Austria, fixed meals by the cold streams, slept in hay huts when they got lost in the mountains, then rested at a farmhouse. "Frieda and I," Lawrence wrote, "have struggled through some bad times into a wonderful naked intimacy, all kindled with warmth, that I know at last is love." Their new bond—and its implied loyalty—would soon be tested.

Lawrence had always liked group excursions to enliven sunny days. Joining him and Frieda in Mayrhofen were Edward Garnett's son, Bunny, aged twenty, and his close friend, Harold Hobson, aged twenty-one. They were engaging, well-read companions. Together the foursome crossed over the steep Pfitscherjoch Pass. One day, while Bunny and Lawrence hunted alpine flowers on the mountain slopes, Frieda responded to Harold's vigorous masculine appeal. Her appetite was strong. She had been repressed by monogamy and would not miss this opportunity. Lawrence must understand her dislike of shackles. Her need for freedom was like his, only expressed differently. He wanted a new morality; she wanted amorality.

Not until Bunny and Harold had departed did Frieda tell Lawrence about the seduction. Although he blamed Harold for not being a gentleman, Lawrence nobly accepted her open aversion to monogamy. He also knew that five years earlier, near Munich, Frieda had participated in a monumental experience: she had given herself to Dr. Otto Gross, the poet of Freudian psychoanalysis, who was addicted to cocaine and morphine. Gross embraced matriarchy and wanted psychoanalysis to overthrow the existing order. He believed that any boundary violated the connectedness of all living things and that love and sex should, therefore, be freely shared.

Lawrence, however, embraced an evangelical tradition that honored the Seventh Commandment and castigated adulterers. Few people in Lawrence's circle tolerated adultery. His family opposed it. Though he very much minded Frieda's disloyalty, he acknowledged her principled differences, respected them, even honored them. He recognized that she had spent summers soaking up the cultural ferment in Munich, where revolutionary ideas blossomed. She revealed a few details about them. He knew that the old Prussian order of patriarchy and oppression was in crisis, uprisings were frequent, and the monarchy was losing ground. Like Frieda, Lawrence believed in revolutionary ideas. What he had written in 1911 he preached to Frieda (who needed little persuading): "My great religion is a belief in the blood, the flesh, as being wiser than the intellect. We can go wrong in our minds. But what our blood feels and believes and says, is always true. [. . .] I conceive a man's body as a kind of flame [. . .] and the intellect is just the light that is shed onto the things around." He boldly repositioned mind beneath the body.

New ideas festered everywhere. The atom had been split in 1910, X-rays discovered, relativity launched as a theory. Pablo Picasso created Cubism in 1912, and Arnold Schoenberg discovered atonality about this time; the two "inventors" broke down established styles of painting and composing. Lawrence and Frieda, having broken from their families and their pasts, were also ready for a different kind of future. Together, as they climbed over the snowy mountains and rough terrain, awakened by the beauty of places like Hennef and Mayrhofen, Lawrence shaped their discovery of love into poems collected in *Look! We Have Come Through!* These poems seem as new as a scientific experiment, breaking down rhythms and meters and turning sinfulness into songfulness. In "Bei Hennef" Lawrence ponders the largeness of their love, now strafed with interruptions and uncertainties:

> And at last I know my love for you is here;
> I can see it all, it is whole like the twilight,
> It is large, so large, I could not see it before
> Because of the little lights and flickers and interruptions
> Troubles, anxieties and pains. [. . .]
> Strange, how we suffer in spite of this!

Other poems show fear, uncertainty, and discordance. What Lawrence discovers as part of their strange suffering is the vital power of opposition, which he bluntly addresses in "Both Sides of the Medal":

> And because you love me
> think you you do not hate me?
> Ha, since you love me to ecstasy
> it follows you hate me to ecstasy.

These balanced lines, broken by a startling *Ha*, neatly reveal the couple's inner antagonism and anticipate the quarrels witnessed later by shocked observers. These spasms of love and hate will recurrently expose the limits of love.

The two travelers slowly descended into Italy. Admiring its friendliness and charm, they made their way to Lake Garda, to the village of Gargnano, where, speaking no Italian, they found the lakeside Villa Igéa, with four huge rooms and a sunny garden, backed by lemon trees and vineyards. On 18 September they moved in. At last Lawrence had found a quiet place to write. Frieda described it to her mother, who by now had accepted the liaison with Lawrence: "We have found something so splendid! [. . .] A flat in a villa with garden and lake, *everything* furnished beautifully and brightly. I am happy with it. [. . .] I've really forgotten that I'm not married to L[awrence]! [. . .] I'm simply sorry for people who slave their lives away when, here, one can live *so* well for so little money. [. . .] I can go swimming in the lake straight from the house, and it is quite indescribably beautiful!" Feeling as if she were newly married amid lush surroundings, Frieda often stayed outdoors to allow Lawrence to write. Her spontaneous delight in the splendid landscape helped her forget the pleas of her distraught children, now living in London with their father's parents, Charles and Agnes, and their aunt Maude. They were too young to comprehend why their mother had left them. Frieda's son, Monty, now twelve, had barely eaten since she left Nottingham in May. How long could she stand to be without her children? How could she protect them while living with Lawrence and recovering her dream of freedom? These questions constrained the joy she had discovered.

CHAPTER 2

England and Germany

In Italy the months passed quickly, giving the Lawrences stimulation and wonder yet also peace. While Frieda worried about how to see her children, either in Italy or in England, Lawrence struggled to complete *Sons and Lovers*. He also wrote travel sketches published as *Twilight in Italy*. One of the best, called "The Lemon Gardens," provides suggestive erotic details that reflect his newly discovered love: "In the morning I often lie in bed and watch the sunrise. The lake lies dim and milky, the mountains are dark blue at the back, while over them the sky gushes and glistens with light. At a certain place on the mountain ridge the light burns gold, seems to fuse a little groove on the hill's rim. It fuses and fuses at this point, till of a sudden it comes, the intense, molten, living light. The mountains melt suddenly, the light steps down, there is a glitter, a spangle, a clutch of spangles, a great unbearable sun-track flashing across the milky lake, and the light falls on my face." The light fuses, then erupts suddenly, intensely, unbearably, onto the writer.

Frieda, fascinated by his creative power, wrote that his words "pour[ed] out of his hand onto the paper, unconsciously [. . .] as flowers bloom." Sometimes she would help him imagine what his characters felt, then argue for her understanding of their integrity. *Sons and Lovers* became a joint venture, full of surprises and disagreements. Frieda had read enough George Eliot to understand social realism, her judgment was sure, and she fearlessly expressed her opinions. Lawrence poured into the novel "a heap of warmth and blood and tissue [. . .] F[rieda] says it's her," he wrote, amused, to Edward Garnett on 15 October 1912. In November he submitted the manuscript to Duckworth, in London, for spring publication. In every way he had made his novel "like life," and Frieda judged him "so plucky and honest in his work," and his writing so vivid, that "it knocks you down." Duckworth generously advanced Lawrence one hundred pounds for the novel—a year's salary for a beginning teacher. He and Frieda were thrilled. They had found love, freedom, money, and months of unfettered time. The fact that they knew no one in Gargnano encouraged them to spend hours talking about their pasts. His was entirely different from hers.

―

From the beginning David Herbert Lawrence, nicknamed Bert, was often unwell. Born 11 September 1885, in the red-brick Midlands town of Eastwood, the fourth of five children and the youngest son, Lawrence joined a bickering, impoverished, unhappy family. Living in a cramped four-room row house, not far from the Brinsley mine where his father, Arthur Lawrence, hewed coal, he loved indoor games like charades, adventure books like *Treasure Island,* and pastimes like landscape painting. Bright and spirited, he avoided the town's rough-and-tumble boys, their crude vigor, and their combat sports. Yet he wasn't weak. He drew strength from the miners' ingrained skepticism and from his religion. With his mother, Lydia, and sisters, Emily and Ada, he attended the Congregational chapel on Nottingham Road, learning to cultivate a bond between himself and God that allowed powerful "unknown" forces to pulse through him. Later his religious rapture sometimes turned to satire. He entertained Frieda by acting out the drama of a revival meeting—the sentimental hymns, the preacher's desperate laments for lost souls, the "saved" wretches creeping humbly forward into the light of salvation. "Lawrence," Frieda wrote, "made me shake with laughter." He loved to mimic.

In his early years he preferred his mother's responsible sobriety and honesty to his father's coarse ways, which included binges of drinking. Lydia valued her personal convictions and passed to Bert her driving ambition—and her iron determination that the dark mines would never see his handsome face. She fiercely protected him.

D. H. Lawrence's family, in Eastwood, c. 1893 (Nottingham City Council). He stands between his parents.

At the age of twelve, Lawrence won a scholarship to Nottingham High School, located eight miles from Eastwood, and—ironically—endured a rigorous discipline. Each morning he left home at seven o'clock, walked two miles to catch the train to Nottingham, mustered attention all day, then did not arrive home till seven o'clock in the evening. He was exhausted. Homework followed. Time was short, and money was scarce. "Every little thing we needed extra," he later told a friend, "meant saving and scraping for, and not having enough to eat." Despite these privations, he worked hard, was steady and able, and behaved well. He excelled in mathematics. But few miners' sons had ever attended Nottingham High School. At a distance Lawrence mingled with the boys of the middle classes but never joined them. Above them in intellect, below them in status, he was always an outsider; when his grades fell in his last year, he knew that a change was coming.

Having no money to pay for college, Lawrence at age sixteen agreed to work—for a few months—as a warehouse clerk in a Nottingham factory called Haywoods. It employed mostly rough young women whose vulgarity appalled him. "They were perfect beasts," he later confided to another friend. He soon left, in December 1901. Listless and pale, he became ill with double pneumonia and, with penicillin decades from discovery, stayed in bed for several months. Since an untreated infection had recently killed Lawrence's ambitious older brother, Ernest, who had gone to London to establish himself, his mother felt keen anguish at Bert's slide into grave illness. She hovered over him, her love intensifying into adoration. Their bond tightened into a grip, astounding but unhealthy.

Once he mended, ever so slowly, Lawrence responded to his mother's urging and agreed in October 1902 to train as an apprentice teacher at the British School in Eastwood. He was seventeen and, to save money, lived at home in the family's cramped quarters. The apprenticeship lasted four years. He taught elementary-age children but also took classes every week at the Ilkeston Training Center. He performed all tasks well. During this time he matured into a fair-haired, fine-featured, thin-shouldered man—sensitive, creative, and disciplined, even as he chafed against the restrictions imposed on him. George Holderness, his supervising teacher, described him as "hard-working and painstaking, energetic and bright in his manner," but also considerate and kind. He added that in his twenty-eight years of supervising teachers, no one had ever showed "greater promise than Mr. Lawrence."

At the Training Center he met a fellow apprentice teacher named Jessie Chambers. They attended the same Congregational chapel, and their mothers were friends. Living on a prosperous tenant farm two miles from Eastwood, Jessie invited him to visit. He found there a feast of fresh experience—fragrant meadows, grazing cows and horses, barn swings, a garden with new potatoes, country walks across open fields, and a gamekeeper's hut hidden in the woods. Jessie's parents, Edmund and Ann, were affable and welcoming. Lawrence discovered there a pastoral escape from worry and work. A new life took root in him there. He trusted Jessie, lent her books, and drew close to her—until, that is, his mother's icy disapproval forced him, in time, to subdue his passion. No matter. Jessie's terror of sex made her too inhibited to incite a young man who wanted to buck Victorian prudery. He could wait.

Stimulated in a variety of adolescent ways, Lawrence began writing sensuous stories like "The White Stocking," in which a married woman, Elsie Whiston, finds herself dangerously drawn to a man with elegance, class, and seductive power. As they dance, "his fingers seemed to search into her flesh [. . .] she felt she would give way utterly, and sink molten: the fusion point was coming when she would fuse down into perfect unconsciousness at his feet and knees. But [. . .] he seemed to sustain all her body with his limbs, his body; and his warmth seemed to come closer into her, nearer, till it would fuse right through her, and she would be as liquid to him, as an intoxication only. It was exquisite." This kind of orgasmic writing ("coming . . . into perfect unconsciousness . . . right through her") introduced an erotic electricity that fellow writers of realism, such as Arnold Bennett, had shunned. Though alien to cautious readers like Jessie Chambers, this kind of writing would prove to be Lawrence's most fertile ground. He specialized in sexual attraction.

Having worked his way up to the level of uncertified assistant teacher, Lawrence, hoping to advance his career, needed a teaching certificate. This he earned in his early twenties at Nottingham University College, from 1906 to 1908. Although he dutifully completed his assignments, he did not flourish. He felt stifled and bored. Jessie remembered that his vital interest "centred on his writing and not on his studies." Except for lessons in botany, he had, he thought, wasted two years on methods and memorization. Preparing to teach had neither challenged nor inspired him. Yet he needed to earn an income. Money was still scarce.

Finally, a successful job interview in 1908 led him to a teaching position, in elementary education, at Davidson Road School, in the London suburb of Croydon. The salary was a modest ninety-five pounds a year, which paid for lodging with a neighborhood family, weekend entertainment, and train fare home when his mother got sick—but no luxuries, no restaurant meals, no European travel. Fortunately, he had learned to economize.

After an initial burst of enthusiasm, however, he soured on teaching. His large class of forty-five boys (many of them from poor families) gave him little time for his own writing. The boys, he said, were "rough and insolent as the devil. I would rather endure anything than this continual, petty, debasing struggle." Refined and well-mannered, Lawrence had never liked "rough" lads; he was intimidated by their physical strength and disgusted by their coarse language. The only struggle he enjoyed was that of shaping his long, handwritten manuscript "Laetitia" into a novel that William Heinemann would publish as *The White Peacock* in 1911. It was a pastoral novel, modified by its realism and marked by its florid use of metaphor—the larches "put out velvet fingers to caress me," a wagon "rode like a ship at anchor," a lighted cigarette became "a ruddy, malignant insect." These experiments in vivid language helped him express the power of his imagination. He felt confident in his talent.

Away from Davidson Road School, Lawrence was an amusing companion, witty and effervescent. He befriended a fellow teacher named Arthur McLeod, who loved books, and he still visited Jessie Chambers, whose sense and stability he had admired; but he was drawn now to a winsome young woman named Louisa Burrows, who had also begun teaching in 1908. Her frankness, beauty, and high spirits inspired him. But no one completed him: no one satisfied his whole being. Feeling torn and sullen, he grew frustrated. He was trapped in indecision. The sudden revelation of his mother's cancer in August 1910 compounded his misery. He began to visit her every other weekend. (Years later, Connie Chatterley's sister remembered that "Mother died of cancer, brought on by fretting.") A mother's painful fretting left an indelible memory.

D. H. Lawrence, in Croydon, 1908 (Nottingham City Council)

Transformed into an emblem of woe, Lydia Lawrence died on 9 December 1910. She had been, Lawrence wrote, severe, straight, and splendid. She seemed to him like a Viking fallen in battle, like an "invincible spear," whereas toward his father he felt astonishingly "hard and bitter."

It is a measure of his own woe that a week before his mother died, he met Louisa Burrows on a train and—sunk by grief, entranced by her dark hair, mesmerized by her tawny eyes—he suddenly proposed marriage.

She was twenty-three, he twenty-five. He was beside himself in trying to drown his despair. In one of the most painful sentences Lawrence ever wrote, he admitted, "I can marry her, and still be alone." He understood his own fierce disloyalty. He knew he must free himself of his affliction. As Frieda later wrote, he was, after his mother died, never whole again.

Months later, in October 1911, an invitation from Edward Garnett, a skilled, worldly publisher's reader, helped Lawrence imagine a life without the drudgery of teaching. That life might somehow allow his wholeness of being to develop. Encouraged by Garnett's praise, he carefully revised the poems he had written. But he was often tired and began feeling anguish and dissatisfied love. He was sinking. After a November visit to Garnett's fine stone cottage in Kent, Lawrence got thoroughly chilled, his hacking cough developed into double pneumonia, and for weeks he lay flat on his back, fast losing weight. His body had rescued his soul. He knew that he could never teach again. An era was about to end.

He shed his old, sick life like a snake its skin. In January 1912 he went to a seaside convalescent home in Bournemouth, two hundred miles south. By the fire in his single bedroom, he worked on a new novel, which would be published as *The Trespasser,* writing it—as he always did—by hand. It addressed his disrupted emotions. The book's protagonist, a passionate man named Siegmund, is a violinist in an opera company. His rich sensuality has been restrained by his need to support a large family. Intensely frustrated, then awakened by a summer tryst with a young woman named Helena, he finally recognizes a hard truth about himself—that for years "he had suppressed his soul, in a kind of mechanical despair, doing his duty and enduring the rest." When his despair overwhelms him, he kills himself. Lawrence had thereby imagined the sorrowful place where a troubled, loveless marriage would take him. It had warned him. He admitted to Garnett that *The Trespasser* had revealed "my most palpitant, sensitive self."

A month later, this insight inspired him to write, at last, to Louisa Burrows to say that his poor health made him unfit for marriage. The old bonds that once held him had snapped. Although he had alerted her six months earlier, "I'll bring you nothing but sorrow," he dismissed her without ceremony. "I am afraid we are not well suited," he told her. No more was she his fiancée. He had sounded flippant rather than penitent, artificial rather than sincere; that was because, after his long illness, he felt emotionally unstable. Louisa had restrained him, had not enabled him to flourish. She was, he knew, not a path to wholeness of being. When they met, in Nottingham, she feigned indifference, then offered friendship, which he declined as a sham part of a life he no longer wanted.

Back in Eastwood—because he had gone home after recovering his health and resigning his teaching post—he felt discouraged and disaffected. He heard the miners' boots on the pavement, heard the clock chime and the church bells ring, listened to Ada's gossip, and saw "liberated" socialists like Alice Dax and William Hopkin, who had earlier opened doors (sexual and political) for him. But his hopes shriveled.

By now, the constraints of Eastwood were becoming unbearable. He was twenty-five and had nowhere to turn—except perhaps to go to Nottingham one day in early March and call upon his witty, sarcastic French professor, Ernest Weekley, who had become a friend. Lawrence wished to inquire about a possible post in Germany, where his cousin Hannah Krenkow lived. He did not know that Professor Weekley's wife, Frieda, was German, one of the aristocratic von Richthofens; that she was an avid reader of English novels; and that she revered writers. She and Lawrence had much in common. At once they found themselves in eager conversation.

―

Frieda von Richthofen's upbringing was entirely different from Lawrence's. Privileged and assured, the daughter of a German baron, she was already the mother of three children. Born 11 August 1879, the second of three daughters, Frieda had been raised in Metz, in a grand house with gardens of rosy fruit, blooming flowers, and rows of vegetables. Unlike Lawrence, she identified more with her father than with her mother; she felt at ease with rough boys. She was rash, displayed the bold fearlessness of a man, and liked to tramp through forests, swim rivers, and hike mountains. She was full of courage and vitality. "At school in Germany, all the children did as I told them," Frieda said later; "they believed in me." They admired her bravery. She was a soldier's daughter, respectful of courage in any form. At a renowned boarding school run by family friends Julie and Camilla Blas, Frieda, though impatient and unruly, studied literature, languages, history, religion, and drawing—as did her older sister, Else, and her younger sister, Johanna—but no science or advanced math. What did it matter? She was destined for marriage.

However, Else had already set an example of how women could liberate themselves from patriarchy. Though women were barred from formal study, Else had arranged to study economics with Professor Alfred Weber, who later described her as a woman "full of unbiased intellectual curiosity." She went on, in 1900, to earn a PhD degree in economics. Frieda had a fine model for thinking differently about herself.

Eventually, her mother, Anna—cultured and graceful—insisted that she become a lady, look pretty, choose flattering hats, sew dresses, learn embroidery, write charming letters, and make lively conversation. Slowly, Frieda—disinclined to study—excelled at such female arts and finished her education in Berlin as the guest of her cousin Oswald, who held a government post. Like Mrs. Bennet in Jane Austen's *Pride and Prejudice*, Anna von Richthofen understood that the business of her life was to get her daughters married. Girls from respectable families did not go to work. At the age of seventeen, Frieda hoped to meet an eligible man and then to embrace an engagement. She thought of marriage as an extraordinary adventure. In 1898 she wrote to her sister Else, "I won't marry without love, I could never do it." Frieda was not brash, but she was naive.

Friends introduced her to an eligible bachelor, age thirty-three, in the Black Forest. The tall man Frieda met was Ernest Weekley, bearded and stiff—and already late to the marriage market. He had prepared himself to fall deeply in love. To Frieda and her parents, he looked very suitable. He spoke fluent French and German. Sober and industrious, he had studied at the prestigious Sorbonne in Paris. A morally good man, he had long channeled his passion into books. He was unusually disciplined. Until he ventured on a solo trek through the Black Forest, he had never had a holiday. When he asked permission to court Frieda, she confided to her sister Else, "I am terribly excited," and added, "I hope that – like me – you will fall in love with him." He wore fine clothes, had a position as lecturer at Nottingham University College, required no dowry from the (improvident) Richthofens, and offered Frieda both security and an exalted sort of love. It was passion without much expression, devotion without much feeling. But Frieda found him strangely appealing. At first he seemed to stabilize her.

In August 1899 Frieda and Ernest were married in the Blases' home. Frieda had just turned twenty and had not yet shed a girl's immaturity. She had much to learn. Moving to Nottingham, the Weekleys occupied small, dark houses on Nottingham Road and Goldswong Terrace. As slowly as a tide, Frieda's marital boredom crept up. She had thought that her husband and children would become her consuming passion, channeling her strong emotions and bringing her solace. Following Montague, born in 1900, came two daughters, Elsa in 1902 and Barbara in 1904. At first Frieda was entranced with them. She shopped for them, played games with them, read English novels, and deftly avoided her husband, who, to supplement his salary, taught night classes in Nottingham. The years passed, lightly bound in dutiful behavior: hers domestic, his professional. The erosion of feeling came on imperceptibly.

Part of the erosion of feeling came also from another direction—from the critiques that German thinkers had mounted at this time. In Schwabing, the bohemian district of Munich, Frieda, during her summer visits to Germany, had met several radical thinkers, mostly unknown today. Ludwig Klages (1872–1956) might have been one of them. His father had insisted that he earn a PhD degree in chemistry. He did, in 1900, the same year as Else earned hers in economics. But Klages, in revolt against patriarchy, turned to philosophy, arguing, for instance, that the decline of the West could be reversed by a return to paganism. He disbelieved in any form of organized religion. So, before long, did Frieda.

In the summer of 1907, awakened by such new ideas, Frieda met Dr. Otto Gross in Munich, near where Else lived. He was a brilliant psychiatrist, privately educated, who had married her childhood friend, Friedel Schloffer. He adored women, mounted them on a pedestal of praise, then seduced them. Frieda soon fell under his erotic spell. His lovemaking surpassed anything she had ever known. She wrote to Else, probably in June: "I know that if you could see me with Otto, you would understand a lot."

She also wrote Otto dozens of impassioned letters. Mesmerized by Gross's intellect and passion, she preserved his many letters, in which he

Dr. Otto Gross, c. 1912 (Wikipedia)

called her magnificent and magisterial and himself "inseparably yours." One letter helped her envision herself as a woman of the future, pristine and unpolluted. Gross wrote, "I know it through you, the only human being who already, today, has remained free from the code of chastity, from Christianity, from democracy – remained free through her own strength . . . [from] the curse and the dirt of two gloomy millennia."

Such delicious warbling gave Frieda a new sense of her potential as a woman with a deep capacity for love. Monogamy, she thought, might simply acknowledge society's fear of openness. She hoped to rendezvous with Gross in Switzerland or in Amsterdam, promising that, when they meet, "the doors to the wonderland of love" will open wide. A magician of romance, Otto Gross had stirred in Frieda a fierce appetite that he hoped to satisfy. His passion was like fire, consuming his beloved. She was prepared for his conquest.

Transformed by his revolutionary ideas, Frieda wanted to free herself to become more enraptured and complete. In Nottingham she quickly became a misfit. To Gross she described dancing around her bedroom in 1907, "dressed only in a shawl, while the worthy Philistines went to church!" She cared little for codes of restraint. Later she wrote that "approving or disapproving are not activities of my nature." She had separated herself from her neighbors, and, like Lawrence, she castigated Victorian prudery.

In Nottingham she felt increasingly lonely. Her need for liberation was mounting, and with it came a fierce marital chill. Ernest took refuge in his teaching and writing, Frieda in married men like Gross, who preferred trysts. Frieda wanted passion without risking her social position. As her feelings of emptiness and loneliness grew, however, so did second thoughts about staying with Weekley, whose sexual skills were crudely male. She had expected finesse from a husband who claimed to adore her. She had therefore been harboring a means of escape. Remembering the emptiness of her parents' loveless marriage, she was tempted to leave and take her children with her. This temptation alarmed Else, who—from her own experience—demanded caution. She sternly addressed Frieda in September 1907: "I am fearfully sad about everything that you write! And [we] can say really nothing, except that we all love you very much! . . . [You surely understand] that a life with Otto [Gross] *and* three children is absolutely unthinkable. [. . .] You do understand, don't you, that I want to hold you back from doing anything that would destroy your life and the lives of your children!"

These bracing words restrained the headstrong impulses in Frieda's character. She soon realized that she could not risk a scrambled, troubled, tumultuous life with Gross. He may have been an incomparable lover, but he was unstable, unreliable, and promiscuous. She would have sacrificed herself to his addictions. As Lawrence had, in fiction, anticipated Siegmund's tragic end in *The Trespasser,* so Frieda had gotten a similar warning from her sister.

Then a surprising gap in the biographical record. What it means is that important documents have disappeared, almost certainly destroyed. Not much is known of Frieda until 1912. What we do know, from newly discovered documents, is that in 1910 Else refused to go on living with her

Jewish husband, Edgar Jaffé. When he threatened to take away her four children, the Baroness von Richthofen intervened. She worried about Else's diminished finances but finally agreed to the couple's permanent separation without a divorce. Edgar, who was rich, bought a home in Irschenhausen for himself and another, nearby, in Wolfratshausen for Else and the children. Else later wrote that everyone preferred "conventional appearances as much as possible." The effect of these complex negotiations on Frieda Weekley was immediate. If she were greatly dissatisfied, she might be able to leave her husband. She would have inferred that her mother might succeed in negotiating on her behalf and thereby perhaps avoid scandal. But in 1911 Frieda was not quite ready for abrupt change.

What we know for sure is that in the spring of 1912, Lawrence departed from Eastwood and arrived in Nottingham to visit Professor Weekley. By chance he made the acquaintance of Mrs. Weekley. They liked each other at once, but only a shrewd observer would have guessed that Frieda would be spending her next Christmas in Italy.

CHAPTER 3

Italian Paradise

Living in exile, in what seemed like a kind of paradise, Lawrence and Frieda spent much of the winter in delicious reminiscence. Both savored anecdotes of the past—of Lawrence tramping across the fields to Felley Mill searching for foxgloves, of Frieda teasing the soldiers garrisoned in Metz. In the town of Gargnano, they walked along the narrow Italian streets, buying cauliflower and goat meat at the market; went boating on the lake that opened like a blue fan below their spacious apartment; and, beside the clear streams, gathered wild Christmas roses, "white and wonderful beyond belief," wrote Lawrence. In the mountains above, at the end of a winding mule track, pretty villages like San Gaudenzio enticed the Lawrences to a day's ramble, to see the violets and grape hyacinths covering the mountainsides. Each week brought challenges that required them to improvise—and compromise. The risk that they would part was "unthinkable," Frieda said. More and more, she added, "Lawrence and I have the deep feeling of love." She had waited fifteen years to find a man like Lawrence. She would not part from him now.

But as Easter 1913 approached, Frieda could stand her dilemma no longer. "I do feel like bursting sometimes about the children," she wailed. They were not allowed to write to her. No one communicated their anguish. In London she would have to see them on the sly. Almost as bad, no one contained Ernest Weekley's rage, and no one dampened his fervent hope that she might return, in person, to comfort the children. He seems to have misunderstood his wife, missed many signals of her emotional distress, and too easily imagined that she would subscribe to Victorian codes of female duty, which mandated unwavering fidelity. But she refused to return to Nottingham.

As each fresh letter of invective arrived from Weekley, Frieda's frustration intensified—she could see them at Easter, she could not; maybe in August, maybe not; perhaps in Baden-Baden, then not. In the divorce suit that Weekley initiated, Lawrence winced when the British consul appeared on their Gargnano doorstep in March, with an official document declaring Lawrence a "Co-respondent" who had "*habitually* committed adultery." Lawrence joked that adultery must be "a nasty habit!" But the couple's happiness wilted with the Christmas roses. Paradise was slipping out of their fingers.

These shadows on their love grew darker. The frictional but joyful infatuation that had delighted both of them modulated into the ease and comfort of stable routines, edged with rivalry. Frieda was especially competitive. A warning flared in a letter Lawrence wrote to his favorite sister, Ada, welcoming "your support just now against Frieda," who claimed he was "difficult and unpleasant." For two people who openly expressed their feelings, marital friction sparked easily, often over trivial matters. But these struggles for power were set aside when, because of the imminent heat, they left Gargnano and—after visiting Germany—reached England.

They went straight to the Cearne, Edward Garnett's cozy stone cottage near Edenbridge in Kent. Socially, they felt so insecure that Lawrence alerted Garnett's housekeeper that, despite their irregular union, Frieda "must be [called] Mrs Lawrence." It is hard for us today to comprehend their fragile position without knowing that in 1913 aggrieved parties filed only one thousand divorce petitions in all of England and Wales. Indeed, Lawrence could not take Frieda to Eastwood, even for his sister Ada's wedding in August. He feared the response. Within his family Ada alone knew of her brother's affair, and she disliked what he had done. Nor could Frieda return to Nottingham. In July, Ernest Weekley, aware of her impending arrival, sought a restraining order to bar her from visiting the children. His anger had crossed into revenge.

The Lawrences, now estranged from their families, did what almost any other couple would have done. When they reached England and then

Katherine Mansfield, 1914 (Alexander Turnbull Library, Wellington, New Zealand, Collection of Pickthall, Charlotte Mary, 1887–1966. Ref: 1/4-017274-F. Photo by Adelphi Studios Ltd.)

John Middleton Murry, 1912 (Alexander Turnbull Library, Wellington, New Zealand, Ref: 1/2-028641-F)

took a small flat in Margate, they made friends mostly with people like themselves who satirized what was respectable and defied convention. Chief among them was an impressive young couple—highly accomplished in their art; as literate as anyone they had ever met; and as liberated as Edward Garnett, who kept a mistress near his cottage. The couple were Katherine Mansfield and John "Jack" Middleton Murry. Having emigrated from New Zealand, Katherine, age twenty-four, sly and satirical in temperament, wrote elegant short stories, had briefly been married, and from her rich father received an allowance of £120 a year. Chic and exquisitely dressed, she appeared lovely and vulnerable but underneath was as hard as a diamond. She always preferred rather feminine men. Frieda found her extraordinary.

Katherine's boyfriend, Jack Murry, was a soft, insecure young man of twenty-three; working-class, like the young Lawrence; square jawed and good-looking; smart and industrious; yet also insensitive to others. His odd sensibility had been warped by his father's wrath (as had Lawrence's sensibility by his mother's love). Murry had studied classics at Oxford and left with a second-class degree. Assisted by Katherine (whom Frieda thoughtfully called "Mrs. Murry"), he had started a magazine, the *Blue Review*, to which Lawrence had contributed two pieces; one was a review of Thomas Mann's *Death in Venice* as a skillfully written but unwholesome book. Alas, the *Blue Review* failed after three months.

Drawn together, the foursome met in July 1913 and were an immediate success, riding on a bus to have lunch in Soho, amazed to find so much common ground; all were ready to knock at the doors of eager publishers. At once Lawrence demonstrated his uncanny powers of perception. "In an astonishingly short time," Murry wrote, "he knew all about me." Katherine helped Frieda try to greet her startled, frightened children as they left school in the afternoons. When the Weekleys objected to her bold overtures, Katherine delivered Frieda's handwritten notes. She was an ally—clever, fun, and underhanded.

The Lawrences' five-month sojourn in Germany and England had been artistically stimulating and emotionally rewarding. Frieda had freshly recognized Lawrence's startling originality as an artist—"he is so much more than one at first thinks," she told Else. She admired his courage and his brave attempt to plumb hidden layers of feeling that contemporary writers like Virginia Woolf had not yet discovered. A new location might stimulate him.

When Italy beckoned, Lawrence responded. He wrote to Murry, "I look to Italy to wake me up." Compared to England, Italy was sunny and yielding; its landscape, people, and climate suited the Lawrences. Edgar Jaffé, Else's gentle and tolerant husband, a professor of economics at the University of Munich who had separated from Else in 1910, had taken a holiday and come to Lerici on the Italian coast. His companion was equally unconventional, a sweet girl from the slums, as Frieda described her. There, on 30 September, the Lawrences joined him and his girlfriend. Together they found a modest fisherman's bungalow in the village of Fiascherino, located between Genoa and Florence, where "pure sunshine" poured from the sky and where figs and grapes ripened on the slopes nearby. The Lawrences delighted in its four rooms, set in a vineyard and framed by tall pine trees overlooking a blue bay, where, Frieda wrote, "the Mediterranean comes in and pitches itself over boulders – quite unbelievable." Braced by the challenge to her healthy animal spirits, Frieda welcomed the freedom that Italy offered. She vowed to seize its benefits. "This winter," she told Else, "I want to translate and write and paint and swim and fish and row – and what else does one want?" Only to assist her partner in his creative work.

The happiness that embraced Lawrence and Frieda slowly expressed itself as Lawrence began to reach for the unconscious forces to which he believed Frieda now linked him. These forces, lying far below the surface, seemed almost inaccessible. Excavation was difficult. No direct route was available, only a jumping of stiles and fences. Lawrence was looking for a way to exonerate Frieda's untrammeled passion—but how? At this time artists all over Europe were bending old forms into new. In 1910, for instance, Georges Braque, in a famous cubist painting, pulled apart a violin and a pitcher and set them on colliding planes. Lawrence, too, was swept along on the wave of experiment, looking for verbal equivalents of primal feeling buried in layers of intuition. He hoped to find—and maybe redefine—the shape of the Unconscious.

Basking seaside in the balmy Italian weather of Fiascherino, Lawrence began to compose "The Sisters," the big novel he was certain he could write. Choosing as his main character young Ursula Brangwen, he used the critical distance that Italy afforded him to judge how her culture had shaped, damaged, and enabled her to be a courageous woman intent on fulfilling her body, mind, and spirit. In its pages he wanted to portray not what a woman *sees* but what her soul *feels* behind the facade of ordinary events. In 1913 this new emotional terrain had not been mapped. As Virginia Woolf said, "The streets of London have their map; but our passions are uncharted." It was Lawrence's task—the hardest he had faced—to lose himself in a woman's pure sense of herself, unshielded by male prerogatives. When he suppressed his inhibitions and composed (as he did) along the seaside rocks, a torrent of words poured out of him. The novel was "so different from anything I have yet written, that I do nothing but wonder what it is like." For her part Frieda, lying all potent in a hammock right there beside him as he wrote, provided the model of womanhood that he needed. At last she could be herself, empowered by his pen; she would no longer be susceptible to codes of convention.

As the cooler months enveloped the Mediterranean coast, the Lawrences preferred being outdoors all day, watching the lemons, oranges, and olives ripen in the bright sun and, if inclined, helping gather the fruit. They might row over to Lerici, with its pink roofs and hilltop castle, or pry shellfish off the rocks. "It is the most beautiful place I know," Lawrence wrote. In the evenings, he said, the sun made streets of fire to the distant islands, and Frieda, accompanying herself on a rented piano, sang German folk songs or asked the peasants below, Luigi and Gentile, to bring their guitar—and their friends—and sing love songs. "The other day," she wrote in January, "we were 18 in our little place." They had created a community in which they were not outsiders but participants.

Into this paradise came dissonant voices. "Mrs Garnett is here," Frieda announced in February without elaboration. Married to Lawrence's mentor Edward, Constance Garnett was a Cambridge University graduate who had won Lawrence's respect as an accomplished and prolific translator of Russian novelists such as Tolstoy and Dostoevsky. Coming to Lerici for the warm winter, she found Lawrence's disturbing cough gone and his voice stronger. He may have been thin and looked hollow eyed, but he worked steadily on "The Sisters." He was immensely proud of it. He had discovered new truths about women, especially about their emotions, ranging from diffidence to aggression. He decided to ask Mrs. Garnett to read a draft of the novel, unwisely trusting that she would recognize its merits. But she was conservative and believed that Lawrence, despite his cleverness and charm, had "no true nobility." Sadly, she thought the draft sloppy, the characters' sexual experiences rendered inartistically, and the whole book in need of major revision. Her appraisal shocked him. But he moved on.

In the vibrant spring weather, scented with anemones and almond blossoms, Lawrence stubbornly began rewriting, page after page. Undaunted, Frieda helped him. From her past she recalled vivid experiences—how she had planted seed potatoes, rowed a boat, and learned to swim. Most important, she gave Lawrence confidence when both Garnetts turned caustic about his new work, Edward now wanting vivid scenes of the lower-middle classes. As the new novel's midwife, Frieda saw what Lawrence alone had seen—that he was fusing the religious impulses of his childhood with the mysteries of the unconscious, found deep inside "the great impersonal." These mysteries, previously hidden, are those she urged him to discover. What Lawrence wrote about Ursula Brangwen characterizes Frieda: "To be [her]self was a supreme, gleaming triumph of infinity." As the Lawrences collaborated on his new novel—Frieda its fierce champion, Lawrence shaping what lay deep inside him—he presented Frieda to the world. She was the glorious, gifted, imperious female that Otto Gross had enshrined years earlier. Breaking the old patriarchal mold, Lawrence had aimed, he said, to make art more fully "the joint work of man and woman." Together they would combine "blind knowledge and suffering and joy" in order to reach "the source of all life." His aim was a daring departure from what had been written.

Lawrence finished his bold, brave novel in May 1914. Following Frieda's suggestion, he retitled it "The Rainbow," then sent it to Methuen, a prominent London publisher that, compared to Duckworth, offered better financial terms—an astounding three hundred pounds. It was a marvelous figure. As Lawrence knew so well, "it is wearying to be always poor." Now good news lay ahead. The Lawrences escaped the Italian heat, Frieda going to Baden-Baden to see her beloved family while Lawrence walked across the Swiss Alps to Heidelberg, where Frieda joined him. Later, in London, they spent a month at Gordon Campbell's flat in South Kensington. Campbell was a dignified and successful lawyer, always elegantly dressed, whose wife, Beatrice, was a painter. Katherine Mansfield and John Middleton Murry shared the house. Katherine wrote amusing sketches; Murry was finishing a dense autobiographical novel called "Still Life." They were fine companions, brilliant but not yet brittle.

Together, Campbell and Murry gladly honored the Lawrences. The men provided legal witnesses at a ceremony that the Lawrences had anticipated for two years. It took place on Monday morning, 13 June 1914. Lawrence, now fully mustached, chose a dark three-piece suit, Frieda a loose, white, flowing dress. "Frieda and I," he announced to Sallie Hopkin, "were married this morning at the Kensington registrar's office." Although Lawrence scoffed at marriage as a mere legal contract, it was much more than that. It made a statement of their enduring commitment.

One day later, on the fourteenth, Frieda wrote to her mother and begged her to come to London and intercede with the Weekleys on her behalf: "I met Maude [Weekley's sister] with the children, and when they saw me, they looked at me in terror, as if I were going to do something to them, and cried, *We mustn't talk to you*. [. . .] Only you can help me. [. . .] So, come as soon as you can." Although Frieda enclosed 100 marks ($425 today) for her mother's fare, the baroness did not come from Germany to arbitrate, even though she had negotiated Else's separation from her husband, Edgar Jaffé. Frieda, surely dismayed, was losing ground with her children.

By now the Lawrences had weathered one crisis after another, meshing their differences, wrangling with the Weekleys, coping with criticism, trying to find loveliness in every landscape and luncheon. It would, however, take all their courage and tenacity to cope with what lay ahead of them, as the lights of Europe dimmed, one after the other, and in August 1914 went out.

CHAPTER 4

A Heart That's Been Smashed

The darkest days in a hundred years lay ahead. For a century Britain had enjoyed relative prosperity and peace. But after Germany declared war on Russia and France on 1 August 1914, Britain joined its French neighbor in the fight. On 25 August, German troops ravaged the Belgian city of Leuven, forcing its ten thousand residents to flee. In one week in September—by which time the Lawrences had moved to a small, damp cottage in Buckinghamshire—battles along France's Marne River began to reveal the casualties to come: 1,700 British soldiers, 80,000 French soldiers, and 250,000 German soldiers were killed. Four years of trench warfare followed. As Europe descended into prolonged chaos, Frieda found herself again in exile, barred from both her children and her homeland. Though she held a British passport, she was a German national and could not leave England. She and Lawrence were forced into a prison of endurance. Italy, like a flickering candle in the darkening winter months, disappeared from their horizon. Although hoping to escape from England throughout 1915, they slowly descended, one rung at a time, into emotional chaos.

Their timing was terrible. Anti-German fervor cast shadows everywhere, army reservists were called up, prices rose, and trees needed for trenches reduced paper available for printing books. If the Lawrences had opened the *London Times* on 23 October 1914, they would have read that the police were arresting "all unnaturalized male Germans [. . .] between 17 and 45" and detaining them in "concentration camps."

In Nottingham fifty enemy aliens had been arrested in one day. At this frightening time, good friends were vital for someone who loved others as much as Frieda did.

A few months earlier, in halcyon summer days, the Lawrences had been the toast of the London fringe, meeting an assortment of fascinating people—some titled, some important, some just interesting. They met translators like S. S. Koteliansky; painters like Mark Gertler; novelists like Gilbert Cannan; poets like Richard Aldington; Cambridge intellectuals like Bertrand Russell; psychoanalysts like David Eder; socialites like Lady Cynthia Asquith; patrons like Edward Marsh; and rich, influential people like Lady Ottoline Morrell and her husband, Philip. Marsh found the Lawrences "very happy together," while Ottoline admired Lawrence's "great passion."

Fired with revolutionary ideas, Lawrence rushed to meet the avant-garde; his staunchest ally, Frieda, remained outspoken and rash. "My country is very strong," she would say. "I am a German woman, and I cannot help feeling proud of German soldiers." Lawrence would then launch into a tirade against the war. "What colossal idiocy!" he would shout. He hated the herd mentality, hated the war, hated its claim on those who wanted a new life in Britain. Inspiring his listeners, his tirades gave rise to plans and schemes for alternatives. He saw himself as a savior, fusing religious zeal with passionate pronouncements.

Now he needed to embody his vision. He proposed to collect a few people who, demanding integrity, would refuse to be isolated from others. They would call for humane values. Two eminent friends helped him. In London, S. S. Koteliansky, a law clerk and translator who had fled Russia's pogroms, gave Lawrence the concept of "Rananim," the Hebrew word for a communal life and all it implied. Koteliansky, with black hair, high forehead, and piercing eyes, valued above all his own integrity. That was a quality Lawrence admired.

Inspired by this vision of renewal and community, Lawrence still needed a location and a second person who possessed money, influence, and a love of art. He found this person in Ottoline Morrell. Tall, titled, strikingly dressed, a woman with grand manners, she responded sympathetically to Lawrence's vision. Frieda quickly recognized her regal beneficence. "Dear Lady Ottoline," she wrote, "I am also grate-

Lady Ottoline Morrell, c. 1899 (Wikipedia)

ful to you that you understand L[awrence]'s *bigness,* you must be big yourself that you can see it. You will be such a moral support and help in what he wants to fulfill in this world!" Twelve years older than Lawrence, Ottoline had grown up a gangly, lonely misfit at Welbeck Abbey, just eighteen miles from Eastwood. In 1913 she and her mild-mannered husband, Philip, bought a three-story country house called Garsington Manor. Sited beautifully a few miles from Oxford, its 360 acres gave it seclusion, its serene pond and graceful elms gave it distinction, and in 1915 its redecorated rooms gave weekend guests ample space.

At Garsington, Ottoline could entertain the London fringe in flamboyant style, with lavish charades, alfresco luncheons, and gossip galore.

She welcomed anyone with talent. She was especially fond of young writers like Virginia Woolf and Lytton Strachey. Though she was married, she was, said one observer, "highly sexed." By now Bertrand Russell had become her lover. A leading pacifist, he complemented Lawrence's radical intuitive vision and lent an academic rigor that neatly muzzled Lawrence's outbursts. It surprised everyone that Lawrence would value Russell's modest vision of the future of England. But Lawrence valued the man's stature and intellectual brilliance.

For a while Ottoline seemed poised to provide the perfect center of this new community that would weave work, home, and religion into one fabric. Lawrence thought her "a great lady," worthy of backing a revolution of consciousness. But Ottoline, though tactful and sympathetic, represented not the future but the graceful, accomplished past. She was deeply entrenched in the assumptions of her class. Despite Lawrence's great hopes, disappointment followed. After a time Russell found Lawrence's voluble passions incomprehensible; worse, Ottoline found Frieda jealous and assertive. Frieda was Ottoline's double: powerful, well bred, and intensely female. In a letter of 2 August 1915, Frieda admitted: "When we came to you last time we were very antagonistic he and I, and I was not at all happy – I thought you idealised him and you had a sort of unholy soulfulness between you that seems to me quite contrary to all good life – Say I was jealous, I may have been." Frieda, acknowledging her jealousy of "unholy" bonds, resented being overshadowed. She proudly declared, "I know you don't mind me saying exactly what I think." She mistrusted the great lady's friendship. The "unholy soulfulness" that worried her was precisely what Lawrence had most disliked about Jessie Chambers a few years earlier. That put him in a muddle.

It was a turning point. Conflicted, he grew disillusioned, and his bitterness poured out even over his wife. "Frieda hates me because she says I am [. . .] a traitor to her," he confided to Ottoline. Frieda saw what he did not—that Russell and Ottoline patronized him. Still, taking a long view, Frieda thought to herself, "Perhaps I ought to leave Lawrence to her influence." Together (Frieda mused) he and Ottoline might do so much to help England. But Frieda loved Lawrence too much to let him be exploited. Ugly scenes followed. Although the Lawrences tolerated each other's faults, repeated stress damaged their intimacy and limited their love. In the tumult of emotional dislocation, Lawrence's sweetness disappeared. The Lawrences felt they must leave wartime London and ensure their loyalty to each other. Maybe America, in the new world, was their Rananim.

Before they left London, Frieda achieved an important goal. Roused into decisive action, she went straight to Chiswick, a suburb of London, found the street she sought, and boldly entered the house where her three children lived. They had no warning. As she wrote to Ottoline in April: "I have been to see my children, I just marched into the house, where they live with their grandparents – They were such dears – so fine and sensitive though they stood like 3 avenging angels, 'you went with another man, you left our father' – The little one [Barbara] quite a Rachel with her head thrown back – But I felt their love staring out of their eyes in spite of everything – "

Despite their love, which their eyes revealed, the visit was piteous and difficult. It had a profound effect. Frieda was a stranger in their home, marching into their midst. Before long, she arrived at a painful but permanent recognition: "When I saw the children I *knew* after all how infinitely more to me Lawrence is and my life with him." This was also a turning point. Frieda had slowly come to terms with her great loss. Lawrence and his friends, vibrant and sparkling, met her emotional needs. From time to time she saw the children again, often in the presence of Weekley's attorney, sometimes for a mere thirty minutes. The visits were artificial, the children embarrassed, Frieda in tears, the venue more like a jail than a home. Everyone felt dismay.

Meanwhile, day after day, Lawrence patiently reworked his novel. The London firm of Methuen, uneasy about publishing books after the war with Germany began, returned all accepted manuscripts for six months. After some thought, Lawrence, always ambitious and resourceful, decided to split his novel in half. He had time. "I am," he told his friend Arthur McLeod in January 1915, "still revising the *Rainbow* – putting a great deal of work into it." In *The Rainbow* he would eventually portray three generations of a family, whereas in the second part, later called *Women in Love,* he would portray women negotiating marriage. The effort of reworking the novel would allow Lawrence to interpret the evolving motivations of each generation.

In his reworked *Rainbow,* Lawrence created, especially in Ursula Brangwen, a more imaginative and resourceful character than either Clara in *Sons and Lovers* or Helena in *The Trespasser.* He did so by fusing his own experience and Frieda's. From Frieda he took a new vision of womanhood that embraced not duty and sacrifice but self-realization and self-determination, not denial and suppression but robust passion. To explore what had been unexplored in women, he liberated Ursula's body and enlarged her soul. "I must," Ursula recognizes, "break out of [the past], like a nut from its shell." From his own experience, he took his childhood alienation from his father and his regimented teacher training, then combined them with a passionate search for freedom that fosters Ursula's capacity for growth. When she finally breaks with her lover, Anton Skrebensky, and discovers that she is not pregnant, she plants herself firmly in the twentieth century, awaiting a stronger man and repudiating the industrial model of work that she had seen in Wiggiston. She will allow no incarceration of her spirit.

The Rainbow is a novel of both transgression and hope. It is a young writer's novel—exuberant and challenging, its parts held loosely together, its development uneven, its ambition tamed by its conception. Yet the novel reaches a steady set of insights: that rhythms of rural life satisfy deep human needs; that marriage is a difficult process of exploration; that a classroom of regimented children resembles a prison, "fascinating and horrible"; that intuition reveals a glimmering mystery beyond all others; and that passion is the truest form of spiritual energy. They reflect Lawrence's ability to create new modes of understanding and to use language in innovative ways. He had created, he told Koteliansky, "one of the important novels in the language." That is a daring claim; it reflects Frieda's audacious capacity to validate his genius.

He also knew that while telling the inner truth of his and Frieda's experiences, he was pushing his novel into unsafe territory. The year 1915 was an especially dangerous year to present such a bold novel to the public. No one knew how long the war would last. Perhaps Lawrence invited the blow that lay ahead. When Methuen scrutinized the manuscript pages of "The Rainbow"—the prized bouquet of Lawrence's love for Frieda—the firm's editors marked passage after passage of high-risk writing. At the novel's center came this surprising passage: "All the shameful things of the body revealed themselves to [Will Brangwen, Ursula's father] now with a sort of sinister, tropical beauty. All the shameful, natural and unnatural acts of sensual voluptuousness which he and [his wife Anna] partook of together, created together, they had their heavy beauty and their delight. Shame, what was it? It was part of extreme delight. [. . .] The secret, shameful things are most terribly beautiful."

How could "shameful acts" create beauty? This kind of coded writing, so dark and personal and suggestive, would—Lawrence must have known—alarm readers. Because he relished the offense to Victorian prudery, he let such passages stand, along with erotic descriptions of two women petting. These "unnatural acts" of sensuality—what *were* they? When Methuen insisted on revision, Lawrence angrily complied. Money was scarce. He had already heard the starving wolf "scratch the door" of the small Buckinghamshire cottage where he and Frieda lived. While apparently obliging his publisher, he refused to mutilate his novel. With Frieda's blessing, he cut few of the high-risk passages . . . and waited. One night he dreamed that the solar system had collapsed and the bright stars, "trooping out of the sky," burned to ash. The dream terrified him. It was a portent he could not ignore. He foresaw a "state of dissolution."

When the damp cottage gave Lawrence a hacking cough and a lingering cold, he realized he could not stay the winter. A rescue came early in 1915. A winsome young writer named Viola Meynell offered the Lawrences her cottage at Greatham, about fifty miles south of London, near the Sussex coast. Not only did she refuse any rent; she also agreed to type Lawrence's new novel. Her cottage, white and new, with three bedrooms and a bath, lay in the Meynell family settlement near the Downs. "I must say I love it," Lawrence wrote to Koteliansky. Lawrence's health soon improved. To welcome weekend guests like Murry and Koteliansky, he would walk the four miles to the Pulborough train station—and home again. He and Frieda liked the low meadows and the trees full of birds and stayed from January till July 1915.

In the months at Greatham, Lawrence excitedly finished the last pages of his novel. His literary standing seemed secure. He wrote many long letters to Ottoline, novelist E. M. Forster, and Bertrand Russell. All were people who could help him test his grand ideas about community, religion, and marriage that might show humans as both brave and splendid.

In Lawrence's hands, the possibilities for change seemed especially rich, freeing men from dependence on material things, giving them spiritual hope, and allowing them to discover Otherness. "The great living experience for every man," Lawrence wrote to Russell, "is his adventure into the woman" and the embrace "in the woman [of] all that is not himself." Lawrence's philosophy burst out alongside the spring flowers and left him unusually vibrant and companionable.

On 30 September 1915 came a day of jubilation: Methuen at last published Lawrence's *Rainbow*—and a month later came the American edition. The next day one reviewer of the book, acknowledging Lawrence's "defiance of all conventions," praised him as a writer of "exceptional strength." Other voices demurred. James Douglas, aghast at the novel's sexual openness, concluded, "A thing like *The Rainbow* has no right to exist in the wind of war."

Then the blow. On 5 November Lawrence heard that the British authorities, alarmed by this review and others like it, had found *The Rainbow* obscene and ordered Methuen to stop selling the book and to deliver 429 unsold copies to be destroyed. Lawrence was given no chance to defend his book. Facing a magistrate, Methuen bowed in shame, acknowledged its mistake in publishing such a thing, and conceded that the novel had "no right to exist." Lawrence's friends protested—but with little effect.

"My heart is smashed into a thousand fragments," Lawrence cried, not knowing how to salvage the pieces, much less how to assuage his hurt. The novel's suppression drove him to despair. "I'm often angry," he admitted to Cynthia Asquith, soon transferring his anger elsewhere. "You cannot conceive how dark and hideous London is today, smouldering in a dank fog," he told Ottoline.

He and Frieda were now eager to find a new footing in a place less hostile. They pined to sail to America, even to the fetid swamps of western Florida, where Lawrence felt he might find a fresh American audience for his work. After the *Lusitania* liner was torpedoed off the coast of Ireland, in May 1915, killing 1,195, violent outrage fell on Germans in London; almost a thousand people were arrested. In the autumn London was cold, foggy, and packed with war casualties. The Lawrences were no longer simply waiting for the war to end; they were victims of rage, desperate to leave. Their collaborative work, patiently constructed month after month, had been destroyed. Although their friends sent them money, their bitterness had no release. In 1915 it festered into a fury never to be forgotten.

But when the Lawrences finally left London on 30 December, they hardly imagined that the place where they were going was colder, hid more anti-German fervor, and exposed their love to darker emotional risks than anything they had yet experienced. The ship they had hoped to take to America left without them. They were stranded in England.

CHAPTER 5

A Map of Passion

The state of dissolution that Lawrence had feared slowly emerged, disclosing the emotional shrapnel of the war. In the distant place where the Lawrences went, boulders, big and small, broke up the fields; gray skies loomed; winds whipped off the Atlantic Ocean with gale force, snapping branches; submarines, lurking near the coast, posed threats of disaster; and the crusty natives, isolated for centuries, rebuffed all outsiders. This was no Rananim. This was Cornwall as 1916 began, at the southwestern tip of England, three hundred miles from London. Cornwall offered the Lawrences a desolate new beginning. The place, though starkly appealing and mysterious, pushed them downward, one more rung, into a welter of strange passions they were not expecting.

From London they arrived at a spacious farmhouse belonging to J. D. Beresford, a writer of science fiction who was a friend of John Middleton Murry. Set back from the cliffs, near the village of Porthcothan, the house, despite its isolation, gave the Lawrences temporary peace. They stayed free for two months. "I love it," Lawrence cried. As the new year of 1916 began, Frieda agreed: "It's wonderful, something magic about it." Eager for renewal, Lawrence also needed to forget the insults of the past. That was a burden. His rage lingered, then festered. Whenever Frieda thought of *The Rainbow,* now condemned and publicly shamed, she bristled. "I am sick with rage too," she told Ottoline Morrell. "I cannot forgive them the absolute rejection of *The Rainbow* – [. . .] I feel a deep and helpless desire for revenge." Her desire only intensified what Lawrence felt. After ten days in Cornwall, he grew ill with what he called, in code, his "wintry inflammation." It was more than that.

This time the illness was different. Creeping up and down his left side came a frightening numbness. He felt paralyzed. The doctor who examined him diagnosed an inflammation "referred," he said, from the nerves. It was a vague diagnosis. The doctor may also have whispered something else, which friends had already guessed: tuberculosis. Lawrence had many symptoms: bouts of coughing, weakness, fever, weight loss. But his spirit was strong. To acknowledge TB was an invitation to defeat, so the word was never mentioned—ever. Instead, Lawrence rested quietly in bed and revised—for July publication—a collection of sixty poems, called "Amores," which were mostly elegies to his mother and to others of his youth. These elegies, freeing him from the past, allowed him to experiment with modes of feeling, illustrated by "The Enkindled Spring":

And I, what fountain of fire am I among
This leaping combustion of spring? My spirit is tossed
About like a shadow buffeted in the throng
Of flames, a shadow that's gone astray, and is lost.

His "spirit" lost in the flaming life of spring, he has "gone astray" and awaits a return to health.

Soon he improved. Although friends wrote letters, sent gifts, and gave money, Lawrence was breaking loose from the old world, including Eastwood, where he had spent his difficult formative years. At Christmastime he had found his family "a great strain," sharing with them only personal connections. "The closeness and intensity of L[awrence]'s family was something almost unbearable," wrote Frieda—whereas with friends he shared books, flickering hopes, and new social directions. In March, Frieda wrote to the painter Mark Gertler, "L[awrence] and I are very happy at present and are full of hope and good things, we will *not* be cheated of a good life, if we have got it in us to live one." They thought they had. But war, Frieda knew, cheated everyone. It would also test the limits of their love.

Later that month, one of his new friends, a composer named Philip

Heseltine, aged twenty-one, drove the Lawrences forty-five miles southwest to the remote village of Zennor, which Lawrence thought "very lovely." Near it, at Higher Tregerthen, only a mile from the coast, they rented a two-room stone cottage. Rough, with an outhouse, it cost only five pounds a year—easily affordable when a wealthy American poet named Amy Lowell, coming to their rescue, gave them sixty pounds, enough for a year's rent.

Lawrence welcomed the crisp sea air that blew across Cornwall in such great gusts that it had contorted the trees in its path. Sudden squalls soaked the fields. Yet the Lawrences found Higher Tregerthen secluded and safe, despite the constant threat of war and conscription. They could live cheaply, getting provisions from the farm below, and watch the mysterious landscape come alive. They could bathe at Wicca Pool nearby and plant a vegetable garden. In the spring sunshine the fields burst with sea pinks, foxgloves, and bluebells. As the gorse thickened into flower, lambs skipped amid the huge gray boulders; blackbirds shrieked; in the far distance a ship might loom; and at dusk came the Celtic magic of Cornwall. Frieda loved it.

Lawrence, entranced by its mystery, came alive too. In April 1916, suddenly and intensively, he began to write. His energy returned with the longer days. He called his new book "Women in Love." Although it was a sequel to (and originally part of) *The Rainbow,* it captured harrowing new passions that erupted like a volcano. Freshly inspired, the novel looked at Lawrence's contemporary society in bold, dark, brutal ways. It was, Frieda said in a letter to E. M. Forster, "so *bitter* and lovely and *dotty* at times, but infinitely the biggest thing he has done." Her joining of *bitter* and *lovely* forecasts Lawrence's fresh insights. The Lawrences' personal experience, also at times violent, melded into a larger analysis of a culture in crisis—not a crisis of war or religion but of purpose and priority. Lawrence took an aggressive stand, observing for himself England's cultural decay and what he called "modern intellectual decomposition." By that he meant the collapse of agrarian values and the rise of machines and industry. The world had suddenly changed. Describing himself as "a brigand," he wanted to write "bombs" that would rid the social system of its rottenness. His new theme—of systemic illness—shaped the inspired prose that once again poured out of him. Finished with a draft in just six months, he knew he had written a masterpiece, published in 1998 as *The First "Women in Love."*

Portraying coal barons, titled women, and unmarried sisters who (as schoolteachers) are hoisting themselves upward, Lawrence's new novel at first sounds like a slow nineteenth-century English novel full of mild domestic conflict over matters of money. It is not. In scenes of striking originality, a destructive energy explodes in his language. In one scene a pet rabbit scratches both Gerald the coal baron and Gudrun the art teacher and reveals surprising secrets beyond pain: "'Isn't it a *fool!*' she cried. 'Isn't it a sickening *fool?*' The vindictive mockery in her voice made his veins quiver. Glancing up at him, into his eyes, she revealed the mocking, blood-cruel recognition of him. There was a bond between them. He saw, with secret recognition, how utterly she loathed the rabbit, how she would wish it and all its kind annihilated. And they were mutually related, he and she, in this secret cruelty." Words such as *vindictive, loathed,* and *annihilated* signal the hidden language of antagonism and hostility, of dominance and submission. That is the language Lawrence had heard in his own troubled childhood and, sometimes, in his marriage to Frieda. He was now recording the subterranean jolts of passion that burst through the mind's fractures. No one had yet mapped passions like the grudge that Gudrun bears the rabbit or the demonic savagery that Gerald—when thwarted—bears toward Gudrun when "she challenged the whole world."

Such intensity made readers uncomfortable. The discomfort appears later in the novel, too, when Birkin, the character most like Lawrence, recoils from women and, to fill the emptiness, engages in a nude wrestling match with his close friend Gerald. It leads Birkin to *penetrate* (it is the author's word) "his body through the body of the other, [...] through the muscles into the very depths of Gerald's physical being." The language is unmistakably sexual. Lawrence was again pushing the limits of tolerance in order to express feelings that had rarely been voiced. He was again enlarging the map of human emotion. To Forster he wrote, "In this book I am free at last, thank God." When Lawrence sent the manuscript to Ottoline Morrell, she read it with "great shock." The novel seemed so reckless that she wondered who would print it. In fact, Cecil Palmer, a London publisher, soon told Lawrence that the novel "would be impossible to publish publicly."

Into this creative inferno at Higher Tregerthen came Katherine Mansfield and Middleton Murry, happy to be with friends and hoping their springtime reunion would inspire their collective creativity. Lawrence, eagerly awaiting their arrival, had already begun his new novel about two unsettled couples anticipating change. The pair of visitors arrived on 6 April 1916, riding atop a cart with their belongings. Wary pilgrims coming to the Lawrence shrine, they took the large vacant house next door and, decorating it with used furniture, made a comfortable home.

For a while Lawrence and Frieda were overjoyed. The foursome spent delightful hours together, playing in the fields, wandering along the sea cliffs, strolling through the crooked streets of Penzance, and scouring the little shops. Once, Frieda remembered, they all went bathing "without any clothes on." They cared not if the neighbors noticed. "I am glad the Murrys are here with us," Lawrence told Ottoline Morrell. Frieda later described to Murry what she remembered about Katherine: "I see her so exquisite when we first met her [in London], then the Buck[inghamshire] Katherine, then in Cornwall – in the cake shop in St. Ives when she had bought me some nougat, you thought it was for you – I can see her 'gugu' eyes at you and she at once bought you some. [. . .] And always there were [memorable] things – funny ones and nice ones – " Still later, in 1932, Frieda acknowledged her love for Katherine. "Yes," she admitted, "I always felt only tenderness for Katherine, there was *never* a vile moment between her and me."

But the camaraderie that bound the foursome in 1916 did not last. The emotional mix was too complicated, the dissonance too alarming, the rivalry too intense. Katherine's exquisite personality buckled under the strain. Always insecure, she couldn't work (the gray boulders oppressed her), and the Lawrences' quarreling upset her (she claimed they were trading punches). From Murry, Lawrence wanted a closeness that Murry's thin emotional range excluded: male intimacy frightened him. Frieda, also growing uneasy, began to sense that Katherine and Murry, who had "never been loyal," had turned viciously spiteful. Katherine, whom Virginia Woolf had found "utterly unscrupulous," was a kind of scorpion. She constantly dissembled, becoming ever more devious.

After only ten weeks, the Murrys left Higher Tregerthen. Katherine soon wrote to Koteliansky to say that she had separated from Murry and felt "free again," finding life "wonderful." But that was far from the truth. Before they departed from the Lawrences, Murry (with Katherine's tacit approval) offered Lawrence a bruising critique of his character. At this time, occupied as he was in writing a cataclysmic work, Lawrence felt emotionally vulnerable and incomplete. That explains why he called Murry "filth," felt "loathing" for him, and later wrote to him: "You shouldn't say you love me. You disliked me intensely when you were here."

Frieda, too, castigated Murry for his treachery and Katherine for her complicity: "To me they have been so mean – especially Jack; wherever they have been, they have turned people against me." The Lawrences' vitriolic response to the Murrys shows not so much bitterness as the shock of betrayal. In the new novel, betrayal is what Birkin feels at Gerald's death: "He could not bear that the beautiful, virile Gerald was a heap of inert matter." Birkin realizes now that he must recommit himself to a woman and make his life only with her. Surely that is what Lawrence imagined he should do with Frieda.

But doing so was harder in life—a lot harder—than in fiction. In life the sensual, handsome man did not die, as Gerald had done at the end of the novel, but lived a five minutes' walk from the Lawrences' cottage. He was single, thirty-three, stubborn, sincere, and still living at home with his siblings and widowed mother. His name was William Henry Hocking. A rural Heathcliff (without Heathcliff's courage or passion), he had tired of farming. He, too, felt incomplete and wanted Lawrence to awaken his consciousness and enrich his understanding. Lawrence met him partway, talked to him by the hour, enlightened him, helped him in the hayfields, and relished his company. He fired Lawrence's creativity. Like Murry, William Henry possessed a sexual magnetism that was difficult for Lawrence to repel. Evening after evening in the winter of 1916 and on into the autumn of 1917, Lawrence would go to the Hockings' farmhouse, play games in the evening, returning home late, uninterested in his wife or her attentions. He suppressed his feeling as best he could, but Frieda, always vigilant, saw it.

At first she sought a convenient fix—find the good farmer a decent wife. When that failed (Hocking waited almost two years to marry), and possibly in retaliation, she began to visit—by herself—the home of Cecil Gray, four miles distant. A composer like Philip Heseltine, Gray was

William Henry Hocking, c. 1917 (Kitty Rogers)

equally young and equally spoiled by a rich mother. Living by himself, he was available to visitors. Writing to Gray in an indirect, overwrought letter, Lawrence linked Frieda and Gray as a couple who (he claimed) "need to go one world deeper in knowledge" rather than inhabiting this "suggestive underworld . . . *felt* between the initiated." This odd letter positions Frieda and Gray in some perverse union that is not "open." At the end of *The "First Women in Love,"* Lawrence creates a similar couple, Gudrun and Loerke, who together are "initiated into the central secrets [. . .] sharers in some religious mystery." In both letter and novel, Lawrence is murky and tantalizing where he could have been clear and exact. He usually preferred directness. What had really happened?

A crisis had damaged the Lawrences' marriage. Had its limits been breached? Whether either of them, or both, had crossed the line of strict fidelity we may never know: the evidence is inconclusive. Frieda had been unfaithful before, and Lawrence had long wanted an intensely close bond with a man. What matters is that some disloyalty occurred, some break in trust, some loss of commitment. If Frieda had earlier felt trivialized in her bid for recognition, now she engaged in a different kind of battle. She liked a good fight and rarely backed down. At whatever cost to her reputation, she would reclaim her husband. A few months after Lawrence's death, she clarified her stance. In an extraordinary letter to Murry, she characterized the unusually close bond between Lawrence and William Henry: "And [about] William Henry, I am *sure,* it was not really nasty there, though I admit abnormal, Lawrence was so *direct* and he was *fond* of him – And I *fought* him out of it, the homosexuality – I got him back – But it was a deep and tragic experience to him."

The nature of the bond between the two men has long invited speculation. Marianna Torgovnick, like some others, claims that it was "a homosexual affair." But Frieda, armed with firsthand knowledge, clarifies the relationship in important ways: yes, it was abnormal, but there was, she is sure, no intercourse ("nothing nasty"). Yes, for Lawrence it was "a deep and tragic experience" that would have reshaped his conception of himself and made him more cautious in his choices. Frieda openly challenged his deep love for another man, fought "the homosexuality" out of him, and won. She "got him back." Skeptics will question her success, worrying that a sexual preference cannot be extinguished by a fight, however brave.

For Lawrence, caught in the grip of guilt, the emotional cost must have been high. His sacrifice would have seemed to him a "tragic" outcome, a cauterized loss. Frieda was a powerful antagonist and, like a soldier, never avoided battle. She demanded that Lawrence give up his intimate relationship with Hocking, a man who was, in word or deed, neither brave nor strong. She was helped when strangers suddenly arrived in Higher Tregerthen on a surprise mission.

Back in March 1916, while still living at Porthcothan, near the cliffs of the sea, Lawrence had hoped (he said) "that the world won't stare in at the windows with its evil face." But his fear was an omen. The suspect "world," which he had hoped to leave behind, hovered near their cottage, even under their windows, listening and reporting. In fact, just a year later, coast watchers in February 1917 were stunned to see two ships go down near Higher Tregerthen, torpedoed by German submarines like the one that had struck the *Lusitania* two years earlier. England seemed very much at risk. All around, fear tightened into ugly suspicion.

One day in October 1917, while the Lawrences were not at home, strange visitors appeared. Two uniformed men knocked at the door, opened it, entered the cottage, and nosed through the letters and papers that lay about, some of them in German, looking suspicious—possibly in code. The visitors were policemen, vigilant and menacing. The next morning they brought a message—most urgent—to the outspoken author and his brave German wife. It would change their lives.

CHAPTER 6

Cornered in Cornwall

The message was an official military order. It demanded that the Lawrences vacate Cornwall within three days. They were barred from living near the coast. They had, in fact, been under surveillance for months: local people mistrusted foreigners. Stunned by their eviction, Lawrence cried to Cecil Gray, "I have not the faintest idea what it is all about." Had neighbors noticed the nude bathers at Wicca Pool? Had Frieda carelessly waved her handkerchief near the coastline? Had she spoken German when they shopped in the village of Zennor? Had the Hocking family alerted the authorities? Had Lawrence's bold red beard, his badge of nonconformity, stirred up suspicion? They didn't know.

On 15 October 1917, like escaped criminals, they crept to London, heads bowed. Richard Aldington's wife H.D. (Hilda Doolittle), whose Imagist poems the Lawrences had admired, lent them her one-room flat in Mecklenburgh Square, at the edge of Bloomsbury. They had no money, no protection, no way to earn a living. And so their emotional fraying went on, though in a different direction. Though still in love, the Lawrences recognized that the space between them had unexpectedly widened. They felt as if they had been swept from shore on a small dinghy.

They lived now like gypsies, moving five times in a year: a few weeks in London, a month or two in borrowed cottages, New Year's Eve in the Midlands, rented rooms in the village of Hermitage—Lawrence irritated and unsettled, Frieda accommodating a life pulled out in pieces from a trunk. Refugees in their own country, they were constantly in motion. Lawrence, still pining for America, wanted to find a fresh audience for his feisty, lyrical writing. Like Frieda, he was determined to leave England. To that end he began crafting essays on American literary figures such as Benjamin Franklin, Herman Melville, and Edgar Allan Poe. In his essay on Poe, composed in February 1918, he continued his analysis of disintegrating selves that had characterized Gerald, Gudrun, and Loerke. He sees Poe as closing an epoch, declining into a "strange decomposition" that finds beauty in "the phosphorescence of decay." Poe's addiction to alcohol and drugs manifests his irresistible decline. The early versions of these essays explore the gap between anxious repression and full expression.

Meanwhile, the Lawrences' emotions, which had simmered for so long in Cornwall, went on simmering but under a tighter lid. In the new balance between husband and wife, Lawrence felt mastered, forced to part from an intimate male friend and bound now by the twine of Frieda's greater strength. Their loyalty to each other shifted to a brokered pact, almost certainly unspoken. If Lawrence snuffed out his interest in other men, so would Frieda. Their pact partly explains why Lawrence's novels over the next several years turned episodic, disorganized, and difficult to finish. They reflect his frustration. The subtle arrangement with Frieda suffocated what Lawrence thought he needed in order to plumb his true self as a writer. He needed to express the rising *intensity* of his conflicts.

Once the essays on American literature had absorbed his analytical self, he began to experiment with jeering voices, flippant tones, ironic registers—as in "Don't grumble at me then, gentle reader, and swear at me that [my character Aaron Sisson] wasn't half clever enough to think all these smart things." Satire became Lawrence's mode of dissent. As he changed, his protective shell cracked—possibly, he thought, "cracked for ever." He tried to fit together the broken pieces of himself but only in a few stories could he do so.

Lawrence confronted the now-familiar crisis of choice in two of his best stories, written in December 1918. In "Tickets Please" John Thomas Raynor, like Lawrence himself, has been given an exemption from military service. Wooing in succession a half-dozen female tram workers, John Thomas, their dashing supervisor, plays the field of opportunity and won't choose one to marry. Enraged by his wandering eye, the girls entice him into their lounge. When they lock the door, they plunge forward, beat him with fists and belt, and humiliate him, unleashing a "terrifying lust," not unlike Gudrun's toward the rabbit. Nevertheless, Annie Stone, their leader, remembers his muscled arms and fine kisses; she would be glad if he chose her for marriage yet feels her pride rebel. When John Thomas—to escape from the vindictive women—finally chooses Annie, she feels defeated and betrayed. Choosing mutilates the self.

In "The Blind Man" the central figure is also rejected, but in a surprising way. Maurice Pervin, blinded in Flanders, can no longer serve his country. He feels inadequate and insecure. When his wife's friend Bertie Reid visits him in the barn, Maurice—out of intense curiosity—grips the man's head and face, "to take him in, in the soft, travelling grasp." Yet Bertie, who has never physically connected with another person—always preferring simple friendship—quivers with revulsion. When Maurice's groping exposes Bertie's secret hunger and blasts him with a sensory overload, Bertie collapses. The intimate connection is so raw and immediate that, in his misery, Bertie finds that his "shell is broken." Maurice, however, is empowered. His knowledge of another man's body, though it comes only through his own fingers, will allow him to approach his wife, Isabel, with renewed confidence. They will find strength in their marriage. Lawrence's inner self had spoken: what ennobles one person may cause irreparable harm to another. Pain is a consequence of choice, and it may be, as it was for Lawrence, "a deep and tragic experience."

Equally vexing, for the Lawrences, was the choice of where to live. Having run out of money and cottages to borrow, they accepted the charity of Lawrence's sister, Ada Clarke, a teacher, who found them a place twelve miles from her house in Ripley. It was called Mountain Cottage. Ada was fine featured, lively, and morally strict. She was devoted to her brother and had earned his confidence. Paying the yearly rent of sixty-five pounds, she gave the Lawrences a home in the English Midlands from May 1918 to April 1919. Lawrence would be near his sisters, brother, father, aunts, and old friends in Eastwood. Despite his misgivings, he confessed to Willie Hopkin that he was glad to be near "all the old people," his boyhood haunts only a short drive away. They would provide solace. The war had made him miserable.

Mountain Cottage, a bungalow with a croquet lawn and two fields, sat high above a steep valley. Lawrence did not mind carrying water from the outdoor well, but now he needed his possessions. Once more forced to choose, he asked his Tregerthen landlord to ship his writing desk, a big rug, a case of books; Mrs. Hocking to send clothes, sheets, towels, tablecloths, silverware; and Cecil Gray to box up the dictionaries, atlases, Bible, artists' paints, and typewriter. Since October, Lawrence had done without them. He and Frieda, having stripped away all but essentials, lived now at the edge of an unstable equilibrium. They were still brokering their allegiances.

Half-settled—and a little frayed—they welcomed visitors for weeks at a time. In relative peace the happy summer days drifted by. Enid Hopkin, the daughter of Lawrence's Eastwood friends Willie and Sallie, recalled a visit to Mountain Cottage in June 1918. For the evening's entertainment, visitors gathered around Frieda's piano to sing English folk songs: "And I remember [Enid wrote] the group around the piano in the candlelight, Frieda singing with a cigarette hanging out of the corner of her mouth. And [sometimes] Frieda [...] would strike wrong notes. After several of these Lawrence would lose his temper and scream at her, Frieda would scream back. [...] The whole scene was very dramatic, as we stood in mid-chorus. [...] Suddenly it was all over, and Frieda would settle down and go back to playing, and we would all start to sing again." The evening's entertainment featured this small spat. It shows how quickly Lawrence and Frieda sparred over a trifle. Frieda cared little for precision or discipline; the ash from her cigarette probably drifted over the piano keys. She might "scream back" to defend herself—and appear rude—but Lawrence admired her even as he scolded. Later that year (she wrote), when "Lawrence's soul seem[ed] one big curse," he jeered at her perfumed cigarettes, mocking her addiction. The "curse" of his soul sometimes ensnared her too. A chafing of temperaments now defined the Lawrences' marriage.

By June 1918, although America had joined the war and boosted the Allies' military power, hardships continued. Rationing of bread had been imposed in 1917, and early in 1918 meat, sugar, and butter were added; Lawrence had welcomed a gift of butter from Beatrice Campbell as "a great kindness, for I sicken at margarine." In March the Germans had pushed back the front line, gaining supremacy, and used railway guns to shell Paris with relentless success. In all, the loss of life was horrific—close to 700,000 dead in Britain alone. Lawrence's first cousin Hedley Berry had been killed in October 1917. Earlier, Rupert Brooke, a friend of the Lawrences, had died on his way to Gallipoli. When David Lloyd George had stepped up recruiting of British civilians, Lawrence himself had been examined—in July 1916 (rejected), in June 1917 (grade C3), and again in September 1918 (grade 3, sedentary work). Ada's husband, Eddie Clarke, had served in the marines, and Lawrence's sister Emily's husband, a soldier, had been in hospital. "It was," Lawrence judged, "a vile sick winter for us all." The past offered no encouragement, the future no appeal.

Occasionally, there was a respite. In October 1918, when Lawrence came to London to visit Katherine Mansfield, who was dying of tuberculosis, she was glad to see him and wrote to a friend: "He was just his old merry, rich self, laughing, describing things, giving you pictures, full of enthusiasm and joy in a future where we were all 'vagabonds' – we simply did not talk about people. We kept to things like nuts and cowslips and fires in woods, and his black self was not." Finding her fearfully ill, he hid his dark side.

Elsewhere the winds of war were shifting. As American soldiers poured into Europe, German morale crumbled. In September, General Erich Ludendorff, chief strategist of the German war effort, demanded a cease-fire. In October, President Woodrow Wilson laid out the conditions for a truce. On 11 November 1918 the armistice, at last signed, opened the door to hope and recovery. All over the world rejoicing followed.

"I long to begin life afresh, in a new country," Lawrence wrote to Harriet Monroe, the American editor of *Poetry*. Given the stress of war and illness and the burden of Ada's charity, it is no surprise that the emotional fraying of the Lawrences' marriage continued. In January 1919 an outbreak of worldwide influenza swept through the Midlands. Before long, Lawrence succumbed, feeling so sick he was frightened. "I have been miserably ill with the Flu and its complications," he told Cynthia Asquith in March. For a month he could not leave his bed. He could barely eat, barely sit up, barely converse.

Frictions now intensified. On 14 March, Lawrence, assessing the damages of illness, wrote bitterly to Kotelianksy: "I am not going to be left to

Frieda's tender mercies until I am well again. She really is a devil – and I feel as if I would part from her for ever – let her go alone to Germany, while I take another road. [. . .] I really could leave her now, without a pang, I believe." In this outburst to Koteliansky, who had long disliked Frieda and thought her disrespectful, Lawrence's animus comes as no surprise. It measures the weariness of being sick as well as the couple's isolation. Tolerance was in short supply. Not a single letter from Frieda survives from March through June 1919.

Ada, alarmed at her brother's plunge into illness, insisted that he stay with her in Ripley. She had helped care for him earlier, in 1911, when he suffered from double pneumonia. Too sick to argue, he acquiesced and left Mountain Cottage. But a proud, headstrong woman like Frieda believed that Lawrence had engaged in sabotage—and did not hide her anger. If she had earlier "screamed" at Lawrence, she would not have spared Ada, whose interference she fought but could not subdue. Worse, unable even to take walks till April, Lawrence sadly realized that he could not make the trip to Germany. Frieda was therefore caught between her obligation to Ada, who quietly paid the rent and often provided food, and her own assertive independence, which directed her toward Germany. The winter had been bitterly cold, Lawrence's soul was still a curse, and the marriage had endured exceptional stress. Frieda's buoyancy and good spirits collapsed but not into inertia.

Eager to escape Mountain Cottage, the Lawrences left in April 1919 for Chapel Farm Cottage, to which they had often repaired. Located in the village of Hermitage, seventy-five miles west of London, the cottage belonged to his beloved friend Dollie Radford and lay hidden in a soft, inviting woods, where spring had arrived. Partly because the Lawrences were by now slowly regaining their vitality, they were also invited to a farm nearby, managed by two young cousins, Cecily Lambert and Violet Monk. The Lawrences enlivened the long evenings by painting tin boxes and organizing the charades they had always loved. In August, when asked to stay longer, Frieda requested separate bedrooms, not wanting, she said, "to be too much married." The words *too much married* announced the steep price of Frieda's arrogance.

Lambert reported an incident that exposes the sad alterations in the Lawrences' marriage. Irritated by a broken sewing machine, Lawrence lambasted Frieda's indolence, "saying she was lazy and useless and sat around while we did all the work. He then ordered her to clean our kitchen floor. [. . .] To our amazement she burst into tears and proceeded to work on it, [. . .] bitterly resentful at having to do such a menial task quite beneath the daughter of a baron, at the same time hurling every insult she could conjure up at D.H."

The couple's allegiance falls victim to diatribe. Lawrence, often ill, had wearied of waiting on Frieda, and she had wearied of his bullying. Together they descended to a new level of contempt. Emotionally, they had been swept apart. No one reports seeing them hugging or holding hands or kissing. To be sure, it was harder now to be in love. Still, all around them, even well-disposed friends must have wondered about the couple's future. What would keep them together within love's new limits?

CHAPTER 7

A Fresh Start in Italy

The Lawrences, distressed and humiliated by their displacements while the war dragged on, were determined to start anew. They wanted to leave England, though they did not apply for their passports until August 1919. Their passport photos show how they had aged. Frieda is heavier, her handsome face now strained, and her suit, cut too large, gives her a hand-me-down look. Lawrence's face has collected long lines, his eyes are dark and sad, his tweed coat hangs loosely, yet his well-trimmed beard and hair show no gray. He looks like a distinguished writer. Their years of being marginalized were passing. With fresh resolve, Lawrence was starting over, aiming toward America, his inspiration coming from his essays on classic American writers. Though still angry and bitter, he was ready to end his long wartime hibernation. He would now, unfurling himself, find new directions.

When the Lawrences left England, they left separately. Frieda went to Germany on 15 October. For months she had been ready for new adventures, even if Germany, war torn and destitute, would not be the happy place she remembered. Food was severely rationed—five pounds of potatoes and a half-pound of meat a week. Her family was "very poor, very hungry," she told Cynthia Asquith. Lawrence, however, hesitated before leaving. He was trying now to reposition himself as a writer and as a man. At first that meant going south—where he had gone before, away from the petty constraints of Eastwood and Croydon. In Italy he had discovered a rich creative ferment at Lake Garda and Fiascherino.

D. H. Lawrence, passport photo, 1919 (Gernsheim Collection, Harry Ransom Center)

Frieda Lawrence, passport photo, 1919 (Gernsheim Collection, Harry Ransom Center)

In wartime England, by contrast, he felt isolated and emptied of resolve by having no one to write for. "I must get out of this country as soon as possible," he said to Koteliansky, and go where he would be valued. Now he would sever his ties to the past, selling even his books. He would fashion a new identity and a richer life.

Before he left, however, he needed to settle publication of two books that reflected years of hard work. Much revised since he finished it, in 1916, *Women in Love* at last found a pair of publishers—Thomas Seltzer in America (who advanced him fifty pounds) and Martin Secker in England; his essays on classic American literature would, he hoped, go to Benjamin Huebsch in America. All three publishers were developing strong lists of bold young authors. Seltzer and Secker would eventually publish many of Lawrence's books.

Before Frieda left for Germany, Lawrence had decided to go to Italy— "for [my] health," he explained to Huebsch in September—and spend the winter with fellow writer Compton Mackenzie on the small island of Capri, not far from Naples. America now seemed too distant, lonely, and expensive, whereas he might easily live in Italy. Its permissive culture also meant freedom. Like the hero of *Aaron's Rod,* the novel he had recently started, Lawrence embraced new forms of friendship. Where they would lead he did not know. Like Frieda, he was ready for adventures. Constraints wearied him.

He now welcomed the friendship of others who were also in transit. He and Frieda had briefly borrowed a cottage in the village of Pangbourne (near Hermitage) that belonged to a woman named Rosalind Baynes. Her husband, Godwin, angry at her admission of adultery, was divorcing her. Toward her three beguiling daughters, Lawrence naturally felt protective and had made them sheepskin coats. Rosalind was Frieda's opposite—demure, useful, and vulnerable. Lawrence hoped that on his way to Capri, he could help Rosalind settle in Italy while her divorce worked its way through the courts. He might, he thought, also stop in Florence. He might visit the kind of openly gay man he had not earlier preferred: untrodden paths were there to be explored.

Before catching his train on 14 November 1919, he stopped to see his friends S. S. Koteliansky and Richard Aldington in London. Both recorded their impressions. Koteliansky wrote to Katherine Mansfield, "When Lawrence was here before going to Italy he was not like his best." Aldington found him discordant and rancorous, in a "state of animosity"; he seemed diffident about Frieda. Uprooted, he was testing every bond that had held him. And Frieda? Chained to the charity of others, she had been held in a hostile country for many months. She now demanded freedom. Both wanted a separateness that had been denied them.

So why did the Lawrences stay together? There were no children, no possessions to divide, no community of friends to repair the fraying marriage, no pattern of forbearance and respect to ease the marital stress. Yet they stayed together, functioning like two meshed gears spinning in opposite directions toward a common goal of discovery and fulfillment. Frieda had been a moving force toward expression. For years she had pulled and prodded Lawrence into flower, had given him confidence, had become a muse for his genius. Both believed that she inspired him.

Beyond this creative balance, the Lawrences shared a view of life that balanced them. Fixed in "oppositional" togetherness, they felt a strong disdain for privilege and luxury, which (they thought) led to spiritual emptiness. They defined success not in having *things* but in asserting a set of shared values—communing with nature, designing handmade gifts, showing independence, sparking lively conversation, cultivating family ties, and scoffing at middle-class conventions. When Lawrence's prose captured the "fit" of their personalities, he celebrated their closeness *and* their friction. Even though he was now in danger of turning away from women, he and Frieda had developed a love deeper than anyone realized. They were attached without being bound.

Change arrived abruptly. Coming into Italy, Lawrence awakened from his bitter paralysis and animosity. He had carefully considered his decision to start over in a new country. On his journey he noticed stands of short, shimmering poplars, saw teams of oxen plowing the fallow fields, and witnessed "lovely lovely sun and sea" and a sky rising like a rainbow into "a brilliant red line." Northern Italy fascinated him, made him feel the stirrings of renewal. The high skies and sweeping plains allowed him to imagine that the walls of England had crumbled. Far from being conservative or puritanical, the Italians were casual, nonchalant, and generous. "Truly, Italy is pleasant to live in," he asserted. Reaching Florence on 15 November, Lawrence thought he had found an appealing place, even if it was not on the sea. "I like it. I've got a really sunny room over the Arno, there is good wine," he told novelist Catherine Carswell a week later, "and there is a nice carelessness [in Italy]."

In Florence he also had a taste of the gay expatriate community. Welcoming him to the city of high culture were two charming men—a couple—who had found him a decent room in the Pensione Balestra, a second-tier hotel on the Arno River. The burly older man was Norman Douglas, a literary acquaintance since 1913, now aged fifty, who had long ago married and had two grown sons. Douglas's boyfriend was the pink-faced, mincing Maurice Magnus, aged forty-three, who had also been married and who described himself as "a very sexual person." Magnus was the kind of man Lawrence had never met, a man who deferentially accommodated Douglas—running to the hotel kitchen to insist that the turkey be stuffed with chestnuts, then selecting the choicest bits for his friend.

Douglas and Magnus were lively, loud, witty whiskey drinkers, reveling in the potent vibrancy of Italy. Around them they had collected a group of men who included Oscar Wilde's friend Reginald Turner. Lawrence's earlier fear of gay men collapsed into wary tolerance and then mild affection mixed with surprise. His attraction to men having provided him with few satisfactions, his own search for "bisexual types," he said later, had ended. Instead, even if emotionally unfulfilled, he now depended on the security and support that Frieda promised. He soon yearned for her stabilizing presence. She was his anchor in the sea of new possibilities.

When she arrived, on 3 December 1919, Lawrence immediately took her for a nighttime drive to see the impressive architecture of Florence: "We went in an open carriage [she wrote], I saw the pale crouching Duomo, and in the thick moonmist the Giotto tower disappeared at the top into the sky. [. . .] We went along the Lungarno, we passed the Ponte Vecchio, in that moonlight night, and ever since Florence is the most beautiful town to me." Its beauty lingered long in Frieda's mind. To Lawrence's sister Ada, Frieda wrote, "How you would revel to look at the jewellery, so beautiful and cheap." But the Lawrences remained in Florence for only a week, then went south, to be situated again on the Mediterranean, a source of endless wonder and revitalizing power. Lawrence loved looking at the sea, the sun sprinkling it with flecks of mirrored gold, the waves rolling rhythmically in the wind. The sea provided forgetfulness and hope, escape and peace. "I feel one *must* go south," he told Rosalind Baynes.

In their adventures through Italy, the Lawrences went first to Rome, which they found crowded and expensive (he despised "the crush and the swindle"), then into the mountains south of Rome to look over a hideaway for Rosalind Baynes; thence to Naples and across the bay to Capri, famous for its rugged coastline and gorgeous views. Capped with mountains and ringed with cliff-hanging roads and tiny villages, Capri was, Lawrence thought, "extremely beautiful." They rode the funicular up to the main square and found a two-room apartment high up in a palazzo near Morgano's Café. From their balconies they could see ships crawling into the bay, Vesuvius smoking in the distance, and, bustling below, the cosmopolitan town smaller even than Lawrence's Eastwood. They could bathe in the sea, a steep mile down, or dine with Compton Mackenzie—elegant, clever, and rich—at his fine villa in nearby Marina Piccola. Mackenzie made the winter days "lively and jolly," Lawrence reported. In early January, Frieda wrote: "We had a high time on New Year's eve, there's a big famous cafe near us where all the world goes, Italians, Russians, Americans, short haired women, long haired men, rich, poor, and then the local people came with a band and danced the Tarantella." Tolerant and genial by nature, Frieda was much amused by the island's diversity, whereas Lawrence denigrated the same evening's "high time." He bashed Mackenzie's swaggering crowd as actors trying "to look wine and womenish" but exposing, instead, "an excruciating selfconscious effort." For Lawrence pretense demanded satire. He was not amused.

Still, Lawrence's letters blaze with descriptions of Capri's exotic island life—the babble of languages, the fields of broad beans, the sudden storms that sent the sea writhing, the magnificent red dawn edging onto the horizon. Both Lawrence and Frieda liked the place immensely; Lawrence called it "one of the most wonderful places in the world." They could visit nearby villas or catch the bright butterflies on the south side of the island. On 10 January Lawrence walked to one of the highest peaks on the island, a hard climb of two hours that eventually yielded a fabulous view to the other islands in the distance and to the restless sea below.

Once Lawrence had sampled all the touristy things on Capri, he tired of it. He had loved the isolation and simplicity of Higher Tregerthen on the Atlantic Coast. After touring around Italy, he knew that he would want his own house farther south. He preferred more space, more quiet, more greenery, less of the gossip that the Lawrences' English friend Mary Cannan delivered daily as if it were the mail. His raw energy festered inside him. He was ready to work. In stories and novels, in poems and reminiscences, he wanted to filter Italy through his pure imagination.

With a Baedeker travel guide in hand, he took a boat farther south to a bigger island—to Sicily, at the southern tip of Italy, whose sunny warmth pulled him like a magnet. The Greek and Roman ruins in tiny Taormina, high above the eastern coast, appealed to him. They linked him to a past of beauty and accomplishment. Unlike Capri, Sicily offered "more space, more air, more green and succulent herbage," he told a friend. It seemed more vital and alive. In Taormina he might live again by the sea, in a house with a garden, and, with Frieda at his side, start to write again. He needed money. Maybe here "the crumpled wings of [his] soul" could unfurl and find the liberation he had long desired.

CHAPTER 8

Intoxicated and Alone

The liberation Lawrence desired—so long in coming—arrived in several forms: a distant location, an urge to write in unfamiliar modes, and new friendships that stirred him with their intoxicating presence. His excitement was infectious but also alarming.

High above the sea, at the crest of a long slope of almond trees, Lawrence found the house he had imagined. An easy walk brought him to the ancient village of Taormina. On 3 March 1920, for only two thousand lire, or thirty-two pounds, per year, he rented the top two floors of Fontana Vecchia ("old fountain" in Italian). Its grand terraces looked far over the Ionian Sea. To the left ran the famous straits of Messina. Behind the house opened a big garden, shaded with almond and carob trees and festooned with scented flowers.

"It is really lovely," Lawrence told Amy Lowell. Far above, Sicilian peasants herded their goats up and down the lane or carried the wheat for threshing. These immemorial rural rhythms were like salve on Lawrence's memories of Europe and a tonic for his restlessness. Unshackled, he prized the freedom and openness that he found. A few days later, Frieda arrived, immediately captivated. "We love this place very much," she wrote. "Oh," Lawrence added, "so much better than Capri." At the southern edge of Europe, he could come alive.

Once again Italy proved fascinating. The hot sun sweetened the Lawrences' tempers so that cross words were rare. The lush surroundings soothed them. They rose at dawn and relished toast and tea on the sunny terrace. They sometimes walked ten minutes into Taormina village, had lunch with Mary Cannan at the Bristol Hotel, looked over the lace and embroidered fabrics that the local women sold on the streets. Sometimes they walked half an hour down to swim in the invigorating sea, then scrambled back up. In their little blue kitchen, they cooked their meals, mostly seasonal fruits and vegetables; the cool interiors of Fontana Vecchia were a comfort. Outdoors, when cloud masses cooled the island, the Lawrences might trek past the almond trees in search of the first green figs. In the evenings they sat on their terrace, waiting for the golden twilight, listening to Mary's tales of her marriage to J. M. Barrie (creator of Peter Pan) or savoring the letters that the slow Italian post delivered in bundles. These were beautiful days of sun, warmth, hospitality, and renewed appetite. "It is very lovely here," Lawrence told Koteliansky. "I feel I shall never come north again." Peace reigned.

After they had settled in, Lawrence began writing freely, experimentally, and sometimes brilliantly. He excelled in every genre—poetry, stories, letters, memoir, novellas, novels, plays. One day in July, sauntering to the old fountain for water, he observed a brown-and-yellow snake drinking alone, "like a guest." The snake

> sipped with his straight mouth,
> Softly drank through his straight gums, into his slack long body,
> Silently.

Instead of killing it, as he thought of doing, he indulged it. He was fascinated as it slithered into its black hole. Like Lawrence, the snake, living "in exile," claims recognition and respect. What Lawrence would once have denied—the snake's creaturely integrity—he now welcomed. The snake offers a message: that all creatures, even the spurned, are "lords / Of life." In this, his most famous poem, Lawrence's compassion for others awakens. He puts himself at risk. He discards petty prejudice in order to embrace what was once unconventional or even forbidden.

In such ways Lawrence was reaching out in new directions—to friends like Rosalind Baynes, whom he hoped to meet "about end of August"; to the gay enclave in Florence; and even to the mincing, parasitic Maurice Magnus, unlucky again, who crept like a thief onto the terrace of Fontana

Vecchia, there—eyes lifted—to beg for money. Astonished and ashamed, Lawrence recorded his uneasy feelings:

> "I came here," he [Magnus] said, "thinking you would help me. What am I to do, if you won't? I shouldn't have come to Taormina at all, save for you. Don't be unkind to me – don't speak so coldly to me – " He put his hand on my arm, and looked up at me with tears swimming in his eyes. Then he turned aside his face, overcome with tears. I looked away at the Ionian sea, feeling my blood turn to ice and the sea go black. I loathe scenes such as this.

Lawrence may have loathed such scenes, but, recognizing some sort of kinship to the suffering man, he paid Magnus's hotel bill at the extravagant San Domenico Hotel. Like Frieda, he hoped he would never see Magnus again.

Soon the sweltering July heat stifled the Lawrences and forced them to depart. Lawrence wrote to Hilda Brown, a child he had tutored: "It has been hot blazing sun for week after week, day after day, and so hot lately it was too much. I have lived for weeks in a pair of pyjamas and nothing else—barefoot: and even then too hot. [. . .] Everywhere is burnt dry, the trees have shed nearly all their leaves, it is autumn. [. . .] The grapes are just about ripe." Desperate for a cooler place, they left Taormina on 2 August. Frieda went to Germany to see her mother; Lawrence went to Como, camping with friends along the Italian lakes, then traveled in September to Florence, to see Rosalind Baynes, warm and inviting and demure, in Fiesole nearby. She rented one villa, he rented another down below, in San Gervasio.

There he celebrated his thirty-fifth birthday. He wrote twice about the exhilarating time he spent with Rosalind, once in poems about fruits, once in *Aaron's Rod,* the novel he finished a year later. Both versions, though expertly coded, tell the same story.

All during August, Lawrence likely thought about Rosalind, six years his junior, in her stately Villa Belvedere. Alone in San Gervasio, he met her often in the three weeks he stayed at the ancient Villa Canovaia, which had once been hers. Refined and artistic but also an intrepid adventurer, Rosalind was the kind of sympathetic, nurturing mother who read Dickens to her daughters, played operatic arias on the piano, and sailed on Lake Garda with the girls. Long after he died, Rosalind described their walks and the Sunday suppers they had cooked. After a special birthday supper on 11 September, they talked intimately, he claiming that "most people [he] can hardly bear to come near, far less make love with." He hated, he said, "the so-called Love – that most indecent kind of egoism." But when he proposed "a sex time together," Rosalind swooned. Two evenings later, at the Belvedere, they held hands in the cover of darkness—"And so to bed," she concluded, leaving to our imagination all but a brief kiss.

Later, Lawrence wrote wistfully, "Wonder where we'll meet next." But when they could have met again, he was traveling with Frieda. The affair, scented with autumn, was already over. Its effect on Lawrence was immediate and powerful. What Rosalind did not put into her narrative, Lawrence put into his September poems about fruits. After each one, he daringly printed "San Gervasio." In part these poems are studies in anatomy. "Peach" reveals a fruit wrinkled with secrets, its groove oddly like an "incision," associated with pain. The speaker rediscovers the beauty and mystery of female genitalia. "Pomegranate" peeks "within the fissure" and, intoxicated, finds it "so lovely [. . .] within the crack." In lines of equal daring, "Fig" has a secret place where "you see through the fissure the scarlet" and delight in the "wonderful moist conductivity towards the centre." Whereas, mesmerized, the speaker had earlier watched the snake wriggle "into [his] horrid black hole," here he discovers a final distressing secret—that women have *burst into affirmation.* In the name of "Love," they have put their sexuality onto a platform of showy assertion and display. They have cheapened their wares with "rottenness."

Then a stunning shift. In "Medlars and Sorb-Apples" Lawrence finds the epiphany of adultery. He crystallizes what his mating with Rosalind had meant, and he reveals how shattering is his hunger for, and satiation by, a woman not his wife. Here is the essence:

A kiss, and a spasm of farewell, a moment's orgasm of rupture
Then along the damp road alone, till the next turning.

The orgasm leads not to shame or regret, or even to the sweetness of ebbing sensation, but to separation and isolation:

> And there, a new partner, a new parting, a new unfusing into twain,
> A new gasp of further isolation,
> A new intoxication of loneliness.

The intoxication hides his own cruel separation. Even for a man of his sensitivity, love does not follow lust. For Lawrence the act of supreme human connection is an act of disconnection, of a "final loneliness." Frieda hated this book of poems, which Lawrence published as *Birds, Beasts and Flowers*. She may have guessed the truth, though in her autobiography she acknowledges that "he guarded his privacy ferociously." Rosalind's discreet revelation did not appear until long after Frieda's death. Whatever the case, it is doubtful that Frieda would have minded much. It is Lawrence who minded.

He minded enough to rewrite the Rosalind affair in *Aaron's Rod*. In this novel Aaron, separated from his antagonistic English wife, feels intoxicated by and then makes love to a marchesa in Florence, just three miles from Lawrence's own San Gervasio. After his orgasm, however, Aaron feels blasted, "as if some flame [. . .] had gone through him and withered his vital tissues. [. . .] His brain felt withered, his mind [. . .] scorched now and sightless." He feels damaged, then disillusioned. Far from showing appreciation or gratitude for this gift of orgasm, Aaron's hostile response is so extreme that Lawrence had no doubt felt similarly violated. In reaching outside the boundaries of his marriage, he felt not so much rejected, as he had with Murry and Hocking, as—now—unfulfilled and cheated. The scorching "flame" had cleansed him of the notion that a married woman might satisfy his loneliness. He had tested one limit of response. Nothing but marriage had really satisfied Lawrence, and even it had yielded deep bitterness. Frieda's autobiography and letters seldom comment on the state of their marriage at this time. The omission suggests that she, married once before, expected less than he, defined loyalty more loosely, and was therefore less apt to be dissatisfied. She regarded a single sexual liaison as relatively unimportant.

From Florence, Lawrence left Rosalind to assess their affair for himself; went to Venice; met Frieda; and on 18 October returned with her to Fontana Vecchia, relieved to be at home again in Sicily. He was glad to recover what he called the "lifted-upness" of Fontana Vecchia. Frieda found the place "beautiful after the rain and [already in October] like spring." She was overjoyed that she and Lawrence were once more together. She wrote to Sally Hopkin in December: "I wish you could come and have breakfast on the terrace when the sun has just risen opposite us out of the sea. [. . .] There is Etna's snow quite near." And all around them, flowers perfumed the air.

Some of this marital joy motivated the brief trip the Lawrences made in January 1921. They traveled from Sicily to the island of Sardinia, two hundred miles northwest. The account of the trip became the book *Sea and Sardinia*. Frieda was exhilarated by the island's potential. (Had Sardinia been at all suitable, it might have become their next home.) At once Lawrence captured in writing—with exceptional verve and fidelity—the island's distinctive vistas; the morning sky and sea "parting like an oyster shell"; the insouciant Italian people they met, casual and affectionate, pouring themselves over each other like "melted butter over parsnips"; the items they saw for sale—cat fur, dangling "like pressed leaves"; but also, everywhere, the callous Italian grab for money.

Frugal travelers by necessity, the Lawrences carried their provisions in a knapsack—utensils, aluminum saucepan, tiny stove, bread and butter. They made quite a sight. Lawrence was mostly quiet but observed all with a jaded eye, Frieda (he slyly calls her "q-b," or Queen Bee) easy and talkative but brooking no disrespect, as Lawrence revealed when, in Palermo, three girls laughed at them. "Suddenly I am aware of the q-b darting past me like a storm. Suddenly I see her pouncing on three giggling young hussies. [. . .] 'Did you want something? Have you something to say?'" she demanded. Their "jeering insolence" crushed, they cower and slink away. As the narrative continues, town by town, it is clear that Lawrence and Frieda have formed an alliance, a partnership; they are brave soldiers used to the discomforts and economies of budget travel.

In *Sea and Sardinia* their marriage shows few hints of strain. Instead, Lawrence captures his many irritations with a pungent humor that could only arise from a comfortably married man. The Lawrences' mutual dependence and solidarity are palpable—in their shared dislike of "pears with wooden hearts," a squalid inn roaring "with violent, crude male life," a drunken man taunting a dog with hunks of bread, Lawrence usually *containing* Frieda's natural exuberance. In truth, however, she is no longer Woman on a pedestal, honored (as she once was) by the creative brilliance of her partner, but a wife at the edge of a marriage, firm and forceful and in the narrative given a thin voice. Despite her energy and passion, Lawrence has redefined their marriage as a form of accommodation. The Lawrences' affection has mellowed into tolerance and mutual understanding.

Still, Lawrence was drifting artistically. His creative sails had unfurled in strange ways. He had started a novel called "Mr. Noon," about a British science teacher who impregnates a girl and then loses his job because a complaint comes to the school's principal. Despite Lawrence's deft, satiric narration, the material isn't funny. He lost interest and didn't finish the book. The surprise is that his manuscript disappeared for fifty years (was it stolen?), then came up for auction in 1972, was purchased by the University of Texas at Austin, and was published in 1984.

Only a few weeks after their trip to Sardinia, the Lawrences, though loving their terrace breezes, were also looking far out over the Ionian Sea, feeling disenchanted with Taormina, tired of its pretentious foreigners, tired of their tea parties, tired of the massive winter rains. They were looking for a land far away. Even the southern tip of Europe was not far enough. Although Benjamin Huebsch, the American publisher of several of Lawrence's books, would warn Lawrence, *"Dort wo Du nicht bist, dort ist das Glück"* (Where you are not, there is happiness), Lawrence would ignore such sage advice. He and Frieda determined to go where they had dreamed of going in 1915, when, instead, they had fled to Cornwall in response to the horrors of war and the suppression of *The Rainbow*.

By 1921 Lawrence believed he was strong enough to go to America. There he would make a new beginning—and find a new public for his work. Full of hope, he welcomed the gamble. "I am very thrilled at the thought of starting for America," Frieda wrote to Robert Mountsier, an acerbic, well-educated man who, having a doctorate from Columbia University, had agreed to become Lawrence's American agent. "We have both had enough of Europe," she added. Lawrence agreed: "I should really like to come to America." There he might find vital raw material.

Needing a place to live, he had learned from Carlota Thrasher, an American widow he had met in Florence, that he could use her ninety-acre farm in Connecticut, two hours from Boston; it had picturesque streams and woods and pastures, but it had all gone wild. "If ever you get a chance and an inclination," Lawrence urged Mountsier, "do go and look at Thrasher's farm." Lawrence was eager to settle there; Frieda, too, was infatuated with the farm—as their first big step toward renewal. At Lawrence's expense, Mountsier drove from New York City to Connecticut to evaluate. "Railroad and trolley fares, hotel room and Ford car on two days' trip to Thrasher's Farm," he explained. He billed Lawrence $22.75 for his expenses. But when Mountsier cabled on 22 March, "*[Come] together [–] hurry [–] buy farm [–] cost [to] repair thrashers impossible*," the Lawrences understood that *if* they had hurried and brought along a young Sicilian couple to help them, they could have planted fruit bushes and acres of peach trees—and become self-sufficient farmers. It would have been a huge step. Lawrence was, he said, terrified of the cost. How could he *buy* the farm? The yearly rental of Fontana Vecchia cost only one hundred dollars.

Suddenly he was unable, he said, to "find my direction." The farming gamble might be very costly. He was worried about money. Frieda had none, and he had published few stories and no books with large sales. He considered alternatives. He might, he said, track down a ship, or even a cargo boat, to make the trip economically. As he was coming unstuck from Europe, looking for an escape from his current life, he was grasping at sails. Now unmoored, he welcomed any possibility. "I itch to go away," he told Koteliansky. He had tired of Sicily but shrank from borrowing money for travel. "This is a sort of crisis for me," he confided to Mountsier; he felt caught now between the desire to travel and the need to economize.

Then Frieda's mother, now aged seventy, suffered a mild heart attack, though Lawrence believed the telegram was "a trick." Nonetheless, Frieda left at once for Germany. A few weeks later she informed Lawrence that she would probably stay all summer, as she often had while married to Ernest Weekley. "With one thing and another," he told Mary Cannan, "I can't manage my plan." The promise of America was gone. Defeated and despairing, Lawrence now had to decide if he would follow Frieda to Germany? or go somewhere else? He was a map of indecision.

CHAPTER 9

Crossing the Seas

The prospect of a long, scorching summer in Taormina killed Lawrence's desire to stay at Fontana Vecchia. Despite its privacy and sweeping views, and despite the way it had empowered his imagination, he missed Frieda. He had gotten used to her cheerful cooperation and exuberant affection. She passed over his prickly irritations and redirected his outbursts. If his books-in-progress had bubbled out of him like a spring, he might have stayed to finish them. They did not. His unfinished novel "Aaron's Rod" would barely budge, and "Mr. Noon" was stuck, too, and would be abandoned. Lawrence had cut his ties to Europe without a full stock of fresh experience to stoke his imagination. By always escaping from his past, he was forced to invent the future. Every tomorrow became a challenge, every week a hurdle. "I [. . .] mustn't look back," he told Frieda's mother, who was recovering her health in Germany. He needed direction. At Fontana Vecchia he sat all alone in the rain, so far off his spiritual course that he even considered going to Palestine and searching there for sudden inspiration.

Though discouraged, he did not sit long. He would, after all, go north to Germany, then return to Frieda's stabilizing presence. In April 1921 he wandered slowly to Palermo, Capri, Rome, and then Florence before he embarked on a difficult journey to Germany, where he hoped he would be "joining Frieda" in Baden-Baden. He had sufficient distance from her to make him long for her again. He also longed (as she did) to discover a culture whose vital impulses had not yet been shackled. While visiting Capri, he had met a cultured American couple—they were Frieda's age—named Earl and Achsah Brewster. Their immense calm stirred his interest. Hidden in a kink of fate was a surprising fact: ten years earlier the Brewsters had lived at Fontana Vecchia. The house connected the two families. Now it was the Brewsters, not Frieda, who gave Lawrence the clue to his future. The call of America, almost irresistible in 1915, was now revived but with a strange twist.

Serene, straitlaced, and thoughtful, the Brewsters were very different from the Lawrences' other friends—from the exacting Koteliansky, the gossipy Mary Cannan, the salty-tongued Norman Douglas, the parasitic Maurice Magnus, the meticulous Robert Mountsier. The Brewsters were painters, living on a small inheritance, whose spiritual life was their prized possession. They lived for their art, which had flowered triumphantly in Italy. They painted animals, Aphrodite, the Crucifixion, the Madonna, the Buddha—and their young daughter, Harwood, who traveled with them. To Lawrence the Brewsters were noble and generous. They calmed rather than stoked his intensity. Yet with them he was also witty and spontaneous; he told anecdotes (Earl remembered) "with a light tactful touch." Deeply reverent, Earl had won Lawrence's respect. He drew out Lawrence's humanity as no one else did. And Achsah later won Frieda's admiration. Frieda wrote to their daughter, Harwood Brewster, in 1945: "[S]he was quite the best woman I ever knew – There was not a particle of vice in her."

In Germany the extended visit from Frieda and then Lawrence had benefited everyone: Anna von Richthofen mended, and Lawrence worked in the woods not far from her retirement home, at last completing "Aaron's Rod." The novel's ending leaves Aaron, like Lawrence when he was alone in Italy, full of indecision, awaiting the future and wondering what to do. Aaron's friend Rawdon Lilly tries to help him distinguish between passion and power. Both are viable, but neither occupies Aaron's soul. He must now ponder Lilly's conclusion: "Your soul inside you is your only Godhead." At the end Aaron figuratively possesses a boat but no oars.

With the book finally finished, Lawrence and Frieda hiked through the Black Forest, ten or fifteen miles a day, then crossed Lake Constance and took a train to Innsbruck. This time, however, their adventure—unlike the

The Brewsters and (*lower left*) Dorothy Brett, c. 1926
(Gernsheim Collection, Harry Ransom Center)

extraordinary trek in 1912—had lost its glamour. Accompanied partway by his humorless agent, Robert Mountsier, they eventually reached the Austrian villa of Frieda's chic younger sister, Johanna; her husband, Max von Schreibershofen, an army officer; and their two children, Hadu and Anita, who were almost grown. The villa was located on a small lake near Salzburg. The family ménage often went bathing, boating, and riding in a pony trap. On 29 July they all visited a glacier that offered Lawrence an exotic setting for a novella he called "The Captain's Doll." This story sketches a portrait of the Lawrences' marriage from the perspective of a middle-aged man like Lawrence, vital but disillusioned, who must start his life over.

The story charts his progress, but it also embraces a new attitude to love and loyalty. After the affair with Rosalind Baynes, Lawrence developed an aversion to romantic love. In June he had urged fellow novelist Evelyn Scott to cast off "love" and embrace "power." "Why not," he urged, "spit in the eye of love?" That is the new story's aim. Alexander Hepburn, an army captain who has left his wife in Scotland, pursues an unmarried woman named Hannele, a penniless Austrian countess, reduced after the war to making and selling dolls (including one of Hepburn). But theirs is no simple courtship. The forsaken wife suddenly appears in Germany, parading her foolish vanity (she's a friendly caricature of Mary Cannan). Before she can rescue her renegade husband from Hannele's grasp, she falls from a hotel window and dies.

Unexpectedly, the captain goes into mourning. He shrinks from Hannele, his emotions paralyzed. When he considers his willing subservience to his wife, he "shudder[s]" to think of enduring "such love again," for in his marriage he had become just a "doll," pleasing his wife. He would not repeat the experience. His decision leaves him—as it did Lawrence—emotionally stranded between revulsion and need. He hated love but wanted what loyalty might offer. It was a new feeling.

Months later, when the Captain meets Hannele again near her lakeside villa, he realizes that she is the woman he wants and needs. She is attractive, secure, independent, and outspoken. Then Lawrence does a strange thing: he uses their journey to a glacier to test their relationship. Stage by stage, from boat to automobile to glacier, their journey exposes their essential selves, uncovering the silent hostility they had been hiding from each other:

> She turned with a flash, and the high strident sound of the mountain [rang] in her voice.
> "If you don't like [the glacier]," she said, rather jeering, "why ever did you come?"
> "I had to try," he said.
> "And if you don't like it," she said, "why should you try to spoil it for me?"
> "I hate it," he answered.

Against this stream of rising antagonism, Hannele realizes that Hepburn wants power over her. She turns from the glacier and ignores his brave, triumphant ascent. He empowers himself. This crisis of separation—she demands he come down, he will not—is the point of the story. A man and a woman, neither young nor idealistic, wrest a bittersweet accommodation out of their joint antagonism. Hannele offers Hepburn a limited sort of love—what he can accept without yielding his self-respect. "I want a woman to honor and obey me," he insists. Hannele, scoffing at everything "but love," eventually yields. Like Victorian heroines, she will, after all, marry him. Lawrence's ending, though hopeful and clever, is nonetheless fragile. It will not take much to unsettle the couple's tentative truce, in which Hannele's spirit and resilience will easily match Hepburn's tenacity.

The Lawrences had discovered this fragile balance in marriage. Although they were often on the edge of a quarrel, that did not prevent many fine moments of shared experience—evening charades, analysis of postwar Germany, games of cards, friends' letters, gentle satire of the Brewsters' idealism. Balanced again, they could depart. Moving south toward Taormina, they reached Florence in late August, spent a month in an apartment near the noisy Ponte Vecchio (the apartment provided a terrace, with lemons, which made Frieda "blissfully happy"), then continued south to Capri to see the Brewsters, who now yearned to visit the tropical island of Ceylon. Not till late September 1921 did the Lawrences reach their beloved Fontana Vecchia. "The very silence is heaven," he wrote, saluting "the peace and quiet of our own house." He would be able to work.

Inspired by seeing the Brewsters in Capri, Lawrence realized he must make money. He needed, he said, to "cross the seas in the early spring" and go east, away from Europe, or west to New Mexico, near the American Rocky Mountains—or maybe, he mused, "approach America from the Pacific." A vague plan was taking shape. The Brewsters' quiet reserve appealed to him because, as Lawrence admitted, "the older I get, the angrier I become." His stance had changed—from offering a forceful challenge to social mores, to espousing a bitter skepticism about human motives. His range had narrowed. The Brewsters, however, soothed his temper and eased his irritation. From Ceylon they threw him a rope of salvation: the source of understanding and peace lay, they assured him, in the meditative East. Skeptical, Lawrence was less sure. "But if you tempt me [. . .] I'll splash my way to Ceylon," he laughed.

Then came a rope flung from another direction. It, too, offered a more tempting form of salvation. It was a scented letter, enclosing medicinal licorice. It offered the Lawrences an invitation to come to Taos, New Mexico, and live under the capacious wing of Mabel Dodge Stern. She was rich and narcissistic but also thoughtful and kind. She begged Lawrence to come and write magically about her hobby, the Taos Indians, a small tribe of six hundred people clustered in a pueblo, outside the town, where they had lived for two thousand years. (Mabel was already smitten with a taciturn tribesman named Tony Luhan.) Physically, she was a smaller version of Frieda, with dark hair, gray eyes, and a low, cool voice. Financially and socially, she was a serene version of England's Ottoline Morrell, with a grand adobe house, a wide circle of friends, and a dominating personality. She was the queen of a tiny kingdom. She lavished generosity but expected a return. All were in awe of her.

It is a measure of Lawrence's desperation that he replied so quickly to Mabel's cunning invitation. He and Frieda would come to Taos, though he could not find it on the map. A town on a high plateau, a furnished adobe house, horses to ride, the spectacular desert at their feet—all of it fascinated the Lawrences. "*There* is glamour and magic for me," he told Brewster. "I want to go." Frieda, too, wanted a fresh start away

Mabel Dodge Luhan, c. 1920 (from *D. H. Lawrence in Taos,* p. 97)

from Europe. Sometimes portrayed as an outsider, cut off from others, Lawrence usually chose to go where there were sympathetic people. In Buckinghamshire, Mary and Gilbert Cannan had lived nearby; Phillip Heseltine had come to Cornwall; Mountsier had joined the hike in Germany; Mabel Sterne *was* Taos; and the Brewsters had made a new home in Ceylon. Despite what Lawrence often said, he much preferred a small community of friends.

Lawrence's letters over the months that followed offer a soiled confetti of irritation with the weather, tea parties, sham of all sorts, publishers both American and British, England's doom. His charity disappears. His letters reflect a deeply felt indecision, even as he labored, almost every day, to shape two important volumes of short fiction, including many new stories, and to compose a masterfully acerbic account of Maurice Magnus, the con man who by this time, deeply in debt, had committed suicide on Malta, leaving his creditors to pay.

In one way, however, conditions were perfect for good work. Lawrence now commanded prodigious imaginative energy; his powers of concentration amazed all who had watched him write. Frieda, acknowledging that he had spent the whole summer with her family, did not intrude: she owed him a calm winter and a respite from annoyance of any kind. At Fontana Vecchia he had come to love his view of the Ionian Sea, the living room stayed warm all winter, the beloved almond trees blossomed early, and the afternoon walks intrigued him. He felt mostly calm. Happy that he was working, Frieda commented in October to Irene Whittley, a friend from Cornwall, "We are enjoying the peace of this – so lovely it has been, not too hot; we have had some long fine day walks! right behind into the hills [. . .] but we have been very quiet and much alone out here – "

Still, Lawrence had made a major decision. He was leaving. He needed only to find a ship to New Orleans or (less acceptable) to New York City. Although he had little money in England, Mountsier had reported eighteen hundred dollars in American earnings, including eight hundred dollars from Benjamin Huebsch's American edition of *The Rainbow*. It was not much for two travelers unless they were gnats of economy. But they were, as their trip to Sardinia had proved. They were not ferociously frugal, but they wasted nothing.

Suddenly Lawrence could not go to America. He had changed his mind. "Dio Mio," he cried to Brewster, "I am so ridiculous, wavering between east and west." He felt "confused to the utmost" by religious and personal insecurity. Frieda explained to Mabel that Lawrence "doesn't feel strong enough [to approach America]!" In truth he had no secure footing in

America, no cushion of comfort, no close friends, only a literary agent who did not greatly admire his work. Wasn't America just a raw version of Europe? Why go there?

Instead, Lawrence responded to a sudden impulse that propelled him to book two berths on the SS *Osterley,* a ship of the Orient Line that held thirteen hundred passengers and would head east. By 20 February 1922 Lawrence and Frieda, in a whirl of activity, had packed four big trunks and assorted boxes for the voyage. Excitement reigned. The ship would depart from Naples six days later. If the Lawrences meant to have a grand world adventure, this was their ship.

CHAPTER 10

Fevers and Fortune

Money was so scarce that Lawrence booked second-class cabins on the *Osterley,* which sailed in October to Colombo, the main port of Ceylon, where the Brewsters had already arrived. Ceylon, a large tropical island off the southern coast of India (it was renamed Sri Lanka in 1972), boasted large plantations of tea, rubber, and cocoa. Earl Brewster had described verdant jungles, breadfruit and palm trees, hulking gray elephants, bright birds, and dark-skinned natives. When these enticing images came into emotional focus, Lawrence and Frieda vaguely realized that they were happiest when encountering a new location and discovering its exotic life. In 1922 travel provided a way to recover some of their intimacy, releasing them from the burden of being "too much married." They could negotiate the demands of a strange territory while actively listening to each other. They had reached the solid footing of a truce.

Their needs had changed. Earlier they had searched for the mystery of relationship; now they searched for the mystery of location. "Lawrence feels so well and at home on a ship," Frieda wrote to her mother later, on 20 May 1922; "today we are pitching and tossing heavily [. . .] We honestly had no idea that we'd want to go farther than Ceylon, and now we're rolling round the world." When the ship left Europe, it took the Lawrences to a land where they had no roots, attachments, or complex past. It was entirely foreign. In "The Captain's Doll" Alexander Hepburn, his mourning having ended, buries his painful past. He crosses the lake to find a new life with Hannele. The Lawrences were making a similar crossing. Their transition began during the two-week journey on the *Osterley*.

The sounds, smells, and sights they encountered on their long journey were so exotic as to seem like dream images—the beggars in Port Said; old men with clay chibouks; the long Suez Canal cut through the desert; the famous Mount Sinai, towering above the Red Sea, where God gave Moses the Ten Commandments; the superb sunsets, gilded with pink and pale lime; the fish leaping on silver wings beside the ship. "The voyage is rather lovely really," Lawrence acknowledged. "I like it so much: everybody pleasant [. . .] and plenty of room. [. . .] And I loved coming through the Suez Canal [. . .] you see the Arabs and their camels and the rosy-yellow desert with its low palm-trees and its hills of sharp sand." The days passed like a sleep, dissolving the old world of Europe and its "tension and pressure."

When Earl Brewster met Lawrence and Frieda at the wharf in Colombo on 13 March, their island initiation began. It was an initiation into the strange territory of Buddhist gods and humid jungle fevers such as malaria. Earl proudly drove them to the Brewsters' hilltop house overlooking Kandy Lake. Inside, the zinc roof magnified nature's weird sounds; outside, the jungle, clamoring with life, crept closer and closer to the wide verandah of the house. Agile monkeys leaped, birds shrieked, animals growled, lizards stared, and strange animals scratched and squealed.

At first these bold, noisy beasts amused the Lawrences. But at night the insects rattled; mating calls morphed into howls; odd creatures slithered nearby; some leaped onto the roof in loud thumps. The constant bestial choir, pitched against the loud music of the insects, deeply distressed the Lawrences. They felt trapped within nature's toxic vitality. Worse, without cooling fans, the humidity and heat prevented restful sleep. How could the Lawrences stay in Ceylon while the country rioted in restless energy? It endangered their health.

Nonetheless, they did their best to find it fascinating. They took long walks into the jungle; admired the temples; joined excursions through plantations, where tea grew on every hill; and bought cocoa, vanilla, and cinnamon as gifts. One evening they watched a special Perahera pageant, attended by the Prince of Wales, which included one hundred elephants, jeweled devil dancers, barbaric tom-toms, and blazing fireworks over

Kandy Lake. "But even at night you sweat if you walk a few yards," Lawrence complained to his sister Emily. The natives frightened them too.

Unable to work in the stupefying heat and worried that he had been infected with malaria, Lawrence wilted. "I [. . .] can't stand Ceylon," he told Anna Jenkins, an Australian woman he had met on the *Osterley*. She had urged him to visit her in Perth. He needed a rescue. He was now "dead off" Buddhism, soon thought the temples to Buddha "hideous," and by April felt sick "all the time"; with no appetite for food or country, he languished. "I loathe the tropical fruits," he admitted to Mary Cannan. He was desperate for the next boat to Australia. After six weeks, he and Frieda left.

If Ceylon had offered a lesson in disillusionment, Perth provided a pleasing two-week interlude on the path to Sydney. The Lawrences arrived in the port city of one million people on 27 May 1922. Australia greatly impressed them. It was an enormous, untamed, unspoiled continent that promised rescue and renewal. "The country is rather wonderful," Lawrence told Mountsier, "with its clear sky and air and sense of emptiness [. . .] where one could lose oneself away from the world." As Lawrence's mood and health gradually improved, so did his marriage. Frieda's letters reveal the satisfying peace and good fortune that awaited them near Sydney.

Their next move altered their usual pattern. Finding Sydney expensive and their money dwindling, they took a train forty miles south. Clutching the "To Let" pages of the *Sydney Morning Herald,* which advertised "Thirroul—Fur[nished] Cott[age]s to Let. Winter T[er]ms," the Lawrences alighted with their four trunks. In the scruffy town of Thirroul, its streets still unpaved, they found a furnished house called Wyewurk. It perched on a cliff that formed a balcony over the Pacific Ocean; the waves below crashed like those in Cornwall. "The heavy waves break with a great roar," Lawrence told Frieda's mother on 30 May. In Thirroul the Lawrences were glad they knew no one. They would have no visitors to entertain.

They felt they had started over—just the two of them—as they had in Italy ten years earlier. When they had evicted the rats, polished the wood floors, cleaned the carpets, and stocked the kitchen with fish, butter, brown honey, and fresh apples and pears, they felt at home. "Here it is winter, but not cold," Lawrence told Frieda's mother. "We have a coal fire going, and are very comfortable." Frieda, equally happy, joined Lawrence for long walks along the coast and discovered exotic shells at the edge of the surf. Their daily ritual honored their preference for order and calm. After Lawrence wrote steadily for hours, they bathed in the saltwater, showered outdoors, wrote letters or napped in the afternoon, cooked the fish and beef the tradesmen brought to the door, and in the evenings took turns reading books.

Still, nothing but their daily swimming and their walks was free. They had spent so much money on ships and meals and gifts, and had so many impressions to digest, that Lawrence longed to sit quietly and write. Simmering inside him was a novel about Australia. He preferred to be alone or with Frieda, who still inspired him as she had in Fiascherino when he composed *The Rainbow*. On 22 June she wrote to her mother, "Here we sit in harmony and peace – don't know a *soul* here." Frieda did not long for anyone else; Lawrence was enough. "I thoroughly like it here," she added, "and feel that I'm years younger in this new part of the earth." Each morning broke miraculous and fresh with the sunrise, each afternoon offered a time of rest, and each evening glowed in the pale light. "I am stingy with every day," she admitted. She had rarely been so contented, acknowledging that "we would like most of all to stay here"; but she also recognized that, as a whole, it was a country too distant and unfamiliar for more than a temporary stay.

Soothed by the ocean's rhythms and shedding his despair at the world's futility, Lawrence worked without interruption on the book he would publish as *Kangaroo*. For details of Australia, he had studied the weekly *Sydney Bulletin* and its quaint articles on outback life—rats that built nests, snakes nine feet long, fish that gobbled humans. The novel's theme revived the idea of stark human isolation that he had explored in both *Aaron's Rod* and the San Gervasio fruit poems; but he spliced into his narrative assorted communications such as letters, bits from newspapers, and conversations overheard, and out of them he wove a novel of strange political intrigue in which one army group clashes with another. These conflicting forces of socialism, democracy, and fascism command no allegiance from the novel's protagonist, Richard Lovatt Somers, who sets himself apart. "Man's isolation was always a supreme truth," the novel concludes. Still today no one knows where Lawrence got all his political information. A week before he finished his novel, Frieda read it and, on 7 July, called it "his dearest book – very striking." With one exception, she would not make such a claim for any of the novels he would later write. Lawrence's portrayal of male solidarity in disarray may have arisen from her claim, made in 1931, that she had discouraged him from "making an outer show with men." She believed that his talent lay elsewhere, in documenting their shared experience of living in Australia.

Kangaroo captures the Lawrences' daily life with absorbing fidelity—what they did, saw, felt, and shared: and how they occasionally fought. They had always tolerated conflict. Frieda loved the book because Harriet Somers, the character who resembles her, shows so much rapt interest in her surroundings. Harriet dresses in Bavarian costume, gushes easily, and communicates "a glamour like magic," but she also shows a manly courage. Most important for her husband, Richard Lovatt Somers—a slight, bearded Englishman—she provides both a woman's sweetness and a man's ferocity. In one of their spirited exchanges, Somers admits that he wants to connect with other men:

> "Don't swank," [Harriet cried,] "you don't live alone. You've got *me* there safe enough, to support you." [. . .]
> "None the less," he retorted, "I do want to do something along with men. [. . .] As a man among men, I just have no place." [. . .]
> "Bah, when it comes to that [*she countered*], I have to be even the only man as well as the only woman [for you]."
> "That's the whole trouble," said he bitingly.

Although Somers believes he must serve a series of male political figures, he is disillusioned by all of them and, at the novel's close, returns to Harriet as the person who most nearly completes him. That is one surprise.

There is another. Privately, Lawrence was no doubt shocked that his sexual desire was waning so fast. After all, he was a man who had celebrated sexuality with vigor and passion. But physical desire, Somers concludes, "would no longer carry him into action." When his neighbor Victoria Callcott hints that she would welcome sex with him, he is horrified. In Florence, Aaron had felt "blasted" by the consenting marchesa;

in Australia, Somers won't risk either a failure to perform or its effects on his fragile ego, badly damaged back in Cornwall during the war. He needed to protect his integrity. At the novel's end, Somers and Harriet, like Lawrence and Frieda, are ready to leave Australia and board a ship to America. Harriet wishes she could stay in Australia: "It's the loveliest thing I've *ever* known."

The ten-week Australian retreat from the world had given the Lawrences' marriage a new intensity and a new purity. They had found the right balance of emotion, disagreement, personal space, and quiet. In short, they rediscovered love—on a different footing. A week before they left, two couples, originally from Nottingham, went with the Lawrences to Bulli Pass, a scenic spot nearby. A photograph taken at this time shows Lawrence and Frieda at Wyewurk, happy and at ease. They have mellowed.

On Frieda's forty-third birthday, 11 August 1922, they left Thirroul and its splendid beach and boarded the *Tahiti*, a ship heading east. It docked overnight in Tahiti—"very lovely voyage [Lawrence wrote] – island and sea magical [...] – Tomorrow we're going by car into the mountains – ." Their fellow passengers were flirtatious and amusing and included a film company shooting in Tahiti. The ship would lead the Lawrences to the last stage of their grand world journey. On 4 September they arrived in San Francisco. "I have the unusual feeling that America is important for us!" Frieda wrote presciently to her sister Else—although Lawrence was more skeptical. He was always less secure than Frieda. But good news awaited them.

For the first time in years, money began to flow. "Our income is growing all the time," Frieda proudly announced in August. On the *Tahiti* they had splurged on a first-class cabin. In fact, from June through December 1922, Lawrence (though not yet informed) would earn—from his American publisher Thomas Seltzer alone—over four thousand dollars (about seventy thousand dollars today). *Aaron's Rod* and *Women in Love* had sold very well in America, where already Lawrence was, Frieda acknowledged, "astonishingly famous." After the war, when the German mark collapsed, Lawrence would gladly assist Frieda's mother, living in a retirement home. The minute Lawrence reached San Francisco and had access to his American money, he sent her a welcome check for thirty dollars—not more because of the plunging exchange rate (in August 1922 one U.S. dollar bought two thousand marks but a year later ten million). The Lawrences' long years of sharp economizing had ended.

Coming by train across the American Southwest, Lawrence worried that Taos, New Mexico, might be full of artist-colony types, whom he had always found tedious and egocentric. He remembered the boring tea parties in Taormina. He did not expect his new patron, Mabel Sterne, to be either petty or self-absorbed: he imagined her as noble and generous. Indeed, she had sent him railway tickets and refused any rent for the new adobe house she had built near hers. And Tony Luhan, though Frieda laughed that he was Mabel's "latest fashion," was more than he appeared. He was once an elder in his Indian tribe, owned land, raised horses, and had wooed, after all, a wealthy American woman. He was uncomplicated and secure. He might help Lawrence discover the profound masculine truths that had—in his friendship with discriminating men such as Mountsier, Magnus, and Brewster—eluded him. Taos itself might offer not only an unspoiled landscape but also personalities unpolluted by European decadence. America was Lawrence's last great hope.

As they came east across the desert, toward Santa Fe, Lawrence felt "glad to be going into a bit of quiet." On 10 September 1922, when the train stopped in the town of Lamy, sixty miles from Taos, there on the platform stood Mabel and Tony, like two pillars at the gate to a new world. This was America.

CHAPTER 11

Mountains in America

In Taos and its surroundings, Mabel and Tony were celebrities. Inheriting money from her father, a banker, Mabel had grown up in Buffalo, New York; toured Europe; attended a finishing school; and briefly lived in Florence with her husband at that time, Edwin Dodge. Later, in Greenwich Village, Mabel opened a weekly salon where talented artists were always welcome. In 1916 she married one of them, a painter named Maurice Sterne, who urged her to move to New Mexico so that he could paint the serenely lavish landscape. In 1919, near Taos, she bought a tract of land and built a big adobe house a mile from the center of town. Gregarious and captivating, she invited friends for long stays. Her newest visitors were the most illustrious she had enticed to come to her ranch. She was sure they would savor the gorgeous scenery when they saw it.

Ascending toward Taos, at a height of seven thousand feet, Lawrence and Frieda sat in the back of Mabel Sterne's deluxe Cadillac and, as they climbed into the Sangre de Cristo Mountains, gazed in disbelief at the river plunging beside the canyon road, the silver cottonwoods catching the fierce afternoon sun, and, later, the sagebrush desert burning to yellow flower. The air was crisp and dry. Under the huge sky, the vistas seemed endless, as if the world might forever unroll. The Lawrences were entranced by this revelation of stark beauty. It was unlike anything they had seen before.

In 1922 Taos was a sleepy village of a couple thousand people—white Europeans, Taos Pueblo Indians, and Spanish-speaking mestizos. Mabel's big adobe house, with its many rooms, was a short walk to the village. This was the land that Lawrence had been looking for. This was the land of primitive rituals, intuitive wisdom, and hard-won serenity. "I build quite a lot on Taos – and the pueblo," he had written to Mabel before he arrived. He hoped that he and Frieda would stay at least through the winter. Maybe longer. Mabel had built them a "lovely adobe house and made it so beautiful. Really we are quite overwhelmed," Lawrence wrote admiringly to Thomas Seltzer.

But beneath the offer of charm and generosity, a different need expressed itself, perhaps over and over. Lawrence wrote to a friend in Australia, "My wife wants a little farm more than anything else, she says." Tired of packing and unpacking, of washing and drying, of waiting and walking, she was ready for roots. For ten years she had wandered the globe with Lawrence. She would not be patient much longer. She wanted a place of her own.

Sucked into the swirl of Mabel's social hub, Lawrence spent five days with Apache Indians; learned to ride a horse (as did Frieda); participated in Mabel's dinners and "drumming" entertainments; joined Tony and Mabel to survey the dark piñon scrub and yellowing aspens; and, like pilgrims to a vast desert shrine, they were "all the time on the go." Lawrence liked America's open spaces, its rough rhythms, its freedom and ferocity. But he disliked America's hard acquisitive edge. It was so unlike Australia's easy comfort and contentment.

Frieda, more thrilled than Lawrence, loved the adobe house, the bright sun, the landscape, the Indians bearing gifts of venison and plums. "It is *indescribably* lovely here," she told her mother, repeating the Indians' claim "that the heart of the world beats here – and I believe it." The enormous spaces around Taos allowed the soul to speak in silence. It could almost have been Thirroul, Australia, that Frieda described, except that, living so close to Mabel, they soon became objects of her gallant generosity. Lawrence had said, in September, that he did not want anyone "to be *kind* to me." He had a horror of condescension, and Mabel wielded her power in subtle, captivating ways.

It was as if, in Taos, the Lawrences occupied the cottage that Lady Ottoline Morrell had promised them in 1915 but discovered now that the generosity of a great lady brought with it a smothering cloak. As their one-month Taos visit turned into two, Lawrence and Frieda chafed under the protective wing of the American cultural priestess. Her good intentions infiltrated their privacy and freedom. Lawrence called her "a little buffalo." In early November, Frieda, distressed, admitted to her mother that "Lawrence [. . .] isn't happy here." Yet Frieda, ever optimistic, was also convinced that the crisp air and clear sun would "heal Lawrence completely" of his respiratory ailments. That was nature's incomparable gift. She believed he must allow it time to work.

In late October the Lawrences learned about the Kiowa Ranch, located in the rugged mountains seventeen miles from Taos, and were intrigued by the possibility of living there alone. When they visited it, on 31 October, Lawrence, mesmerized, saw its potential at once: it was isolated and rustic yet had neighbors nearby. He announced to Elizabeth Freeman a surprising intention: "Frieda wants us to go and live there."

The Kiowa Ranch, which belonged to Mabel, was a 160-acre homestead of three ramshackle cabins. Pinewoods lay behind, the rolling desert below. Lawrence and Frieda loved its mountain location. In early November they stayed four days. With snow all around, "Lawrence felled trees by day," Frieda wrote, "and in the evening learned Spanish with Sabino [his Mexican friend]." He donned a work uniform of tan corduroys and a blue shirt. But the ranch, distant and deserted, was still too rough to be habitable. The bitter cold would soon arrive.

Neighbors offered a rescue. Below the ranch, only two miles away, was a place called Del Monte Ranch, where the newly married Hawks, Bill and Rachel, lived. Young cattle ranchers, unpretentious and kind, they offered the Lawrences a five-room log cabin set amid tall pines. From December through March they could rent the cabin for one hundred dollars, the same as they had paid for a year at Fontana Vecchia. Like Mrs. Hocking at Higher Tregerthen, the Hawks would supply milk, eggs, and meat from the main farmhouse five minutes away. The Del Monte location offered the perfect blend of distance and proximity. The distance enabled Lawrence to work; the proximity enabled a small community to flourish.

But instead of finding there a handsome, unmarried farmer like William Henry Hocking, the Lawrences imported his double. They approached two painters from Denmark, also single, who had recently arrived in Taos. Knud Merrild, aged twenty-eight, and Kai Götzsche, aged thirty-six—always called "the Danes"—were best friends. Good-looking and self-sufficient, they were taciturn but companionable, thoughtful and intelligent, and avowedly straight. They liked to make lively musical evenings with their flute and fiddle. They were gregarious but not meddling. The Lawrences urged them to spend the winter at Del Monte Ranch, stay in their own three-room cabin adjacent to the main house (for only fifty dollars), help split wood, clear the snowy roads, fetch supplies, and keep the Lawrences company in the long winter evenings. In the mornings Lawrence would write, condensing his "Studies in Classic American Literature" to make the book aggressive and sharp—as in his comment that, although charity appeals to everyone, "you don't have to force your soul into kissing lepers or embracing syphilitics." He adopted that pugnacious tone as being "American." But his many insights are far-reaching, and today his studies constitute a vital (if idiosyncratic) analysis of American literature and identity. He understood, for example, that "Europe and America are all alike: all the nations self-consciously provoking their own passional reactions from the mind, and *nothing* spontaneous."

Then came a spat with Mabel that led to a break. For weeks the Lawrences had been dissatisfied, Lawrence feeling pressured to write a novel at Mabel's direction, Frieda having caught the toxic scent of Mabel's sexual interest in Lawrence. Alarmed, they decided on bold action. In Cornwall, Frieda had already rebuffed one competitor for Lawrence's affection; she would not tolerate another. The confrontation on 6 November had a major consequence. Lawrence sent Mabel a written declaration— he did not care "a straw" for her money, she was an emotional bully, and she would damage his marriage. "I believe," he wrote, "that, at its best, the central relation between Frieda and me is the best thing in my life." His *credo* was a vindication of his marriage. The Lawrences would not be divided. They would leave. They would, once again, start over.

Just as the sticky heat of Ceylon framed the ocean's rhythmic appeal at Thirroul, so did the spat with Mabel frame the peaceful winter at Del Monte. On 1 December the Lawrences, using Sabino's wagon, brought their belongings to what seemed like another world. Living amid the thick forests and snowy mountains, Lawrence confided to Koteliansky, "I feel very different [here]." He had won a measure of security. A few days later Frieda, writing to her mother, rhapsodized about the bare but beautiful country that spread out below them, the huge indoor fires stoked with hand-sawed pine, the long afternoon rides on horseback, the fruit cellar bulging with apples. "Everything is so good and unspoiled – thick cream on the milk, and as much veal and pork as we want." Amid all this plenty, she and Lawrence baked big loaves of bread.

The country seemed to be a primitive paradise. In the marvelous mountain air, she believed, "we have not had a winter when Lawrence was so well!" The physical challenge, the Danes, and the climate invigorated them. Although they had few conveniences and were often snowbound, they stripped themselves to the essentials of shelter and food. They had no electricity, no indoor plumbing, no car, no typewriter; groceries were miles away by horseback. It was a life of survival. And yet they made it a joy, living every moment intensely. At the edge of civilization, they found exhilaration. At the core of existence came self-sufficiency.

After they had made Del Monte their home, important visitors—a publisher and then an agent—arrived. On Christmas Day came Thomas Seltzer and his wife, Adele, Russian immigrants, tiny, well-read, Jewish—and thrilled to be Lawrence's American publishers. They had stumbled onto gold. In 1921 and 1922 Seltzer had proudly issued eight of Lawrence's books and had, though it cost him dearly, fought off a legal action to suppress the novel *Women in Love*. At Del Monte the Seltzers had a glorious time, singing songs with the Danes, eating fresh chicken and mince pies, making aromatic apple cobblers, traveling ten miles to the Manby Hot Springs for a long, healing soak, and at night hearing the coyotes howl, horrifyingly, by the front gate. A week later the Seltzers left, utterly charmed by the Lawrences' spartan life. The visit was the apex of their lives.

On the Seltzers' heels came Lawrence's agent, Robert Mountsier, solemn and, by comparison, dull. He remained a whole month at Del Monte, then moved down to Taos. He disliked Jews, constantly belittled Thomas Seltzer, and demanded long, detailed contracts. Seltzer thought him "impudent" and "meddling" and found him simply itching "to pick a quarrel with me." Lawrence and Frieda, as mediators, were torn. Mountsier, while offering candid literary advice, always followed Lawrence's instructions and had tried to secure a good income for an author who often needed money. However, Mountsier irritated Lawrence and soon exhausted his welcome. After Lawrence had listened to protracted grievances from both sides, he agreed that Mountsier should go. In a stiff letter, Lawrence fired him on 3 February 1923. "Nothing Mountsier ever did was helpful," Seltzer had urged. Lawrence reluctantly agreed: "I wish finally to be rid of him." But to evict a friend had been difficult and hateful. Mountsier had tried.

The pattern of Lawrence's response to a wound is clear. He moved forcefully to rid himself of assaults on his fragile psyche. Rid of that "liar" Mabel. Rid of Mountsier, who, at bottom, "did not believe in me." Rid of America, which Lawrence "can't stand any more." Rid even of the consumptive Katherine Mansfield, who at age thirty-four had recently died of tuberculosis. These sharp breaks with the past had been going on since 1919, with one major exception: Frieda. It was she who held together Lawrence's fractured self once he had turned away from love to loyalty. "To me, loyalty [comes] far before love," he had asserted. For now Frieda simply accepted the gradual loss of romantic love. She accepted, instead, the gift of companionship, which offered sweet compensation and many hours of camaraderie. But she also knew that her own capacity for love was still undiminished. "I know I can love," she declared. It was her gift. It had no limits.

The long winter months had wearied the Lawrences, and they reluctantly agreed to leave Del Monte. "This cold and this primitive life are really tiring," Frieda observed as the snow continued to pile up higher and higher in March. The battle against the wind and ice had taken its toll on Lawrence's physical health and on Frieda's good spirits. On the eighteenth, Lawrence reported to Adele Seltzer: "[We] left Del Monte in deep snow and the tail end of a cyclone. It was rough." But their departure for a warmer climate opened a new and difficult challenge.

By this time Lawrence had come to prefer the simple Mexicans like Sabino to the silent Indians or the bullying Americans. Ready for change, he and Frieda were drawn to Mexico, partly to feel the sun's warmth, partly to test Lawrence's belief that a strong peasant life could unveil the religious mysteries of a culture, but mainly to compose a new novel. In Taos he could not write about America—Mabel had poisoned his creative well—but he might write about people south of the border who lived harmoniously and spontaneously and might reveal grand spiritual truths. He wanted to be empowered by their knowledge.

Again, two men—Santa Fe friends of Mabel's named Witter Bynner and Willard "Spud" Johnson—decided to accompany the Lawrences. Together they would form a little expatriate community. The two men, a couple, were openly homosexual—like Douglas and Magnus back in Florence, except that Bynner and Johnson were much less promiscuous in searching for partners. Bynner was middle-aged, balding, rich; Johnson was young, thin, and clean-cut. "We might have a good time together," Lawrence urged. "Tell Bynner to splash about and get ready to come along." Lawrence and Frieda liked the men's humor and openness. Far from choosing to be an outsider, Lawrence had invited five people—including the Danes—to join him and Frieda; only Bynner and Johnson would follow. To be alone in Mexico was neither his wish nor his expectation. He always favored a small community—for diversion and safety. His diffidence toward gay men had disappeared. He felt kinship.

Leaving Taos on 18 March 1923, the Lawrences hoped to find an exotic locale populated by peasants who were less secretive and more genial than the Taos Indians. After consulting *Terry's Guide to Mexico,* Lawrence had tentatively set his sights on the city of Guadalajara, twelve hundred miles south, one hour from a huge natural lake. One detail about the area would have had special appeal. The climate was reported to be "almost perfect" for tubercular types. The Lawrences welcomed the opportunity to go south and see Mexico and its beauty for themselves.

CHAPTER 12

The Mysteries of Mexico

Traveling by slow trains guarded by armed soldiers, the Lawrences reached Mexico City on 23 March 1923. They were surprised by its noise, its size, and its contrasts. Poverty jostled with wealth, savagery with refinement, revolution with peace, greed with charity, political betrayal with religious grace. But the Mexicans seemed more interesting and alive than the Taos Indians, whose sad decline had been evident. After Witter Bynner and Willard Johnson joined the Lawrences at their little Monte Carlo Hotel, they all went to see the major sights—the floating gardens of Xochimilco, the grand government buildings with Diego Rivera's murals, and the unique pyramids at Teotihuacán. They also wondered where they might spend the summer away from the country's violence and instability.

The Lawrences feared for their safety. Bynner had earlier introduced Lawrence to a novelist named Wilfred Ewart, who, as he stood on his hotel balcony in Mexico City, had been shot through the eye and died soon afterward. It was a frightening death. Lawrence concluded, "It's an evil country down there." He worried that violence might be pervasive.

There was more to fear. A week after the Lawrences arrived, they witnessed a bullfight that sickened them when the bull gored the blindfolded horse; they watched helplessly as the bloody entrails piled onto the ground. Frieda found the spectacle "vile and degraded" and—with Lawrence in tow—fled. Hence, death and horror framed their visit to Mexico. But within this frame Lawrence wrote one of his most evocative and unforgettable novels. It exists in two complete drafts, outwardly similar, inwardly very different.

Both Lawrence and Frieda were wary of Mexico's beguiling charm. They found the country "very savage underneath." Although its history was rife with fearful episodes, Lawrence was bewitched by it. He loved seeing the short, handsome natives working under their huge straw hats, cutting ripe wheat with sickles; they stirred his wonder and compassion. In Mexico he was looking for a revelation—and believed he would find it in writing a novel. It might express the conflicted feelings that the new country aroused in him.

After the four friends visited several Mexican cities in April, Lawrence took a train by himself to Ocotlán, then by boat went to Chapala, thirty-five miles from Guadalajara. He wrote hopefully to the Danes, "I think we may settle [in Chapala]." A simple village beside a huge lake, Chapala boasted three hotels, a twin-spired church, a train station, and, at lake's edge, shade trees and motor boats. It seemed idyllic. Lawrence rushed to send Frieda a telegram: "CHAPALA PARADISE. TAKE EVENING TRAIN." Bringing all the luggage, she eagerly came west. Two blocks from the lake, Lawrence found a large house with oleanders, scarlet hibiscus, and orange trees. (It still stands today, though much remodeled, and offers guests a "D. H. Lawrence Suite.") With the house came a Mexican woman to cook and clean—along with her grown son to guard the house at night, when bandits, looking for easy prey, stalked the lakeside haciendas where foreigners lived. Chapala offered a fertile mix of quaint beauty, quietness, waterfront access, and real danger to inspire Lawrence.

Needing an income, he soon began to write, sitting every morning under a pale-green pepper tree at the lake's edge. Steady breezes, coming off the water, cooled him. Within just five weeks he had written enough for Frieda to declare the novel "the most splendid thing he ever did." He called the new novel *Quetzalcoatl,* after the feathered serpent-god of the Aztecs that he and Frieda had seen when they visited Teotihuacán. The title refers to the eagle caught within the snake's coiled body. Out of that tension arises the uncertain future that the novel's main character, Kate Burns, struggles to shape in a foreign land. Feeling unfinished and alone, bruised and diminished, she must forge a female identity that will unite the fragments of her past life.

Lawrence was now adept at synthesizing what he *knew* with what he *imagined*. Kate blends distinctive traits of both Lawrence and Frieda. Like Ursula Brangwen coming into her maturity in *The Rainbow*, Kate has Lawrence's questing intelligence and intuitive understanding (though not his difficult intensity). She has Frieda's assertiveness and womanly essence (though not her lack of focus). Irish by birth, twice a widow, her two children almost grown, Kate is ambivalent about the future, but she is also free to reinvent herself and to satisfy her craving for some ennobling belief. Like Lawrence, she declares herself finished with love, vowing "to be in love with nobody"; and like Frieda, she accepts the loss of romantic love but has found no viable replacement. In short, her soul is withering. Her quest for recovery depends now on her ability to explore the ideas of love and power that Aaron Sisson had, earlier, struggled to understand.

As her quest begins, Kate finds her challenge in two handsome Mexicans, Cipriano Viedma and Ramón Carrasco. "Mysterious" and "not quite fathomable," they reveal an exotic masculinity that nearly overpowers her. As leaders of a nascent religious revolution, they point beyond themselves to the kind of revelation that Lawrence himself sought. He wanted to pierce the veil of mystical knowledge hidden in the "wild" Mexican natives, whose "wildness [was] undreamt of," Frieda said. Ramón—who is noble, sensual, and cruel but also "beyond and above all love"—is the man she chooses to guide her. He has a mystical, entrancing vision. Married, he is also unavailable for romance.

To Lawrence, now at another turning point in his life, the novel soon meant "more to me than any other novel of mine." It gradually showed him how to connect to others—not with charity or "self-sacrificing" love but with the bond of brotherhood, man to man, arising from deep within his psyche. Spiritually exhausted, Lawrence needed to find a path out of himself, out of his own unstable lethargy. As for Frieda, she had changed too. She began to display an attitude of feisty antagonism toward Lawrence (which Witter Bynner had slyly encouraged); as a new opponent, she could no longer point the way forward. The Mexican Indians, still in touch with the sacred life of the blood, could—but only if Lawrence could weave for them a myth of resurrection. In New Mexico the Taos Indians and their primitive dances had given him a clue. Now finally he understood. Marriage could no longer provide a clue, as it had in *Kangaroo*. He would take sexuality out of the body. He would make it impersonal yet also mysterious and unknowable. He would bring back its divinity.

To put Lawrence's insight into action, Kate embarks on a journey to spiritual enlightenment. Weary of life as she has known it, she retreats to an isolated location (Chapala) where she can learn what the natives value, how they live, and what might redeem them. Awakened by the stirring of a Quetzalcoatl religion, she quivers in response to the music that Ramón inspires in his followers. The poignant hymns—of men singing in unison—create a "spell" over her, as "the hot-blooded soul" of the men rises up dark, deep voiced, and wild. She is entranced. Tears of relief fill her heart. Ramón and his soul brother Cipriano, both of them drawn to Kate's womanly charm, rejoice that she, in turn, is drawn not only to the inspired Quetzalcoatl hymns but also to its dances, ceremonies, and sermons. These rituals, though resembling those that Christians celebrated, now include an erotic component. When Ramón fills Kate's cup of salvation, she trembles "with strange excitement and with fear. She felt her heart would die." The sermon that follows is like a serpentine fugue, an incantation to the earth's creative forces, but now disrupted by the "great machines" that have taken control of the world.

Irresistibly drawn to this new religion, Kate learns to sublimate her sexual attraction to Ramón into emotional ecstasy. Aroused from her torpor, she becomes a female Somers—mesmerized by the passion of handsome men but refusing to serve, even as muse, their male solidarity. At the novel's end, she understands the high cost of her "Mexican" salvation—the loss of her essential female self, which strips away her identity. She cannot stay in a country where she will submerge her identity in male forms of worship. She stops just short of fulfillment. Her experience ennobles but does not sustain her. It makes a finer woman of her but diminishes her pride and her confidence. At the close her transformation is incomplete.

The novel may seem overwrought and florid, but its deeper purpose is clear. It offers a blow to the sterility and lack of spontaneity that Lawrence had hated in both Europe and America. In the experiment of *Quetzalcoatl*, he had boldly drawn a map of the hostile "demons" he so often felt, had located their fury, and, by redirecting their energy, had saved himself from spiritual extinction. Given a voice, the demons were mollified. Lawrence had recovered his equanimity and his resolve. He felt he was in possession of his fate—though not of Frieda's. For now it was enough. But it was also a difficult turning point.

Almost finished with the novel and now facing departure from Chapala, Lawrence expressed intense ambivalence. He had changed, felt freshly empowered, and better recognized his own needs. "I don't really want to go back to Europe," he wrote to Thomas Seltzer on 15 June. Though he realized that Frieda deserved to see her mother again, he wavered. "I think I like Mexico best of all the places, to live in," he added. Frieda, in turn, sensed that Lawrence was uncharacteristically resisting her desire that he accompany her. He seemed obstinate. But he had embraced a different idea. He imagined that in Mexico they would later make "a little life here on this lake," where the country's unhurried rhythms had soothed him and where he had felt revitalized.

In July the Lawrences left Chapala and, ten days later, arrived by train in New York City, then escaped to a country cottage near Morris Plains, New Jersey, which Thomas Seltzer had rented for them. It was a serene place. Lawrence immediately set to work correcting proofs of *Kangaroo*, a collection of his poems called *Birds, Beasts and Flowers,* and a translation of Giovanni Verga's *Mastro-don Gesualdo* about Italian peasants. Though intensely busy, he felt weighted with indecision. He told Willard Johnson that he felt "desolate inside." Was he considering new limits on marital love?

His desolation soon shaped itself into resolve. He bought Frieda's transatlantic ticket but refused to buy his own. Aghast at his disloyalty, Frieda was—this time—helpless to combat his will. Writing *Quetzalcoatl* had given him new strength: he rebuffed all her entreaties. The break came in August. On the seventh he informed Koteliansky that "*she* will sail [to England] on the 18th." The Lawrences still had eleven days to grind out their protracted conflict. Their affection and commitment had slipped into the shadows. "I will stay here, till my feeling has changed," he declared without much precision. But he did not back down. He told Frieda that he could not return to Europe and perform as a celebrated writer. He could not be lionized, could not "stand on the old ground," could not "come with a cheerful soul." But Lawrence's explanations fell short. They were only symptoms of the unspecified malaise, the crippling numbness, that he felt. There was perhaps another reason why Lawrence would not accompany Frieda to Europe.

The alternate explanation for Lawrence's refusal comes from *Quetzalcoatl*, in which women assume roles outside the circle of power. For Lawrence camaraderie had now replaced love. "I want men with some honorable manhood in them," he had urged. He wanted a new family grouping, mostly without women. Above all he wanted to re-create his life at Del Monte Ranch with the Danes, who grounded him in their balance of work, silence, and physical solidarity. When Adele Seltzer met the Danes in December, she described them more than once as "Norse gods." And more than once, Lawrence had told the Danes that he imagined his future with them. "I hope you will both come down [to Lake Chapala] and help us manage [a little banana farm]," he implored. There in Mexico "we could make a life," or if all else failed, "we might take a donkey and go packing among the mountains."

The dream was sad and unsustainable. Although Frieda participated—and also imagined the foursome building a life together—she may not have understood her role in it, nor could Lawrence easily explain it. In this new family group, Frieda's presence was essential. She was the "safety" that protected the men from emotional entanglements, real or imputed. Her presence helped Lawrence sublimate his erotic feelings. In imagining Kate's experience, he had discovered that she could be near handsome men without feeling aroused. It may have been Lawrence's need too.

In New Jersey these issues came to a forceful conclusion. Whereas Lawrence wanted Frieda to go back to Mexico with him, she insisted on going elsewhere. Often putting out her mother's gifts (thimble, tablecloths, cookbooks, opera glasses) in each new place where they lived, she was far more attached to her mother in Germany than to a new family model that populated Lawrence's dream. In a surprise move, full of anger, he must have charged her with disloyalty. A week after she sailed to England on the *Orbita,* she wrote an important letter to Adele Seltzer, charging her husband with selfishness and animosity: "I feel so cross with Lawrence, when I hear *him* talk about loyalty – Pah, he only thinks of himself – I am glad to be alone and I will not go back to him. [. . .] I will *not* stand his bad temper any more if I never see him again – [and I] wrote him so." Both had reached the end of compromise. Neither would yield. Their growing dissonance had matured into hostility and contempt.

In truth Lawrence cared less than Frieda about family bonds. His memories were saturated with disillusionment. He remembered painfully the constraints of Eastwood, the unending dissension in his family, and the cramped house he had shared with Emily and Sam (her husband), Ada, and their father in early 1912. Although he often wrote to his sisters, he never wrote to his father or elder brother, George, and rarely to aunts or uncles; and about his character Kate Burns, he had written, "She wandered to avoid a home, a group, a family, a circle of friends." Frieda, however, wanting to validate her family ties, insisted on reconnecting with her mother, her children, and Lawrence's friends—in that order. She had not visited England for four years. Now, in 1923, she felt she must go. She must make the difficult choice. And now the colliding temperaments of husband and wife had cracked the marriage wide open.

CHAPTER 13

Her Ship Goes East

By the time Frieda groused that she would never go back to Lawrence, he was halfway across the United States, on his way to Los Angeles, where the Danes were living and working. They were now his hope. Recently discovered letters from Lawrence to Frieda show that during September he was at first amused, if irritated, by his surroundings. The noise and chatter of the city jostled with the splendor of the palm trees and wide boulevards. Near the Danes, he stayed alone in a single room. They were busy decorating the library of Harry Johnson, a wealthy geologist in nearby Santa Monica; Götszche was quiet and self-contained, Merrild sulking and unresponsive. Lawrence rarely saw them. Still, he had clung to the hope that, together, they might hire a ship "and sail off – perhaps to China" or even, if possible, "sail into the void for a little while." The "void" is a strange destination for a voyage. But since 1915 Lawrence had hoped to "sail away from this world." He was pitching about, his direction unclear, his emotions in tumult while he awaited change. He and Frieda had not reconciled. He wondered if they would.

His most inspiring experience in Los Angeles came when he went to the Barnum & Bailey Circus with a new friend, Anna Forsyth, on 14 September 1923. The performers astonished him. He wrote to Frieda, diverting his loneliness into a fantasia on the circus performers whose daring and skill were ravishing:

> The circus is great fun. The *courage* and physical beautiful skill really impress me. [...] The [performers] have beautiful cool daring and lovely achievement. [...] There is something handsome and manly about the tiger tamer, and something weird and sharp-eyed, like birds, about the trapeze flyers. These last *very* beautiful. [...] One has to admit [...] their strange, abstract, bird-like faces and *marvellous* movements. [...] Afterwards we saw all the lions and lionesses and tigers and panthers and leopards fed: and that was impressive too. [...] One could stand quite close, almost touch them. It brings back to me the unfailing glamour and fascination of life itself.

The circus performers and animals gave him an alternate vision of beauty—elemental, disciplined, exotic. The performers' courage and grace inspired him. Could he somehow replicate this vision in western Mexico, around Guadalajara, over the mountains to the south? If he could not, he would feel aggrieved. He then offered Frieda a surprising pledge: "If I find nothing [there] I'll come to Europe." He did not know that five days earlier Frieda had written to her mother, "I miss Lawrence very much." Though separated, even alienated, they were closing the gap between themselves.

Lawrence waited patiently but tentatively for the Danes to decide if they would join him for the winter months—in a ship on the sea or somewhere down in Mexico. Though he searched hard, he could not find a suitable ship in the Los Angeles harbor. Merrild, pressed for a decision, declined to join him. Though a staunch ally, he was seeking a career in art, not an adventure in Guadalajara.

Hugely disappointed, Lawrence left Los Angeles with only Kai Götzsche on 25 September, going south, to endure one of the hottest and most arduous journeys of his life. He and Götzsche moved slowly—stubbornly—along the windy, barren western coast of Mexico, toward Guadalajara. Late in September they took the train to Tepic, in the Pacific coastal highlands, then spent two hard days on horseback, catching the train again at Etzatlán. Though worn with fatigue and dazed by the heat, they eventually crossed a majestic plateau, ringed with high mountains, and entered Guadalajara. In his letters Lawrence rarely mentions his Danish sidekick except to tell Merrild that Götzsche "looks at these broken, lost, hopeless little [Mexican] towns, in silent disgust. He speaks not one word of Spanish and is altogether an onlooker."

Disenchanted, Götzsche had become an acerbic, brusque companion who soon found Lawrence "difficult to live with." Idella Purnell, a young poet who observed them together in Guadalajara, judged their bond "casual," without much affection. It did not survive their next move. Quickly disillusioned, Lawrence never again mentioned his dream of a new life with the Danes. Every parting, Lawrence knew, was "a new unfusing" of sympathy—and a test of loyalty. When his Mexican dream died, another was on the way. It would involve a triangle—but not a triangle that he would have expected.

While Lawrence, mostly bored, wandered the narrow streets and sidewalks of Guadalajara, he greeted Frieda's infrequent letters with dismay. She would not, she said, come back to Mexico. Her family came first. Back in August, when Frieda arrived in England, S. S. Koteliansky and John Middleton Murry had met her and taken her to Mary Cannan's flat in Hyde Park. Later, Frieda found a large room in Hampstead, in the house where novelist Catherine Carswell lived, not far from Koteliansky in St. John's Wood. As for Lawrence, who had cashed in his return ticket, he would not, he assured her, come back to Europe. Instead, he had insisted on 22 September, "It's time now we found a place for the winter," reassuring her that America had recognized Mexico as "very safe." He referred to a story in the *Los Angeles Times,* which reported President Obregón's assurance that Mexico would renew its diplomatic relations with Great Britain. But Frieda, alone now, had other things on her mind.

After she arrived in England, she must have written to Lawrence about Murry's kindness, about his misery that his wife, Katherine, was now dead, and—who can say?—maybe about how she was feeling. Whatever she said, Lawrence was disturbed. Did she offer him an ultimatum? His reply suggests that she did. She may have hinted that in case he did not return, she was being innocently wooed. In his reply he demanded caution. Give nothing away! he admonished her. "Keep your heart safe hidden somewhere," he added. He surely guessed that her affections were at risk. His postcard of 22 September, which is strangely and surprisingly cool, expressed no loneliness, no longing for her, no affection. He and Frieda were still estranged, maybe permanently.

Buttressed by Murry, who was now editing the *Adelphi* magazine in London, Frieda assured Lawrence that he should make his literary home in England and that, though he might resist, he "must come back." Stay in Mexico at your own risk, she implied. His resistance, once so firm, thinned into hesitation. "I might be driven to make a visit," he acknowledged to Seltzer. On 21 October, when he visited Lake Chapala by himself—and felt "alien" in the luminous landscape—he reconsidered his earlier decision. Frieda's cable of 2 November, urging his return, ended his wavering. He needed her strength.

In Frieda's life this was a tangled, uncertain time. At first she gladly sought out others, Murry in particular. Flush with money from Lawrence's earnings, she bragged to Adele Seltzer, "I have a banking account of my own and feel an important female." She may have been priming herself to live independently; she could not plumb the future. For all she knew, Lawrence, no longer guided by her strong presence and likely influenced by the Danes, might have bought a small farm in Mexico near Lake Chapala. He still wanted to "start a little centre – a ranch"—and could have spared a few thousand dollars for it. He still assumed that Frieda might come back. But she was very clear about the Mexican farm. "I do hope he won't find one!" she told Martin Secker, his British publisher. "I don't want to go to it!"

Farm or no farm, if she refused to return to Mexico, she would be alone in Europe and would need her own "sidekick." He was, of course, Murry, who had for six weeks lived beside the Lawrences in Cornwall in 1916, then had returned once for a visit. Unlike the brusque Götzsche, Murry was a vine that could wrap around anyone, be attentive, cling. Catherine Carswell admired his fine talent "for eliciting emotion in others." In some ways he was Frieda's type—intellectual, diffident, emotionally insecure: in short, a man who needed her strong protection, as Lawrence had. Still smarting from Lawrence's defection, Frieda gently stirred Murry's emotional stew and listened raptly to his declarations of Lawrence's genius. Murry had at last realized Lawrence's stature and had realized, she proudly informed Adele Seltzer, "that Lawrence was a greater man than he was and how bitter it was for him to come to that conclusion [. . .] but now he had forever accepted him, no matter what Lawr[ence] did [in the past]—After all it almost takes greatness to see that another

Dorothy Brett, 1931, photo by Dorothea Lange (National Gallery of Art, Washington, Alfred H. Moses and Fern M. Schad Fund)

man is greater than you – " Carried away in her rhapsody, Frieda innocently reveals Murry's self-serving strategies. In April, five months earlier, Murry had finally seduced a lonely, middle-aged painter named Dorothy Brett (always called just Brett), who had experienced a sad childhood and felt rejected by others and now clung to a man who had fired her passion and even charmed her with the prospect of marriage. And now he may have shown an equally vivid interest in Frieda.

So, of course, did her three children, living in London, awaiting her return. They could now visit her as adults, aged twenty-three, twenty-one, and eighteen, and reassess her for themselves. When they saw her in September, she was bowled over with happiness. They had changed, grown up without her, and become "very tall and like Prince and Princesses," looking "absolutely distinguished," she told her mother. Barbara, the youngest, was full of grace; Elsa delicate and reliable; and Monty, well educated, already at work in a museum. Seeing them every week, she knew she wanted them to live freely. Long ago, she learned, Monty had been "terribly attached to me," then felt betrayed—now must "learn again that I am here!" Her reunion with her children made her life "complete and more lovely than I had dreamed." She had missed them more than she had realized.

Unable to gauge Lawrence's next move, Frieda stayed busy. After a weekend spent with Martin Secker outside London, she went to visit Lawrence's sisters in the Midlands. Her friendship with Koteliansky, Catherine Carswell, Dorothy Brett, and the painter Mark Gertler gave her confidence that Lawrence, if he returned, might thrive in London. Murry had promised to assign him reviews and essays in the *Adelphi* magazine.

On 28 September 1923 Frieda left for a month in Germany to see her mother, now seventy-two. Murry discovered that he and Frieda (already "chummy," according to Carswell) could go together by train; he to Sierre, Switzerland, to retrieve the belongings of his dead wife, Katherine, and Frieda to Baden. Here the story gets tangled. The evidence precludes firm conclusions, but during the trip Frieda and Murry may, some writers believe, have become lovers. For her it would not have been so much an act of disloyalty as an act of generosity to a miserable man. She liked Murry "very much," she told her mother. But in a 1931 letter, she said that *he* had made the decision to avoid a sexual entanglement: "I was so happy [. . .] going to Germany with you – And then I accepted your decision: 'I owe myself to the Brett and there's Lawrence' – I accepted it without complaint even to myself and put my feeling to sleep like a hurt child." Murry may have been in too much pain to initiate an affair; he appears to have been unwilling to dishonor Lawrence; and he may also have recognized that, as Frieda worried, "he doesn't care much [for me]." She knew, or at least guessed, that he was emotionally deficient. His generosity expressed itself in a shrewd display of concern.

Lawrence's plans remained vague. He had fallen into the abyss of being alone—and hated it. Having experimented with his options, he had everywhere been defeated. He therefore went with Götzsche to Veracruz, Mexico, then boarded a slow ship to England. Their camaraderie without Merrild had cooled into modest friendship. On 12 December, Lawrence finally arrived in London, where he was met at Waterloo Station by Frieda, Murry, and Koteliansky. He judged for himself the intimacy between his wife and Murry and, sensing their unusual closeness, was likely distressed. A limit may have been crossed. Lawrence had long distrusted Murry as diffident, without integrity. Much later, in 1934, Frieda wrote that Lawrence "should not have come [back] to Europe"; rather, she ought (she said) to have "[met] him in Mexico." That is a hint, but no more than a hint, that in his absence she may have compromised herself emotionally, ignoring Lawrence's plea that she "keep her heart safe hidden." At this time safety was foreign to Frieda.

On arrival Lawrence despised England—the foul weather, the lack of freedom and openness, the fawning Murry (still, after eight years, a source of emotional addiction). "Here I am – in bed with a cold – hate it," he told Idella Purnell on 17 December. "Just hate it all. It's like being in the tomb. [. . .] I swear at [Frieda] for having brought me here." In London he felt tired and diminished; he yearned for the tonic of New Mexico.

In late December, however, once his health improved, he allowed Frieda to invite his closest friends to a welcome-home supper at London's Café Royal. Meeting in a private room, Lawrence was a gracious and entertaining host. Frieda was delighted. But the gathering turned from a convivial exchange to a tense test of loyalty when Lawrence, laced with liquor, asked each person in turn to go with him to New Mexico to create a community bonded in trust and support. Frieda, holding herself aloof, said little. But Catherine Carswell, a careful observer, caught the jealous male flavor of the evening. Koteliansky declaimed heroically that "no woman here or anywhere [Frieda was exempt] can possibly realise the greatness of Lawrence." Murry, spewing effusive love for Lawrence, reminded Catherine, with masked malice, that "women can have no part or place" in the procession of male bonding. Lawrence was, however, unmoved. He sat "still and unresponsive." Initially, he was impressed but also skeptical. Elsewhere he had argued that one must "eschew emotions – they are a disease." He had in mind Murry's enticing brand of pheromones.

All the guests—save one—sooner or later made excuses. They could not leave England. The exception was Dorothy Brett, a Slade-trained artist, forty, unmarried, mostly deaf, and, by June, pregnant with Murry's child (though she soon lost it). She had ample money (five hundred pounds a year from her father, Viscount Esher), a pedigree (she was the *Honorable* Dorothy Brett), much talent, a sweet if saucy temperament, and a genuine fondness for Lawrence. She agreed to go to Taos in the spring. Glad for her company, Lawrence now argued that, for genuine living in the United States, "Taos is about the best place." It was a place of tranquility, marvelous scenery, and few visitors.

As 1924 began, Lawrence (depressed) and Frieda (exuberant) took a two-week trip to Paris, visiting Malmaison and Chartres; they went on to Baden-Baden to spend February with Frieda's mother. Travel absorbed their uneasiness. Far away from London, Lawrence wrote a bold, courageous story called "The Border-Line," which, while it adopts Frieda's point of view, is a thinly disguised letter to his wife. Lawrence brazenly calls her "Katharine," the exact misspelling he had always used for Murry's wife.

The emotional codes are straightforward. After ten years of marriage, Katharine (Frieda) and her husband, Alan (Lawrence), stop living together. After his death, she takes up with Alan's close friend Philip (Murry), a journalist who wraps Katharine in "subtle, cunning homage" and marries her, offering her no critique of her behavior (he is too cringing for that). He succeeds in inflating her female ego. Suddenly Lawrence brings into the story Alan's ghost (a wondrous mouthpiece), who walks beside Katharine and whispers words of wisdom: "And dimly she wondered why, why, why she had ever fought against [Alan's comradeship]. [. . .] The strong, silent kindliness of him towards her, even now [in the afterlife], was able to wipe out the ashy nervous horror of the world from her body. She went at his side [. . .] walking in the dimness of her own contentment." The story, a subtle form of love, exposes Lawrence's crisis. He acknowledges his fears of adultery, then (in disguise) shares them with Frieda. His very personal message, however, is far from oblique.

"The Border-Line" is one of the stories that comment indirectly on Lawrence's difficult conflicts. He wanted his marriage to survive. To do so he would indirectly urge Frieda to reevaluate his courage and kindness.

Whether or not Frieda and Murry ever consummated their "chummy" bond does not matter. Lawrence wrote *as if they had*. That is what mattered. His dark assumption colored, arguably affected, and probably damaged the rest of his life. His trust in others gathered a mold of cynicism about human motives. Though Lawrence did not hold grudges, he never forgot a slight. He blamed Murry more than Frieda—Murry had professed love and loyalty, Frieda just love.

Lawrence, weaker now, begged to return to America. "God get me out of here," he had pleaded in December. His spirit was being crushed. But even in America, all was not well. Despite strong sales of his books in 1923 (which provided money for travel), Lawrence had not been getting letters from his esteemed publisher, Thomas Seltzer, or Seltzer's wife, Adele. They had been close friends who were bound to Lawrence in mutual trust. However, Lawrence was aware that Seltzer procrastinated—put off writing important letters—and so Lawrence did not fret until his American taxes were coming due. Since August he had heard once from Seltzer, then nothing at all about his American royalty payments. But Seltzer had firmly promised Lawrence to be a loyal ally, and that meant paying accounts promptly and providing full transparency. It was a point of honor.

Uneasy, even anxious, but without panic, Lawrence decided to return to Taos by way of New York City, bringing along Frieda and Brett. He would appraise the Seltzers' financial affairs for himself. On 5 March 1924 they boarded the *Aquitania*, speeding across the Atlantic to escape "the doom of Europe."

The doom lay in wait. The Lawrences had spent thousands of dollars. Their fountain of money had supplied Frieda's German relatives and paid for train tickets, ship fares, hotel rooms, expensive meals, lavish gifts, new shoes, and stylish Parisian clothes. They could not afford to let the fountain run dry. The thought of being poor again was unbearable.

CHAPTER 14

Frieda's Rustic Ranch

When Lawrence arrived in America and got off the ship, he found that his fears were confirmed. Thomas Seltzer, his esteemed publisher, was headed to ruin. In a tight fiction market, he had invested a lot of money on the wrong novels and had accumulated huge legal fees defending from prosecution books such as *A Young Girl's Diary*. He had taken staggering risks, then suffered many sleepless nights. Lawrence, mostly unaware of his plight, was stunned by Seltzer's collapse.

"At the moment," he revealed to Catherine Carswell, "I have no money at all in the bank. Seltzer had a bad year." It was a painful admission, though Seltzer, showing concern, paid the Lawrences' train fare to Taos, where they went for the spring and summer of 1924. There, in the land of promise, they could live courageously (and now very frugally) in a landscape that might still inspire Lawrence to write. Seltzer, contrite but defensive, offered advice. He asked Lawrence "to be as economical as you can." He desperately wanted (he said) to "keep you on my list. You seem to belong there naturally." But there was nothing natural about insolvency, and Lawrence balked at promises. Once again, he felt betrayed by a man he had trusted.

He was also determined that Taos would be different this time. Europe had wearied him "inexpressibly," driven him into a "depression," and made him recoil from big cities. The trip west, which began on 22 March, took the travelers from New York City, through Chicago, to Mabel Sterne's desert compound, where the Lawrences occupied the two-story structure across from her big house and where Brett—thrilled to be in America—took the studio nearby. Mabel, who had also endured a bitter winter, at first seemed mellow and kind. The new beginning in Taos promised genuine happiness for these bruised people who had come (or returned) to Taos to heal. Above all, the tenants needed peace.

After the misery of London, Lawrence welcomed the hot sun and the singing birds, loved riding the mustang ponies again, and, after all his upsets, felt he was finding contentment. Even Frieda, he said, was "growing lively again." Away from high costs, away from living in hotels, away from emotional temptations and disturbing revelations, the Lawrences could, as the snow melted and spring roused their spirits, begin to mend the torn remnants of their marriage. As they brokered the lingering tensions that stood between them, they recognized that healing might take months. For a man like Lawrence, sensitive despite his protests, the healing was slow and never complete.

Dorothy Brett (still called Brett) both eased and complicated the Lawrences' transition from nomads to settlers. She eased it by buffering two sparring personalities but complicated it by treating Lawrence as a sacred idol hidden under Frieda's cool gaze. Mabel also sniffed competition. After meeting Brett, Mabel called her a "grotesque." Brett carried a brass ear trumpet in order to hear better, whirling it in all directions to catch scraps of conversation. Undaunted, she examined Mabel with hostile, questioning eyes. She was "curious, arrogant and English," Mabel wrote. Brett got up early, worked hard, and regarded herself as a serious painter. She had never married. Lawrence reminded everyone that Brett was a viscount's daughter. Her haughty, staccato accent distinguished her from all others.

But the surprise is what Brett became. Away from England's class snobbery, she could daringly reinvent herself—not as the prim, drawing room spinster that Mabel or Frieda would have preferred but as an American cowboy. She turned herself into what Lawrence had long been wanting. She became his sidekick—a Kai Götzsche whose admiration, passion, and love never wavered. Earlier, when Brett agreed to accompany him to America, he had called her (approvingly) "a real odd man out." Now she wore a wide sombrero, baggy men's trousers stuffed into cowboy boots, and sometimes a dagger thrust into her right boot. A tough sport for every adventure, she later rode horses with Lawrence (mostly in silence), felled trees, chopped wood, wielded a hammer, caught fish, shot rabbits and pack rats: in short, she masculinized herself, partly to adapt to a freer culture, partly to display her independence, and partly to prevent sex from coming between them. When finally it did, they hardly calculated its sudden, traumatic effect.

After a month of Mabel's organized festivities, which unfolded in growing discomfort, the Lawrences yearned for the quiet, savage beauty of a mountain ranch like Del Monte, their home a year earlier. Still attuned to their needs, Mabel offered Frieda the Kiowa Ranch two miles above Del Monte. In 1923 the Lawrences had loved its stark simplicity. As payment, Frieda proudly gave Mabel the gorgeously handwritten manuscript of *Sons and Lovers*—"worth fifty thousand dollars," Frieda claimed—which she and Lawrence had carefully recast in Gargnano, Italy, as they explored the first stages of their love. The Kiowa Ranch—160 acres of pine trees abutting the sage desert below—comprised a cluster of three cabins. All three needed major repair—buttressed foundations, new roofs, rebuilt chimneys, chinking of walls, coats of paint. On 6 April 1924 the Lawrences and Brett, driven by Tony Luhan (not yet Mabel's Indian husband), visited the ranch. Amazed at its primitive splendor, Lawrence vowed to move where he could be "away from the world," in a rustic place among the hills that felt like a real home. Though long refusing to own things, Lawrence nonetheless swelled with pride at what he called "Frieda's ranch." They had finally arrived where they knew they belonged.

When the day of possession came, a month later, the Lawrences brought along three strong Indians—Geronimo, Candido, and Trinidad—and a Mexican carpenter named Richard. Lawrence, Frieda, and Brett set up camps near the three cabins: one camp for themselves and another camp, higher up the mountain, for the Indians. Frieda cooked their meals while Lawrence and Brett organized their work. Despite the altitude of 8,500 feet, he had never worked harder in his life, from morning till night, day after day—cleaning, hauling, constructing, supervising. The effort was exhausting. As the sun set, all would gather around a campfire, the Indians plaintively singing and drumming and dancing, the firelight flashing over the whites of their eyes. Frieda admired the Indians' way of making a game of their work—inefficient but enjoyable—and Lawrence admired their skill in rebuilding, plastering, restoring the barn, and making adobe bricks for a new chimney and an outdoor oven.

Moving into the finished three-room house in late May was, Lawrence wrote, "great fun." Apart from the big kitchen with plank floors, Lawrence had a small separate bedroom, while the sitting room doubled as Frieda's bedroom. Brett enjoyed a tiny cabin nearby, all to herself. Rebuilding the ranch cost less than five hundred dollars, far less than Brett's yearly allowance of five hundred pounds from her father. Frieda, surveying her renovated ranch, called it "simple and stylish."

Lawrence wasted no money on stylishness, but he loved simplicity. Now that Seltzer's royalty payments had ended, the Lawrences agreed they must, once more, curb their expenses. They picked their own strawberries and raspberries, bought vegetables like broccoli and cauliflower, ate chicken sparingly, and, without refrigeration, pickled their beef. Given the limited supply of water in the high desert, they had not planted a garden. Still, the summer passed in a comfortable rhythm. Brett painted, Lawrence wrote every morning and sometimes baked bread, Frieda sewed, cooked bacon and eggs, and read books, a cigarette not far from her lips. Every day at dusk all three saddled their horses and rode two miles through the woods to Del Monte, going for fresh milk and the mail. Later they could gaze at the big moon in the desert sky or listen to the prowling coyotes. Mabel's interference, always a risk, had been minimized. No longer could she disturb them with her machinations.

All summer the spirit of the ranch had impressed them with its raw challenge. Its bristling energy had awakened Lawrence's creativity. He wrote to Frieda's mother, "Here, where one is alone with trees and mountains and chipmunks and desert, one gets something out of the air: something wild and untamed, cruel and proud, beautiful and sometimes evil, that really is America." At last Lawrence had found the echo of his deepest self. This wild, cruel, proud spirit defined a story he wrote during one sunny week in June. He called it "The Woman Who Rode Away." It is a brilliant but disturbing work, a distilled version of love. Its disillusionment and hostility are rigidly controlled.

It is disturbing because of the cool anger that percolates through it. On the surface the anger arose from Mabel. She had a diabolical gift for insult even when she proffered kindness. That infuriated Lawrence. The luminous landscape around him, though it eased his irritation, could not dispel his belief that American women, like America's spirit, were sometimes evil. The woman in Lawrence's story, not given a name (because she's a type), leaves an unsatisfying marriage—as Mabel had. Both are fascinated by Indians. Back in October, Lawrence and Götzsche had seen an ancient tribe of Mexican Indians coming down from the far mountains into Guadalajara, dressed strangely; older and more primitive than the Taos Pueblo Indians; a "pristine race," Götzsche thought. Lawrence too was fascinated. It is to these Chilchui Indians that the Woman "rides away" from her children and marriage, compelled to find "the secret haunts of these timeless, mysterious, marvellous Indians."

The secret hidden from her is that the Indians have suffered a grave loss of power. They need a sacrifice to propitiate their angry gods of sun and moon. Finding her ascending the mountains alone, apparently in search of their gods, they assist the Woman in undergoing a transformation from willful arrogance to complete submission. To them she is not a female but an essence, a spiritual conduit. She has no sexual appeal and can, in that way, enable their spiritual rebirth. Given herbal drinks, she gains transcendent new knowledge and hears the heavenly stars sing like bells to the charmed cosmos. She is now their servant, unafraid of death. Gradually, when their silence and sexless power disable her will, she is carried to a sacred altar inside a cave; and just when the sun shines deepest into the cave, the priest raises his phallic knife and, as the whole tribe watches, prepares to reclaim the racial power his people have lost. He will sacrifice the Woman.

Now the men of the tribe, like Lawrence himself, have rechanneled their sexual drive outside the body. Their arousal, no longer sensual, is driven by a psychic hunger. The men are fulfilled not by an act of compassionate love but by an act of cold violence. After the disappointments of the past—Lawrence admitted having been "badly hurt"—he was left with a residual fury that affected his remaining work.

Lawrence's love for Frieda had modulated into complex friendship, and in Frieda's soul, too, came "a steady suppressed growl." Acknowledging her limits, she had put her sexual longings into low gear. To do so was small penance for her dalliance with Murry a year earlier. Turning forty-five on 11 August, she had tired of foolish pettiness, her own included. She wanted love, not hostility. Brett's vivid account of the summer months of 1924 does not record a single instance of the Lawrences showing affection for each other; it reveals only a brusque camaraderie. Lawrence had disowned love. He wanted it reinterpreted as if it were the sun without heat, as if it were a presence, even a powerful presence, but not an embrace. He no longer wanted to be touched, except by the same cosmic forces that inspired the Chilchui Indians to empower themselves.

Yet in the story the Chilchui are dying. Lawrence does not say if the Woman's death makes a difference. Their poignant, sacrificial call to their gods comes with a violent but passionate plea for rescue. In this they resemble Lawrence himself. That summer he told Brett, "To bring the gods, you must call them to you." Lawrence's proud, lonely call had not brought them. He needed to go where they might hear him. In Old Mexico he had heard of the Zapotec Indians, who had preserved their ancient culture around the city of Oaxaca. He wanted, he told E. M. Forster, to "see the gods again," there in Mexico, in the south, and perhaps rewrite his novel *Quetzalcoatl* with fuller knowledge of their cosmic insights. He wanted to know what—beyond violence and silence—they might demand of him.

And what did Frieda demand? Admitting in September that "this country has become part of me," she would have preferred going to Germany but—this time—would wait. The marriage still invited bouts of compromise. By themselves the Lawrences were mostly busy and companionable, though probably no longer "intimate." In her book on Lawrence, Brett portrays Frieda as mostly disagreeable and contentious in the summer of 1924, but Frieda's outbursts of hostility usually arose when Brett took Lawrence's part in a dispute. In her unpublished letters, Frieda appears surprisingly brave and optimistic: reporting, for instance, that "Lawrence looks so good." Whereas Brett often describes Lawrence's illnesses (headaches, fatigue, coughing, spitting up blood), Frieda concluded that the mountain air "has been good for him"—"lungs and heart are excellent," a doctor had said. That is what she preferred to hear. Frieda looked resolutely forward. She would neither pamper Lawrence when he was sick nor traffic in words of pity or defeat. She was, after all, a soldier's daughter. Her strength lay in knowing how to let Lawrence, without doctors, rescue himself. And so he tried. He listened valuably to the voices inside him. When Frieda did once call for a doctor in July, Lawrence was furious. He stubbornly believed he could heal himself.

Before leaving to go south, the Lawrences took a long, hot, tiring trip to visit the Hopi Indian Snake Dance. Lawrence disliked the crude spectacle he saw there, but after Mabel complained that he had written dismissively about it, he later reassessed what he had witnessed. He saw that the Hopi Indians of Arizona did whatever they could—even gripping shiny rattlesnakes between their teeth—to appease the inscrutable "cosmic beasts" of sunshine, thunder, wind, and rain. These potent powers, more like dragons than gods, awakened Lawrence's questing spirit. He nobly persisted in searching for personal salvation. Although America's Indians, tainted by Mabel's special pleading, had offered him limited spiritual nourishment, Frieda later said that the "real, religious, reverent attitude to all life, we got there [in Taos], affirmed in the Indians." Lawrence's religious awe, however, had not yet reached its conclusion. Unlike Mabel, Lawrence was not inspired to save the Indians from their inner decay; he wanted to be inspired by their rituals and by what he saw as their need to understand forces beyond love. Farther south he might find what he sought. It was a gamble. He finally persuaded Frieda, who was hesitant, to come with him.

After wintering in Mexico, Frieda firmly intended to return to the ranch in April, when the deep snow had melted. She acknowledged Brett and Mabel's mutual dislike as well as Mabel's compulsive need to interfere with Lawrence, yet she looked forcefully ahead. In the spring she had a vision of her own. She wanted to grow a large vegetable garden; cultivate strawberries, currants, and gooseberries; raise ducks; and milk a cow. "There is so much space," she exclaimed to her mother. "I *love* this whole area." It promised many possibilities: Kiowa Ranch might become Thrasher's Farm in Connecticut, which Lawrence had dreamed of in 1921 and sent Robert Mountsier to investigate.

Now, in New Mexico, that vision of self-sufficiency could become a reality. Far from cities and towns, the stark grandeur of the ranch supplied a unique kind of comfort, offering "the unfailing glamour" that Lawrence had witnessed at the circus in Los Angeles. The ranch resembled other isolated places where the Lawrences had lived—Gargnano, Higher Tregerthen, Mountain Cottage, Fontana Vecchia—but there was a difference: the ranch belonged to Frieda. It was the first property she had ever owned. From Mexico she could return with Lawrence, sick or well, and know that they were coming home to a place both of them loved. Its power to unite them offered great comfort.

Grieved to abandon their horses, Lawrence, Frieda, and Brett left the ranch on 11 October 1924. They spent the early autumn days packing trunks, shuttering windows, tying up boxes of books and manuscripts, covering furniture, and moving winter clothes to Del Monte below. "F[rieda] weeps for her Ranch," Lawrence told her mother on the fourteenth. Who would have guessed that Lawrence would return to the ranch just five months later? By then he was a different man.

CHAPTER 15

Menace and Malaria

Mexico promised renewed vitality. But Mexico was still a polarized country of peaceful peasants and mob rule, of Catholic piety and pagan preference, of staggering beauty and dreadful disease. On 20 October the Lawrences boarded a plodding train, secured by armed soldiers, which headed south from El Paso, Texas, to Mexico City. Days later it jolted through the state of Puebla, lumbering across the wild, hilly, dusty country before crawling down toward the huge plain around the southern town of Oaxaca (pronounced *Wa-HA-ka*). "You don't know how different and strange it is until you see the people," Lawrence alerted Brett as they approached the town. He foresaw the dangers in the country, then after a time embraced them for the inspiration they provided.

The ancient Zapotec Indians made up two-thirds of Oaxaca's population. Short, stocky, black haired, and broad faced, they were farmers who used oxen to harvest corn and sugarcane; they were also superb craftsmen who wove intricately designed wool rugs and blankets. Although these people had developed a culture of heroic patriarchy, Lawrence sensed that the postcard images of the smiling Zapotec Indians hid a sad reality. Ten years earlier, rebel violence had compromised their cooperative stability and weakened them. Their stoic vitality was so eroded that Frieda described them as "these dying, apathetic Indians." Even so, the Lawrences' second Mexican adventure began in great anticipation.

In Oaxaca, a sleepy town of thirty thousand, the Lawrences, with Brett, stepped off the train on 9 November 1924. Lawrence wore a black-and-white checked suit, paired with a tie from Frieda's mother in Germany; Frieda wore a cotton dress and a plain bowler hat. They looked distinguished and European. The town, quiet and orderly, offered a perfect climate. The hot sun shone all day. At five thousand feet, the elevation was "just right" for Lawrence's damaged lungs. In the fields, workers—as they had for centuries—cut sugarcane by hand and piled it on big wagons. In the hot afternoons they rested.

At first the Lawrences chose the grand Hotel Francia, near the main square and the big covered market. They soon moved to the edge of town—to an adobe house, solid and flat roofed, on Avenida Pino Suárez, with a handsome wide verandah facing an enclosed garden with big orange trees. They could enjoy all their meals outdoors and employed a cook, Natividad, to prepare their food. (In 1995 the owner of the house proudly showed me the foot-thick walls: *"Mire! Pero mire las paredes: tan gruesas que nunca se han derribado en un temblor!"* [Look! Just look at the walls: so thick they've never crumbled in an earthquake!])

The Lawrences settled in comfortably. They always preferred to experience a place at first hand. When they wanted an excursion, they would take a mule-drawn tram to the crowded covered market. There they perused the local pottery, black and gleaming; the heavy sterling silver jewelry; pyramids of limes and oranges; boldly designed serapes; roses in profusion; even live chickens. At long counters, vendors prepared and served fried grasshoppers, a Oaxacan delicacy. Smells and colors mixed with varied dialects. Sometimes the Lawrences—with Brett—would sit patiently in the main square, waiting for a band to play or a silent film to start. They liked to be entertained.

Despite recurrent rumors of violence and disruption, the trio would sometimes bravely walk to an Indian village like Huayapa, their Zapotec servant Rosalino carrying their picnic basket. Because Frieda and Brett spoke little Spanish and because Rosalino was extremely shy, Lawrence was their leader. It was a role he liked. He insisted on asking questions wherever he went: *Can they drink the water in the village? Are the custard apples good to eat? How much do the sweet limes cost? What is the noisy crowd of men doing in the shed?* The answers baffled him. "They are listening to something," Lawrence wrote about these men shrouded in their groups, "but the silence is heavy, furtive, secretive. They stir like white-clad insects. [...] Rosalino mumbles [about them] unintelligibly." The countrymen remained oddly alien, inhospitable, and unknowable to outsiders. They were like Mabel's Indians.

One day a friend named Donald Miller suggested driving to Mitla in his car. After several hours the trio arrived—"battered and shattered," Lawrence laughed—to see an ancient Zapotec burial site many miles away. Mitla's central chamber walls were covered with repetitive geometric patterns, like hoofbeats in stone. One of Brett's photographs shows the Lawrences intently examining the high stone walls. The place awakened Lawrence's interest in what the living do to protect the souls of the dead. But he had a bigger job ahead of him.

Lawrence had always intended to rewrite *Quetzalcoatl,* the novel that both he and Frieda had liked. Its rococo design intrigued him. And so he worked quietly in the garden during the winter months of 1924–25, rethinking the quest of his main characters. He didn't recopy his draft; he reimagined all of it. It is clear that Frieda influenced many revisions that Lawrence introduced into the novel, published as *The Plumed Serpent.* Primed by her months of living independently in London, Frieda's aggressive behavior had roused him—in response—to make the main female character, now called Kate Leslie, more eagerly receptive and to make the admired males, Cipriano and Ramón, more masculine, dominant, and godlike. They are pillars of power.

Lawrence's revisions, of course, also reflected his clearer understanding of both his characters and his waning strength, which worried him. Something festered inside him. He grew fearful that malaria, the toxic fruit of mosquitoes in Ceylon, might have attacked him, then wondered if the disease was returning. He slowly lapsed into illness. He confessed to William Hawk in January that he had long "wondered why I wasn't well down here." While his lassitude lingered and his energy flagged, he pushed forward, working harder than before. He was desperate to finish.

As he worked, he altered his novel in surprising ways, creating the ritualized poetry of the Quetzalcoatl religion and reconstructing his characters to serve stronger gods. As he patiently rewrote, Frieda recognized her own growing jealousy of Brett, whose camaraderie with Lawrence seemed to promise more than friendship. She acted swiftly and forcefully. She demanded a break. Never intimidated by Frieda (or anyone else), Brett could at times be arrogant and mocking. Despite Lawrence's mediation, she was Frieda's adversary. At last Lawrence, weaker now, made his move.

Hating domestic "scenes" like those he had encountered with Maurice Magnus, he asked Rosalino to deliver a surprising letter to Brett: "You, Frieda and I don't make a happy combination now. The best [solution] is that [...] you should go your own way," he insisted, then added: "Better you take your own way in life." Lawrence could no longer broker a truce between two hostile women. They refused to be compatible. However, Brett—unwilling to agitate Lawrence or to fight with Frieda—agreed to return to Del Monte and, despite the high winds and drifting snow above Taos, to become a cowboy again and occupy the Danes's small cabin. Miserable but undefeated, hiding her great sadness, she left Oaxaca, by herself, on 19 January 1925.

Frieda had won this skirmish. But in another sense she had not. Lawrence's revised novel, newly pocked with irritation, reveals his emotional crisis. A month earlier he had written to a friend that his new novel "is just beginning to digest its own gall and wormwood." This bitterness is a new ingredient as Lawrence reshapes Kate to become yielding and submissive—less like Frieda, more like Brett. Turning forty (as Lawrence would soon do), Kate crosses the line from trust to bitterness, from congeniality to loneliness, from health to worry. She is easily discouraged. Much of what she sees around her—the bullfight, the peasants, the dirt, the lice—disgusts her.

Only strong men awaken her. To charm them, she shows not her penetrating intelligence but her "soft repose" and her "mystery." She becomes demure. Craving completion, she begs the gods "to put the magic back into her life, and to save her." The magic is now redefined in *The Plumed Serpent*. The magic Kate craves is not love but an urgent force embedded in religion and embodied in Ramón. More powerfully than in *Quetzalcoatl,* Ramón perceives that Mexico needs an indigenous spiritual revival, a rebirth springing from the vital roots of peasants. In this man's presence Kate feels dazzled, honored to serve, and grateful that, as a married man, he is unavailable for sex. That was Brett's position exactly. Kate is ennobled but not entangled by Ramón's religious fervor.

Lawrence risked a great deal in reshaping Kate. Mesmerized by men and their religious enterprise, she lacks the brilliance or complexity or resistance of Lawrence's earlier heroines. Exhausted in spirit, she yields her body not to Ramón but to his lieutenant, Cipriano, whose brusque masculinity grips her in its urgent power. She becomes now "just a woman," her core gone soft. In intercourse the journey is his; it leads to his climax. He expects her to gush "noiseless and with urgent softness from the volcanic deeps," where the clitoris has no role. She must respond to his mastery. As he teaches her the erotic potential of passivity, she becomes a pale photograph of her former self. With Cipriano, Kate will enjoy "no personal or spiritual intimacy whatever." She will function in a male-powered machine. It is therefore puzzling to learn that Frieda liked Lawrence's new work because, despite its occasional brilliance, it is so profoundly marked by systemic illness. His creative imagination had faltered. His publishers, when they read it, knew it would not be popular. Later even Lawrence concurred. It was not the masterpiece he had hoped to write.

By January 1925 he had worked so feverishly on the novel that Frieda found him weak and exhausted. The novel, she observed, had grown bigger and bigger, "like an enormous cactus." But when he reached the end of his book, his intestines erupted, whether from malaria, influenza, or typhoid, no one knew. He was soon dehydrated. Brett having been sent away, Frieda valiantly nursed him herself. In February he got worse, lost weight, and could not stand. The Mexican doctor whom Frieda summoned failed her. Later she wrote: "The Mexican doctor *simply* did not come, [either] from laziness or from fear of being responsible [for a death]; so all fell on my shoulders. I did what I could and [now] have pulled him through." She had done so before. She moved Lawrence back to the Hotel Francia, where the Americans living in Oaxaca could help. For ten days he lay prone, incapacitated, at the brink of death. He and Frieda now hated Mexico. "I never wanted to be here," she told her mother, "but [Lawrence] was as if bewitched by his Mexico." Its infectious charm had led them to disaster.

In late February they departed. Lawrence, now dosed with quinine, and Frieda, battling fierce depression, boarded the slow, rattling train for Mexico City. Dust and pollution swirled everywhere—no tonic for lungs that easily hemorrhaged. In the city the Lawrences stayed for a month at the expensive Hotel Imperial. Lawrence got thinner and thinner, turning, he said, into "a perfect rag." His X-rays were ominous. The doctor came to his room and told Frieda that her husband was unfit for the long sea voyage to England. Then came the dreaded words: "Mr. Lawrence has tuberculosis." It was a sentence of death.

Frieda shrugged off the hateful verdict and, though shocked, agreed to take him back to the Kiowa Ranch, where, despite the brutal cold, he might recover. It is where he wanted to go. It took all of his courage—and all of Frieda's energy—to climb aboard the heavy, jolting train to El Paso, Texas. Uneasy when people stared at his thin body, Lawrence had bought rouge and told Brett, "I used the rouge [. . .] till I reached New Mexico – until I got past that terrible doctor at El Paso." When the doctor at the border heard Lawrence cough, however, he would not admit him into the United States. Frieda made a horrible scene. They were, she complained, "tortured by immigration officials."

When the American embassy in Mexico eventually intervened and released them, the Lawrences fled north from El Paso. In Santa Fe, New Mexico, almost four hundred miles north, Frieda did not take him to a nursing home to recover. The new expense—and the delay—deterred her. Thomas Seltzer's payments had stopped. Feeling impoverished again, Lawrence knew that he needed to publish a lucrative novel—yet he must have wondered if the elaborate rituals of *The Plumed Serpent* would entice, or distress, readers. However, once the Lawrences reached the Del Monte Ranch, they were almost home. Brett, along with Rachel and William Hawk, graciously provided for them while the howling winds battered the mountains and piled the snow into ridges and drifts. Roads closed.

Lawrence's illness was another turning point. He was never the same after Oaxaca—weaker than ever before. That he might still write another novel seemed unlikely. He had gone from a disciplined writer staring illness in the face to a fragile, frightened man who, every day, pleaded with the gods to give him strength. "The only gods are men," Ramón had, in *The Plumed Serpent,* understood. The message they offered was part of Lawrence's slow recovery. The gods that Lawrence had been looking for in Mexico, emerging from his own heart, told him two things—that love might be expressed not in passion but within the limits of tolerance, and that loyalty might include betrayal. The gods offered bracing truths—hard to hear, impossible to shirk.

For now the big risk was the collapse of his health. He hoped the dry, pure air of New Mexico would help to heal his ailing lungs. In early April the Lawrences, slowly gaining confidence, moved two miles up from Del Monte to Kiowa, where Trinidad Archuleta and his wife, Rufina, came to build big fires and carry water. The ranch's isolation and pristine beauty were miraculously soothing, and the tall cottonwoods slowly opened into green flame. Home at last, Lawrence spent every hour trying to get well. "It made him deeply, almost religiously happy to feel better again," Frieda wrote. Her ranch had purchased his recovery.

CHAPTER 16

The Route to Spotorno

Lawrence had always liked risks, challenging whatever lay outside him. But the risks had altered dramatically. Death had issued him a solemn warning. At the ranch far above Taos, he lay quietly on the narrow porch that Brett had helped him build, listened to the songs of the spring birds, and heard the patter of gray squirrels on the roof. Frieda advised her mother that he is "decidedly better," so much so that "I don't worry about [him] any more." While she cooked and cleaned and helped keep him calm, he slept for hours and hours. The healing April sun seeped into him like a potion. Indoors he watched the blowing snow pile up in the trees. "Really," he had cried, "one ought to be able to get a fresh start." But a fresh start was less likely now. He was "only half awake." In 1925 both Lawrence and Frieda longed for change: Frieda, to share Kate Leslie's desire that the gods "put the magic back into her life"; Lawrence, to return to a place, even if only in his imagination, where he had been well. It was difficult to know which route to take.

As a couple, they had different but equally complex journeys to make. Very early, Lawrence knew that his journey to recovery would take him back into his past—to England and the Midlands, then to Italy and the Mediterranean. He imagined moving from the arid mountains to the sea and from an elaborate Mexican novel to a series of short pieces. Frieda's journey, though parallel to Lawrence's, would diverge in startling ways. She might, like Kate, meet someone attractive, someone resembling the masculine Ramón in *The Plumed Serpent*.

At the ranch the Lawrences' orbit contracted. They rarely went to Taos and were rarely visited. Lawrence, still ghostly pale, believed he would regain his health simply by resting: for, as Frieda lamented, people "make him tired, because he pours himself out to them." Remaining below, at Del Monte, Brett often rode up—sometimes for tea—and brought the mail, chatting easily about the past, about Katherine and Murry, about the horses and all the local gossip. She soothed Lawrence as few others did. She did not soothe Frieda.

Brett's sketch of Frieda at the ranch that summer is mostly hostile. Frieda appears rough, rude, and temperamental, ordering Lawrence about, dismissing first Rufina and then Trinidad as servants, Lawrence powerless to stop her. Half in jest, Brett threatened to "rope her to a tree and hit her on the nose." Though Frieda liked the busy ranch, she was also discontented, having uneasily "reclaimed" Lawrence in Oaxaca, where she had written angrily to Brett: "You know I wish you well, but my life is my own and I don't want you to boss either my life or my ranch – And you would soon do both as your will is stronger than mine." In fact, Frieda was still the *wife,* able to play the marriage card whenever she felt threatened. Whereas Lawrence preferred a triangle with Brett, who validated him, Frieda felt diminished by it and fought for her status, as she had in Cornwall in 1917.

The hard work at the ranch required the help of strong men. When spring arrived, Scott Murray, who charged fifty dollars, constructed a good irrigation system so that the ranch, usually parched, would have water. Before departing, Trinidad, turned part-time coachman, hitched the horses Aaron and Ambrose to a new buggy and, while singing softly, would drive the Lawrences downhill for an afternoon. Fred Alires, a young Mexican from nearby San Cristobal, came and worked for two dollars a day. On 19 May arrived Frieda's nephew Friedel Jaffé, her sister Else's twenty one-year-old son, who had been studying at American colleges. He surprised Frieda with tales of anti-Semitic hazing during the time, between 1914 and 1922, when he attended an elite boarding school in Bavaria. He fit easily into the rhythm of the ranch and remained for two months. Tall, good-looking, and highly intelligent, he lived in Brett's tiny cabin, chopped wood, and helped the Lawrences with their daily chores. Frieda had acquired chickens and Lawrence a cow named

Susan; he milked her every morning at 6:00 a.m. and every evening after tea. The Lawrences now had milk, butter, and eggs—and tended a small garden. At last, no longer relying on Thomas Seltzer (who hoped yet to resume "our old relations"), they were again becoming careful and self-sufficient. Lawrence told Willard Johnson in July, "I am very well: really much better than I was last summer," although he reported that his "malaria comes back in very hot sun."

Sick or well, Lawrence acknowledged that he "never felt less literary." Unwilling to deplete his remaining strength, he wrote only a few dozen letters the whole summer. Any effort carried the risk of collapse. Any upset might induce a calamity. Still, his creative life went on. For a Santa Fe friend named Ida Rauh, an actress with masses of curly hair, he began to work on a biblical play he called *David*. When Ida listened to Lawrence read through the whole play and sing its songs, she responded with cool appreciation. At forty-eight she felt too old to play the young Michal, though she supported Lawrence and Frieda's enthusiasm for the play. Dotted with archaic language, it captures Lawrence escaping the evil spirits in King Saul, to embrace the simple love between David, soon to be king of Israel, and Michal, Saul's winsome daughter. Frieda liked the play so much that she translated it into German. Though never published, her translation celebrated Lawrence's slow return to health.

He also wrote a strange, meditative essay about power relations called "Reflections on the Death of a Porcupine," which contemplates the life of an animal he shot with Brett's .22 rifle. At the ranch, killing rats, chickens, chipmunks, and at times porcupines (because they gnawed the tops of pine trees) was necessary. But it stirred Lawrence to consider the natural hierarchy of creatures and their compensatory capacity to attain heaven (what he calls the "Fourth Dimension"). That the strong will vanquish the weak was a given. Lawrence now argues that inequality has a purpose rarely acknowledged—to provide every creature with a meaning beyond itself. Every living thing, he says, while striving to become more than itself, "quivers with strange passion to kindle a new gleam, never yet beheld." The key word is *passion*. Long ago Lawrence had found passion in the human body. Now he abstracts it from the body and endows it with a spiritual dimension. Having in Oaxaca come so close to death, Lawrence redefines Christian ideas of everlasting life: sacrifice no longer ennobles, nor does equality. What ennobles is the capacity to embrace *hierarchy* on the route to fulfillment. Fullness of being replaces good works or reverent meditation.

His turning point, however, was temporary. It lasted only until his waning sexual feeling forced upon him, by 1926, a renewed appreciation of the body. The curve of his writing began now to follow the curve of his marriage. In his career he had modulated from passionate love stories; to marriage conflicted, soured, or doomed; to a fascination with spiritualized landscapes, as in the porcupine essay. The perennial favorite of all Lawrence's short stories, however, bends backward, along the curve of a child's toy. The toy is a rocking horse. As the story opens, a marriage lies in crisis; its familial love has collapsed into cold duty. A failed father, depleted of value or interest, complements a materialistic mother whose selfishness she cannot hide. Their young son, Paul, silently pleads for love. He is in crisis, too, having lost the protective power of love.

This story, "The Rocking-Horse Winner," came to Lawrence ten days before he gave up the ranch in September 1925, although he delayed drafting it for several months. A journalist named Kyle Crichton had sought Lawrence's advice on portraying a young boy. "You've got to use the artist's faculty of making the sub-conscious conscious," Lawrence advised him. Look beneath the boy's "unending materialism," he added, to find "the hidden stuff."

"The Rocking-Horse Winner" follows this advice. In the story Lawrence returned to his painful Eastwood past to portray a boy obsessed with pleasing his mother. For Lawrence it was a bewildering topic, since "the hidden stuff" would require him to see himself in Paul's bid to win his mother's love. Paul's bid becomes more and more difficult. Her heart "could not feel love, no, not for anybody." To give Paul confidence and inspiration, he begins rocking and riding his nameless wooden horse. His quest, unusual in its intensity, becomes desperate. He must win his mother's love.

All the while the walls of his family home mock him (as the subconscious becomes conscious) and cry ever more urgently, "There *must* be more money! [...] There *must* be more money!" The maddened walls stir Paul to ride harder and harder, in a masturbatory fantasy that leaves him exhausted—but also knowing, in a sudden revelation, who will win horse races like the Derby. With an agent, Paul bets money and wins—more and more money. Like the Woman Who Rode Away, Paul rides after new knowledge, finds it, even invests on the strength of it, then discovers its cost: "[H]e fell with a crash to the ground." Though unconscious, he utters the name of the Derby's winner before he dies in the night. The boy's unselfish attempts at love, defeated by the materialism of his culture, are rebuffed by harsh, insurmountable barriers to fulfillment. The boy leaves life believing he was lucky. The story is a parable of defeat.

For Lawrence, however, the story's defeat was personal. It was an ending. Leaving the ranch in September, when his six-month American visa would expire, really meant leaving his life in America. The autumn days were especially fine, the nights cool and scented, and the aspen leaves touched with gold. But life at the ranch was hard, despite its blessing of independence; the daily round of work was taxing; and the management of four horses, even with Frieda's help, was difficult. Weakened by illness, Lawrence did not thrive. Frieda, determined to see her children in London, had fueled his annoyance. He was, Brett reported, exhausted by his "incessant feeling of hostility." Brett accurately gauged the change. His courage remained, but he wanted to shed his constant irritation. The next step? The Lawrences would go back to Europe, back to the marvelous Mediterranean.

Arriving in New York City, they saw well-to-do people like Alfred and Blanche Knopf, now Lawrence's American publisher, as well as friends like Nina Witt, who lent them her apartment in Washington Square. Frieda had lunch with the Seltzers but found them horridly condescending, hanging by a thread over the collapse of their publishing business. Their many attempts to become solvent had failed. For Lawrence the doom of the city fell with "a weariness beyond expression – so nerve-jumpy, and steamy hot." He was grateful to depart.

The Lawrences' summer visits delayed their decision about where to settle for the winter. In London during September, they spent a weekend with Martin Secker, Lawrence's committed British publisher, who, along with Knopf, gave him a comfortable advance on *The Plumed Serpent*, now in production. In America, Lawrence's account at the Chase National Bank of New York showed a balance of $1,002 on 30 September;

six months later it stood at $2,254. Lawrence had been paid well enough that in Italy he thought he could afford a house on the Mediterranean, whose comforts would offer rest after the rigors of the ranch.

At last, in London, Frieda saw her children, although she complained to Brett of jealousy: "I rejoiced in the children, but alas, they are jealous of L[awrence] and L[awrence] jealous of them, can you believe it? And I between." William Gerhardie, a new acquaintance, also complained—of Lawrence's "girlish, hysterical voice" and his flippant judgments—whereas Catherine Carswell found her fine friend looking "pinched and small" beneath his wide-brimmed Mexican hat yet bearing toward her family the same kindness and concern as always. She appreciated his tact. But the two dreary weeks that Lawrence then spent in the Midlands, motoring to see his boyhood haunts, depressed him. They made him see the paltry, petty life he had left behind. "I'm weary of past things – like one's home regions – and don't want to look at them," he confessed to Carswell. His pleasure in returning to the past would have to come in whatever fiction he might now write.

The Lawrences escaped to Germany for two weeks, where in November they celebrated Anna von Richthofen's seventy-fourth birthday. She was fond of Lawrence, who played whist with her and her friends at the retirement home where she lived. Frieda had her hair bobbed and fluffed, to make a splash on the Italian Riviera. She was fortifying herself, staking a claim to more freedom than she had enjoyed at the ranch. As before, the Lawrences still pined for Italy, and in November they followed Martin Secker and his wife, Rina, to Spotorno, a coastal village with an appealing indolence, forty miles from Genoa. Facing the Mediterranean, the village rose steeply behind, its square houses shaping a slow staircase to the ridges above. But the emotional staircase went in a different direction.

The Lawrences' journeys around four continents were ending: Frieda would not leave Europe again during Lawrence's lifetime. For Lawrence it was a journey back home, not only to the Midlands but also back to Italy, the European country he loved more than any other. But if he had known what lay ahead, he might never have chosen Spotorno. Within weeks of their arrival, Frieda—now distant from the ranch and the animals she loved—was already reporting to Brett that in Spotorno, "I feel happy – for no reason." As Lawrence soon guessed, there *was* a reason.

CHAPTER 17

Rage and Compassion

In Italy the rigors of the ranch were only a fond memory. For Lawrence, Italian sunshine was a pleasure beyond most, bringing color and warmth to his frail body. Wearing the new suit that Eddie Clarke, Ada's husband, had made for him in his Midlands tailor shop, Lawrence had arrived in Italy on 15 November 1925. He was greeted by "good sunny days, with blue sea – [. . .] much better than the damp darkness of England," he reminded his sister Emily. Unlike Frieda, who had relished visits with her three children, Lawrence gladly left behind both the oppressive cold of the Midlands, where he had "coughed like the devil," and the brutal winds of Switzerland, where he and Frieda, coming from Germany, had stopped to visit a doctor named Max Mohr.

They went straight to Spotorno, set on the frayed edges of the Riviera, which Martin Secker, Lawrence's publisher, had recommended—and then to the Villa Bernarda, the four-decker house that the Lawrences soon rented. It sat high above the village and overlooked the Mediterranean, which sparkled as always in the sunshine. "It's Italy, the same forever," Lawrence told Blanche Knopf, "whether it's Mussolini or Octavian Augustus." In the Bernarda's huge garden, the last leaves were dropping from the grapevines. Behind them rose hills where he could stroll when the wind wasn't blowing. Mostly he rested. Frieda, with her fine appetite, was soon preparing lavish lunches. "I must go [now] and cook some rice and artichokes and fish," she wrote to Emily; the second course included "Gorgonzola and figs and nuts and pears." By 8 December,

Frieda was chortling to Brett about someone she had met at the Bernarda. This man, hearty and fine, enticed Frieda to put at risk the safe limits of her marriage.

Around Christmas 1925 Lawrence, whose eyes were not yet open to the new risk, wrote a satiric novella dissecting the Ernest Weekley family who, after 1912, had tended assiduously to Frieda's three children. The novella, published posthumously, is called *The Virgin and the Gipsy*. It skewers the family matriarch, Granny Saywell, a dominating widow who aims to crush the freedoms that her two lovely granddaughters seek beyond provincial life. Daring to go away from home, Yvette, the younger girl, meets a gypsy who exudes a magnetic appeal: he is tall, aloof, handsome, and clad in forest green. He proudly "robbed her of her will." She and the gypsy are separated by class (she is a vicar's daughter, he sells brooms and brass) but separated also by age (she is seventeen, he over thirty). Yet Yvette's attraction is profoundly physical: "He [. . .] makes me feel – different! . . . as if he really, but *really, desired* me." When she sees him again, she admires "the slim lines of his body in the green jersey, the turn of his silent face. She felt she . . . belonged to him, in some way, for ever." Before their strong attraction can turn into intimacy, a nearby dam bursts, a flood descends, and, although the gypsy saves Yvette, her house is destroyed. After he and his family decamp, he sends her a note: "I hope I see you again one day."

Most readers doubt the two will meet. On 30 January 1926 Lawrence received a typescript of the story but did not try to publish it. The reason is clear. His worry about Frieda's infidelity grew into alarm, and he lost interest in a book that would honor her decision to leave Weekley in 1912. He considered rewriting it but refused. Discarding the book's central idea, he remembered the sexually aroused woman and the handsome married man and shelved them both. He could return to them if he chose.

A different topic now dominated his attention. Frieda had been aroused by a man wholly different from Weekley or Lawrence. He was Angelo Ravagli, the agent who, in October, had showed the Villa Bernarda to the Lawrences. He was a peasant from a large farming family inured to a rough frugality. Stocky and genial, two inches shorter than Lawrence, he was a robust, handsome man of thirty-four who had risen from poverty into the ranks of the Italian Bersaglieri (they were infantry marksmen) and was now a lieutenant. During the war, probably in 1917, he was taken prisoner by the Germans. He was charmingly frank and secure. He managed the Villa Bernarda for his wife, Serafina, who had inherited it; they were raising two young children, Magda and Stefano, in the nearby town of Savona. Serafina was a high school teacher who had long ago acquiesced to her husband's frequent dalliances.

The Ravaglis' marriage was more open than most. Stefano remembered his father as a man who naturally attracted women and acted on his impulses. Frieda, in turn, described the thrill of seeing Ravagli's dress uniform, with a hat trimmed in black cock feathers, a short jacket, and a dagger at his hip. He displayed some of Frieda's courage. Candid and assertive, virile and expansive, guided by the raw edge of his emotions, Ravagli resembled Otto Gross, who, back in 1907, had sent Frieda to the altar of love and made her a madonna of the flesh. Both Gross and Ravagli were seducers. They had little respect for marriage.

Lawrence, increasingly wary, sensed that Ravagli looked at Frieda as the gypsy had proudly looked at Yvette, and he was troubled. Together, Lawrence and Frieda had rebuffed Mabel's cunning advances; she was destructive. Yet Frieda had been patient for many months. She had never hidden her emotions—she allowed others to cultivate restraint—but she was also careful. She simply waited. She once said to Murry, "Genuine living people are free to do as they like." She knew that the freedom to be herself was a desirable goal and that it demanded strength of character. As Christmas approached, however, she saw less of Angelo Ravagli because her younger daughter, Barbara, had come to the Bernarda to visit and required her mother's attention. Now twenty-one, Barbara "went for walks and swept and set the table," Frieda wrote, "and in the evenings we drew and sang." Lawrence, too, was enchanted by Barbara, who was cultured and beautiful. Still, as he sat outdoors on the terrace, bundled in a new overcoat and scarf, he was watching and wondering. The beginnings of a novel, unlike those he had written, were slowly taking shape. They were buds of the flowers of disenchantment.

Beside the Mediterranean, Lawrence, while keeping one eye on Frieda, also blessed the glorious sun, which danced all day over the water below. In the peace and stillness, he wrote short stories, which were typed by Brett, now staying on Capri near the Brewsters, who had returned from

Ceylon. But his suspicions about Frieda's newly discovered romantic interest explain his subsequent behavior as little else can. One evening, for instance, the topic of love elicited an outburst. Frieda, giddy at being reunited with Barbara, had annoyed Lawrence. Already uneasy about Ravagli's long weekend visits to Frieda, Lawrence suddenly challenged Barbara. "Don't you imagine your mother loves you," he hurled at her. "She doesn't love anybody." Then followed the crowning insult: "Look at her false face." Where, Frieda must have wondered, were his charity and love? Had he a firm claim on her sexual fidelity, when she had so long ago recognized—in her father's distress over his mistress, Selma—the emotional risks of simple monogamy? Did she have no right to fulfillment? Had her early experiences taught her nothing?

No easy answers were available. Only doubt. February 1926 brought more tumult to the Bernarda. Lawrence's adoring sister Ada came for a two-week visit, bringing a friend. Frieda's daughter Elsa also came for a visit, also with a friend. Add Barbara—and that made five strong women and one weakened man, and on 5 February he was hit with what, though coded as flu, was a bronchial hemorrhage—"worse," he told Brett, than at the ranch in August. Downcast, he lay in bed for six days. "The doctor says just keep still." For weeks a cold rain poured, escalating tensions at the Bernarda, where the atmosphere grew toxic. At last Frieda and Ada collided over how to nurse Lawrence. When neither would budge, he could no longer mediate. He was too sick.

Offended by Ada's insults (Ada had locked Lawrence's door against Frieda) yet determined to enjoy the company of her lovely daughters, Frieda decamped and fled with them to a nearby hotel. Weary of hostility, she had tired of the abuse. Lawrence, still feeble—and still miffed—rose from his sickbed on the sixteenth and left the Bernarda with Ada and her friend Lizzie. They went together to Monte Carlo before the two friends went home to England. "I'm so awfully sorry there was that bust-up to spoil your holiday," he told Ada a few days later. "I had so wanted you to have a nice time." Clearly, the fragile bonds linking husband and wife had once again broken. Love had tested its limits.

Alone now, where could Lawrence go? He seemed, Barbara said later, "really shattered." In times of acute distress, he always went south. Suddenly, rising like a phoenix, he too fled. On 26 February he sent Brett a telegram. He had written her such entertaining letters, and so many, that she had formed an illusion or two of her own. She adored him. His telegram read: "Vengo a Capri" (I'm coming to Capri). She was astounded.

After a jubilant reunion with Brett and the Brewsters, Lawrence, despite looking wan and collapsed, put his maleness to a test. It was a profound mistake. As February ended, Lawrence surely believed that he and Frieda had separated again—though this time Frieda's girls were, he may have guessed, only a diversion from Ravagli's persistent affections. Lawrence fretted that he was "tired to death" of the Bernarda's friction. During the 1923–24 separation, Lawrence had found no one except the taciturn Götzsche to share his nomadic life, but on Capri he found the Brewsters, the eager Brett, and others. Feeling now a warm sense of accord, he spent many blissful days on the narrow beach at Marina Piccola and at the Brewsters' villa, though one evening he complained bitterly about Frieda's disloyalty to him: "Women are hardly ever true to themselves"—and consequently "they are not true to others." He minded her disloyalty, not because she felt entitled to sexual fulfillment but because he could not see the shape of his own future and therefore could not decide where to go. He hated possessing so little money for travel when he still wanted to hire a yacht and "go away for a time." He had illusions of his own, of freedom and fidelity.

On 14 March he and Brett went off by themselves to the mainland to visit Ravello, a picturesque town high up over the Mediterranean, where they took adjoining rooms in the Hotel Palumbo. Having spent hours roaming Ravello's narrow streets, setting up their easels to copy statuary at the stately Villa Cimbrone, hiking high in the hills behind the town, talking and resting under the shade trees, Lawrence and Brett naturally drew close. Closer than before. They shared many acquaintances; both felt disadvantaged (she by her loss of hearing, he by his difficult childhood), and both had ignored the narrow demands of their families. In different ways both had freed themselves. He was glad for companionship without friction, she for the opportunity to cover him in the glow of her love. Sweetened by opportunity, their time together was like a honeymoon without the life ahead.

Then one night, after saying good night, Lawrence—his courage aroused—went into Brett's adjoining hotel room, got into her bed, offered her a kiss, and made tentative sexual overtures. She responded as best she could, but Lawrence could not sustain his overtures and, feeling disappointed and diminished, he abruptly left her room. The next night he visited again, more confident of the outcome. "I felt desperate," Brett recalled. "All the love I had for him, all the closeness to him spiritually, the passionate desire to give what I felt I should be giving, was frustrated by fear and not knowing what to do. I tried to be warm and loving and female. He was, I think, struggling to be successfully male. It was hopeless." It also produced intense humiliation, the kind that a sensitive man never forgets. Whether suffering from physical dysfunction or fearing failure, Lawrence endured a brutal blow to his ego and, blaming Brett, fled to his room. He was deeply ashamed, and though Brett was as kind and forbearing as ever, he was relieved when she went to Naples to check on her immigration status. She wanted to go to America with Lawrence, traveling with him into a future of happiness. He had a different idea.

He never saw her again. Nor did he wish to. When Brett wrote to him, probably to declare her passion and her misery, and to beg him to meet her somewhere, he lashed out in anger. He ordered her to be valiant: "The greatest virtue in life is real courage, that knows how to face facts and live beyond them. Don't be Murryish, pitying yourself and caving in. It's despicable. [. . .] Rouse up and make a decent thing of your days, no matter what's happened." She would have been mortified by his letter. But in one sense he had had his revenge on Frieda without, in this instance, being unfaithful. In another sense he had freed himself from imagining a future with Brett. She was not what he wanted.

It was, he understood, Frieda or nothing. That was also a painful truth. Yet Lawrence knew that despite their intense and prolonged struggles, he loved her as he had loved no other woman. In such a mollified frame of mind, confident that the bonds of marital love had rescued him from serious danger, he meandered by way of Florence back to the Villa Bernarda. Frieda had raised a white flag. She wanted him back.

He was welcomed with joy. Luckily, Frieda's daughters, still at her side, had assumed Lawrence's role as antagonist and sparring partner. On 11 April he wrote to Earl Brewster: "I find Frieda very much softened. [. . .] Finding her own daughters so very much more brutal and uncompromising with her than I am, she seems to [have changed] her mind about a good many matters." Still, for Frieda the ground on which to resurrect their love—and their marriage—had become unstable. To herself she would have admitted that the strength of her love had deteriorated, while her sense of loyalty to a famous man, who enhanced her standing as no other man had, checked her tendency to dominate him. A departure from Spotorno might put them both on higher, safer ground.

On 20 April they gave up the Bernarda and, together, went to Florence. They loved the quaint city, with its Basilica of Santa Croce, its Uffizi Gallery and its incredible treasures, and the beautiful Boboli Gardens. Frieda especially wanted her daughters to see the masterpieces of European art. Florence also offered the advantage of not being near Ravagli and Savona. Early in May, from the Lawrences' temporary home at the Pensione Lucchesi, they heard from a new friend, Arthur Wilkinson, a tall, bearded puppeteer, about a sixteenth-century villa that was for rent. Nestled in the rolling hills outside the city, it was called the Villa Mirenda.

When the Lawrences saw the Mirenda, they were entranced. It was larger, more impressive, and more nobly situated than any house they had ever rented. They opted for the upper floor and took a year's lease, then extended it to two. On 3 May, Lawrence wrote, "It is quite lovely

The landscape of the Villa Mirenda (Lynn K. Talbot)

The Villa Mirenda, near Florence (Michael Squires)

in its way"—a big villa, perched on a hill, with two gardens, and, nearby, three peasant families to work the land. Frieda liked it too. "My heart," she wrote, "went out to it. I wanted that villa." The house, almost unchanged, still stands today. In 2001 Alessandro Mirenda, gazing out from the high windows of the villa he owns, told me, "*Questo è il panorama che i Lawrence potevano ammirare; si estendeva per molte miglia*" (This is the view the Lawrences had; they could see for many miles). For Lawrence it was a thrilling view of the valley spreading out below. The rent was only twenty-five pounds a year. (By comparison "The Rocking-Horse Winner" had sold for the equivalent of fifty pounds to a magazine in America.)

Below the windows of the house, neat rows of grapevines fell away from the knoll on which the house sat, sloping past the olive trees to the gentle stream below, near which, after the summer heat had passed, Lawrence sat, his back to a tree, to begin the novel that made him famous the world over. In it appears a gamekeeper who, though he owes much to Lawrence and the English Midlands, has some of Ravagli's sexual appetite and skill. The titled lady at the center is as unfulfilled as Frieda. The novel became *Lady Chatterley's Lover*. It is Lawrence and Frieda's story, carefully disguised. Out of it comes the most eloquent portrait of disloyalty ever written. It is full of rage, compassion, and profound disappointment.

CHAPTER 18

Revealing the Secret

This fictional portrait of disloyalty festered for months. Lawrence wondered if he could write another novel but also guessed that if he became seriously ill, he might need money. He chose, instead, to write a series of travel essays on the ancient Etruscans, whose art he liked. A travel book is what Martin Secker, in London, had long wanted to publish. Still, Lawrence hesitated, unwilling to repeat his collapse in Oaxaca.

In the fragrant Italian spring of 1926, the Lawrences watched the peasants at work in the vineyards and happily anticipated the ancient grape harvest in September called *vendemmia*. They had seen the huge open vat squatting in the basement of the Mirenda, where, each year, barefoot men took turns treading the ripe grapes, squishing out their sweet juices, and preparing them for wine.

While Lawrence waited for the torrid summer drowse to pass—it was too hot to write—he and Frieda hoped to travel across northern Europe and escape the Italian heat. What they could not escape were the altered boundaries of their marriage. Limits had been reached. In the flow of unpublished letters that Frieda wrote to her mother, there is a strange two-year gap in 1926 and 1927. Soon after Frieda met Angelo Ravagli, in 1925, her letters home probably became too candid for preservation— and may have been destroyed. A reference in a later letter from about 28 April 1928 shows that her mother, Anna von Richthofen, knew all about Ravagli. Intrigued by his strong passion, Frieda had welcomed his romantic overtures. Tired of nursing Lawrence, she did not believe that wifely duty was a sacrifice worth making; it was not what she understood by life, she told her mother. She wanted more freedom. In 1926 the Lawrences' intimate feelings probably went unexpressed. They had rebuilt their marriage on a smaller foundation.

While the thin, toughened strands of their feeling came together again, the Lawrences spent their early days at the Mirenda buying cookware and furniture in Florence (the villa had "very little furniture," Lawrence wrote), painting shutters, whitewashing the walls, and carpeting the living room. They carried picnics down to the stream, admired the willow trees (which Lawrence later painted in vivid reds), picked the wild yellow tulips, and, as the nightingales sang, walked among the soft pinewoods nearby. Alone, they relished these joyful times together. To their neighbors Frieda, boisterous with laughter, described Lawrence at the Taos ranch chasing his cow Susan, scolding her, and shaking his finger in her face. The Lawrences' deep companionship had become a compensatory source of strength.

They went to Germany to celebrate Frieda's mother's grand seventy-fifth birthday, then to England for Lawrence's family reunion, which was complicated by the ugly feud that had disrupted the Bernarda gathering. That feud left Lawrence going alone to Scotland, to see a friend; to the English coast to see his two sisters, who for now avoided Frieda; and then to a bungalow he had rented at Sutton-on-Sea, where Frieda, joining him, could swim vigorously in the surf. "England seems to suit my health," he told Brett. "But I don't write a line, and don't know when I shall begin again." He was mediating a lot of conflicted feelings. "I am so bored by the thought of all things literary," he confided to Koteliansky.

Surprisingly, the visit to England empowered rather than oppressed him. Lawrence had liked being immersed "in my native Midlands," he admitted to Koteliansky. In long conversations his sisters had denounced the horrors of England's coal strike—called to protest the miners' wages and working hours—and the damage it was continuing to inflict on Midlands families. The aftermath of these conversations renewed Lawrence's vision. He began to sympathize with the common people—the very people, after all, who were his ancestors. In his rich creative imagination, two strands of material were joining. The theme of adultery, recently so familiar and disturbing, and the theme of England's conflict between miners and mine owners, now so much on his mind, were coming together in a story different from any he had told before. He needed Italy's warm, quiet, sunny days to write it. "Italy is always lovely," he told Brett, who had returned by herself to America.

Arriving home in early October, immersed now in the final days of *vendemmia,* the Lawrences relaxed in the Mirenda's cool interiors. The weather was perfect, more like summer than autumn. They savored the peace of the old villa, strolled through its grounds, and in the fields watched the masses of grapes being harvested. "The grapes are very sweet this year," Lawrence commented. "We've got them hanging in festoons in the rooms – eat them as we go," he told his sister Emily. The sour smell of fermenting grapes gradually filled the big, tall-ceilinged rooms. It was a tonic.

Then a change. The man whose response to the coal crisis had intensified to a maddening pitch ("I am always thinking about the strike") could no longer contain his fury. The coal strike, he said, seemed "like an insanity." A general strike in May had been called off after nine days, but miners had refused to participate. When their demands were not met, most miners—by October—were drifting back to work, acquiescing to longer hours and wage cuts.

On Saturday, 23 October 1926, Lawrence picked up his padded cushion, notebook, and fountain pen and walked down into the pinewoods to write. The proof of what occupied him comes from his English neighbors, Arthur and Lily Wilkinson, radical expatriates who tirelessly kept a diary. They invited the Lawrences to tea a day later, on 24 October. When the guests arrived, they were ready to quarrel:

> The talk soon got on to Revolution and stayed there and was really impassioned. We all generalised a bit – but [Lawrence] did so tremendously and swears by his class, and death and damnation to the other class. He's done with them.
>
> "They're hard – cruel, cruel" (crescendo). He was so rude and cross to [Frieda], and she retaliated with spirit –
>
> "Why didn't you marry one of your own class then?" she said. "You'd have been bored stiff."
>
> Says he, very sad and vinegary: "I may have my regrets."

And she retorted: "Well, you can be off – you can go *now* if you like."

It was rather tense – but we got them off that tack and, though the talk on their part was so savage, we daresay it did them good to let off steam.

Two things seem surprising—how easily Lawrence could become agitated and how his exaggerated claims could still cause Frieda (who could have ignored them) to retort. Their exchange is "tense" and "savage," alarming the Wilkinsons. A week later Lily Wilkinson acknowledged that Frieda "speaks up for herself boldly." Lawrence, of course, resented her quarrelsomeness, even though he provoked it. Despite always wanting to "change the subject," the Wilkinsons reveal that class conflict had wormed its way into the Lawrences' marriage and formed a wedge. Did Lawrence "damn" those with power? Did he have "regrets" about his marriage? Had it scaled its limits? In his new novel he could explore class divisions, the selfish arrogance of mine owners, and the restrictions that a noble sacrifice might impose on a wife. If Frieda was "bold" in her speech, so was Lawrence—and he was about to reveal the secret that separated them.

Lady Chatterley's Lover came out of Lawrence's powerful imagination in three parts (1926, 1927, and 1928). Each part is surprisingly different. Each justifies adultery, but each increasingly understands the high cost of crossing class boundaries—as Lawrence and Frieda had done—in order to find personal fulfillment. Lawrence's early novels had been explorations of emotional discovery and extreme feeling; his middle novels, adventures into other cultures undergoing a crisis of values; *Lady Chatterley's Lover,* the most explicit, discovers with increasing precision the stages of sexual bonding outside of marriage.

The novel's first version, written in just four weeks, glimpses the Lawrences' secret with the least guile. In rapid episodes it dissects a conventional, upper-middle-class marriage rooted in compatibility and entitlement. The couple share assumptions about civility and refined tastes. But beneath the couple's assumed happiness lies a profound disappointment: Clifford Chatterley "had always hated sex." The war injury that leaves him impotent only supplies the outward justification for the asexual friendship that defines their marriage. The result? An excess burden of "personality" that leaves Connie strangely dissatisfied. Although Clifford has had every advantage—friends, education, servants, productive mines, privately held land, an inherited baronetcy—he lacks the one potent power that would hold his wife. He is D. H. Lawrence in disguise.

Connie Chatterley, however, now twenty-five, refuses to be a victim of her marriage vows. Educated like Frieda partly in Germany, she has come to love her husband as Frieda loved Lawrence: "She was very good to him, loved him in her peculiar, neutral way. And he, of course, felt he could not live without her." The couple become "true companions." He articulates ideas with éclat; she listens, comfortable in her own private thoughts. Clifford, acknowledging that Connie, a fully sexed woman, has always felt "a heavy, craving physical desire," finally agrees to a lover "if you have to!" He accepts his sexual handicap as a fact but worries about its consequences.

Connie's needs are therefore uncomfortably close to Frieda's. Later, Frieda wrote to Murry: "Can you *see,* how Connie is *me,* though outwardly younger[?]" Connie's forays away from a big house where her husband is an invalid are Frieda's; Connie's budding love for a married man of a lower class is Frieda's; Connie's decision to see him secretly is Frieda's; Connie's sister's stinging advice on such an affair echoes Else's rebuke of 1907, when Frieda wanted to leave Ernest Weekley. Such parallels make Lawrence's story the boldest, most daring, most provocative he had written.

In time Connie moves toward rescue. She shocks herself (and everyone else) by taking as her lover a lowly gamekeeper named Parkin. A brown-eyed Ravagli of the woods, he has also served in the army, has the bearing of a soldier, carries a gun over his shoulder, does not speak proper English (in Spotorno, Lawrence had tried to improve Ravagli's English), and fights the Midlands coal strike by becoming a communist. He, too, has been hurt by a big, florid, insolent wife, named Bertha, who, like Frieda, had "gone loose while he was away." Lawrence had no direct way to send Frieda a warning, that phase having passed. But if she had taken an Italian lover on the sly and if she thought he hadn't guessed, he could surreptitiously write her into his novel as the slut Bertha. Even more slyly, he could salute her with a coded last name, Coutts, which easily becomes Coonts and then Cunts; she might never guess. His code was not so much a form of revenge as a "gotcha" sign that he *knew.* He knew, and he *minded.*

In the novel the three main characters—Clifford, Connie, and Parkin—suffer from their wounds yet crave relief from them. Clifford has the life of the mind—books, newspapers, literate conversation, painting; like Lawrence, "he had once had a passion for painting." That leaves Connie and Parkin, disillusioned and lonely, keenly feeling their emptiness. Only one experience can awaken them. That is sexual intercourse. Since *The Rainbow,* a decade earlier, it had been Lawrence's forte. In a pivotal scene Parkin arouses Connie to ecstasy:

> For the first time in her life, passion came to life in her. Suddenly, in the deeps of her body wonderful rippling thrills broke out where before there had been nothingness; and rousing strange, like peals of bells ringing of themselves in her body, more and more rapturously, the new clamour filled her up, and she heard and did not hear her own short wild cries as the rolling of the magnificent thrills grew more and more tremendous, then suddenly started to ebb away in a richness like the after-humming of great bells.

Rescued from a mechanical life of duty, Connie reaches a wondrous state. Her wild cries signal her first-ever orgasm. She is filled with rapture beyond words, thrills beyond comprehension. Similarly, Parkin kisses her unconsciously, directed by an instinct that profoundly connects the two. Male and female fuse, achieving a sort of divinity.

Although the novel's two later versions will introduce Connie to a richer vocabulary of the senses, this first stage of her education allows her to recognize pure passion. At once she can begin to cleanse impurities from her mind: class bias, patronage, philosophical abstractions, elitism rooted in privilege. Yet Connie and Parkin rarely talk: Lawrence's narrator speaks for them. He gives Connie's body a voice, a stream of beautifully articulated feelings like flowers opening in sunlight. Beyond that, he gives the couple's bodies *a sacred voice* that commands respect. For most readers, that was new. Connie and Parkin try to preserve the religious awe they feel inside themselves. Their future hinges on their ability to sustain their sacred connection. Though the novel's first version ends hopefully, it does not propose a future between them. Lawrence could not hand the unfaithful woman a pass to happiness. For him that outcome was still too disturbing and painful to contemplate.

Having quickly finished the first version, Lawrence welcomed the mild autumn at the Mirenda and saw a few friends whom he especially liked. One was Giuseppe "Pino" Orioli, the center of Florence's gay enclave—a rotund, worldly bookseller who was as excited by scandal and smut as was Norman Douglas, his bawdy, boy-loving companion. A few years later Frieda remembered Orioli's "marvellous imitations of Florence['s] English people!" His mimicry rivaled Lawrence's. When *Lady Chatterley's Lover* altered its course and went private, Orioli would make himself famous as Lawrence's publisher.

Giuseppe "Pino" Orioli, Florence, 1935. Library of Congress, Prints and Photographs Division, Carl Van Vechten Collection, LC-USZ62-127742

Matthew, Maria, and Aldous Huxley, c. 1932
(from Sybille Bedford, *Aldous Huxley: A Biography*, 1974)

Other friends, far more conventional, came too. Driving up to the Mirenda in a new car (an Itala) were a married couple Lawrence had known for years—Aldous and Maria Huxley. Aldous was tall (six feet, four inches), an Oxford graduate who, like Lawrence, had been a schoolteacher. Taught by his mother till he was fourteen, he was now a writer of great distinction, having published fifteen books, including *Crome Yellow* and *Antic Hay*. Maria, his petite Belgian wife who had been Lady Ottoline's protégée during the war, had a special liking for Lawrence, who admired her "peculiar long cheeks, and rather nice eyes." The Huxleys, living on an income that Lawrence envied, had traveled the world. (They also provided intimate portraits for two characters added to the novel's final version.)

At this time, Frieda confirmed, she and Lawrence savored the autumn months in Italy. The Mirenda was a refuge from upsets. "Our lives, Lawrence's and mine, are so easy, if nobody makes any mischief," she informed Mabel Luhan. Christmas 1926 brought the local peasants to see the Lawrences' tree, decorated with shiny ornaments. After handing out wooden toys to all the children, the Lawrences enticed the girls to sing, then served cakes, candies, and dessert wines. They loved such festivities. A month later the Wilkinsons observed that after all partook of tea and Lawrence's hot potato cake, "Mrs. Lawrence was in great form and just went for the piano in the most relentless way, and sang as well as played the accompaniments." She had a strong, husky voice. No doubt she was smoking one of the cigarettes the Wilkinsons had given her for Christmas. Later she stayed busy sewing blouses, jackets, dresses, and a coat for herself. She would look splendid in her new wardrobe, Lawrence told her mother.

All the while, Lawrence was working steadily on the second version of the novel, making it splendid too. In January 1927 he reported to Brett: "I've kept very well, on the whole: have got a cold now, but if the sun will only shine, it will go. I've been quite happy painting my pictures, and doing my novel." One of these paintings, called *The Villa Mirenda*, perhaps influenced by Cézanne, is reproduced on the jacket of this book. Two figures, likely Lawrence and Frieda, relax on the lower lawn of the Mirenda, he keeping an eye on her as she reads a letter. On the left, Lawrence's bold brushstrokes overpower the figures drawn in stark black and white. The painting celebrates the rustic scene as a villa worker fades into both landscape and house, leaving startling, powerful pine trees towering over the scene.

Lawrence finished the second version in February. This time he wrote slowly, exploring the "bottomless pools" of his imagination. In this version, nearly twice as long as the first, Lawrence makes the love story far more persuasive. He introduces Cambridge intellectuals who debate the concept of immortality and therefore, because of their contempt for the body, neatly motivate Connie's escape into the woods of Clifford's estate. Lawrence also begins to lift the gamekeeper out of the working class. He makes him an anomaly—a sensitive, suffering man who has gone back to his Midlands roots because he refuses to "get on" in the world; he resembles Lawrence, though his "medium build" and "military erectness" resemble Ravagli's. But Lawrence's rage—now intensified—feeds new diatribes from a narrator who castigates money, class hatred, power, and gossip. "Our society is insane," he rails, his tone sometimes shrill. "Insanity can only be cured by death."

In the second version the sexual scenes, much expanded, are shaped into stages of developing sensual exploration, from intimacy to religious revelation, from daytime encounters to nighttime experiments. Lawrence had grown more daring. When Connie sees the gamekeeper approach her, "a queer fire would melt her limbs." And when she sees his naked torso, she feels a "queer, fluid maleness [. . .] flow out of his eyes into hers." He gradually assumes divine attributes that arise from his "mysterious phallic godhead" and awaken her with his power. More surprising, Lawrence adds a night of sensual passion with a bold anal dimension, when Connie feels consumed by the flames of the keeper's keen passion and wants to be "put perfectly" to sleep. Still . . . Lawrence, though he had carefully revised the manuscript, decided not to publish it. He worried about the inconclusive ending, and he feared the book's rejection and mutilation. He would never forget the destruction of *The Rainbow*.

A slow realization emerged. With Pino Orioli's professional help, he might issue the novel privately, in Florence, in which case he could print exactly what he had written. The text could remain whole and uncensored, and he could avoid the strictures of publishers like Secker or Knopf, who (he knew) would certainly demand cuts: cuts such as Edward Garnett had forcefully imposed on *Sons and Lovers* and as Methuen had stipulated (but not required) in *The Rainbow*. But after Lawrence finished the second version, whose tender love story he liked, his health worsened in the damp February weather—his flu, he wrote, "not bad, but beastly." The second version was put away in a chest. There it would lie, untouched, for months.

All winter Frieda noticed how well Lawrence had felt. In the late spring they found red tulips hidden in the corn and, below the Mirenda, the last of the purple anemones. Then came the almond blossoms, and soon the corn turned pale green. Beside the front gate, choruses of nightingales sang in the horse chestnut. Sunny days returned. Feeling surprisingly better, Lawrence decided on a different path. It was a path into the wonders of Etruscan Italy, deep in the heart of a country he loved.

He agreed to a walking trip with Earl Brewster, whose tact and wisdom had made him a trusted companion. Like Arthur Wilkinson and Aldous Huxley, Earl possessed stamina, some inherited money, and a strong marriage built on affection and respect. Above all, he valued a life devoted to art. While Frieda went to Germany for a month (she left on 17 March 1927), Lawrence went to Ravello, Italy, to visit the Brewsters at their Palazzo Cimbrone. On 28 March he and Earl set off for ten days to see the Etruscan ruins north of Rome—"very interesting, very attractive," he observed. He would write sketches of the sites where the ancient Etruscans had lived, describing the decorated tombs at Cerveteri, Tarquinia, Vulci, and Volterra. In the wall paintings that had been preserved, he saw the quick ripple of spontaneous life expressed in dancers who "know the gods in their very finger-tips." Their sensuality jolted him with its energy.

The glowing nakedness that Lawrence found in the Etruscan tombs came to him as a "phallic shock" similar to that which Connie feels on seeing the gamekeeper's half-naked body in the *Lady Chatterley* novel that lay in manuscript at the Mirenda. He had not yet had it typed. In discovering the Etruscans' physical vitality and their sensual freedom ("I was instinctively attracted to them," he wrote), Lawrence rediscovered the distant past, as he had also rediscovered the Midlands from his sisters' vivid, disturbing descriptions of the Eastwood miners on strike.

Yet the past was fast slipping away. His frailty was in full view, his mortality ever more evident. "I've had a perfect hell of a time this last year with [my] bronchials," he told Phillis Whitworth, a London theatrical producer. "It's sickening." Like so much at this juncture in his life, the walking trip with Brewster was the last of its kind: like the last trip to America, the last novel to be issued by Secker and Knopf, the last glimpse of Brett, the last visit with Murry, the last evening with Frieda's son, Monty. The doors were closing.

CHAPTER 19

The Third Version in Florence

The third (and final) version of *Lady Chatterley's Lover* arose unexpectedly. When Lawrence returned from his Etruscan walk with Earl Brewster, he rested at the Mirenda, took long afternoon siestas, relished fresh peas and asparagus for supper, strolled in the evening among the scented pines below, and watched the fireflies emerge. "It's summer," he told S. S. Koteliansky on 27 May 1927, "so I'm not doing much," only some of his Etruscan essays, which were not emotionally demanding. The month of June turned so hot that he "lounge[d] about all day," he told Ada. July was worse, sending all living things into a prolonged and stupefied drowse. On a day early in July—probably the sixth—Lawrence picked all the ripe peaches in the garden, then, coming inside, cried out from his bedroom. He could barely speak. Blood gurgled from his mouth. He and Frieda were terrified. His lungs had hemorrhaged.

Full of anxiety, Frieda did what she could and called a doctor, but Lawrence's hemorrhaging persisted, made worse by the heat. Every effort was carefully measured. Weak and often exhausted, he mended slowly. Giulia and Pietro, their servants, ran errands and cleaned the house so that Frieda could take care of him. A mustard plaster, used in the past, provided little relief; and at night, she reported, Lawrence dripped with sweat. Coming daily from Florence, Dr. Giglioli demanded bed rest; Lawrence, too feeble to resist, cooperated. The Wilkinsons found him "so good and patient that one hardly knows him." Eventually, when treatments of any choice barely made a difference in his health, Frieda decided to move him to a cooler climate, where she would have the support of her family. A month later, in the fierce heat of 4 August, they got into a taxi and went to the train station in Florence, there to catch the all-night train to Austria. Lawrence would have remembered the difficult, dusty trains in Mexico that had proved so daunting to endure.

The cooler weather of Villach, the Austrian resort town where they met Frieda's sister Johanna, offered a tonic. At Irchenhausen they stopped at Else's wooden chalet, their temporary home in 1913. Hoping to treat his tuberculosis, Lawrence drank tumblers of goats' milk. Then the couple went to Baden-Baden to visit Frieda's mother. There a doctor described Lawrence's bronchial tubes as inflamed and recommended a ten-day inhalation cure. Every day for an hour, Lawrence stoically endured the cold steam from radium springs. He also took Junicosan to loosen his phlegm, which stuck to his lungs like plaque. Still, he hoped "to get well as soon as possible." After so much hemorrhaging, he understood that the tissue of his lungs was damaged beyond repair. He knew he would have little time to write. He must hurry.

As he traveled home to Italy, he reflected on Eastwood and the Midlands, where he had spent his childhood. In a sketch written at this time, he shows a scornful cynicism that anticipates Connie Chatterley's disenchantment as her chauffeur drives her through the heart of England: "But nothing can save [Eastwood] from the poor, grimy, mean effect of the Midlands, the little grimy brick houses with slate roofs, the general effect of paltriness, smallness, meanness, fathomless ugliness, combined with a sort of chapel-going respectability. It is the same as when I was a boy, only more so." Lawrence will soon take this "general effect" of ugliness and pretense, and make it the shell of the story that had been festering in his imagination.

His novel, untouched for months, now occupied him. As he gained a little strength, he reconsidered what he had written. But now he was seething and truculent. "My business is a fight," he had told Brewster in May, "and I've got to keep it up. [. . .] I want subtly, but tremendously, to kick the backsides of the ball-less." If he were going to rewrite the novel—already (he knew) "pornographic"—he could not delay writing the final version. He had held back his "kick." Now he demanded "dauntless courage."

On 19 October he and Frieda returned to the Mirenda in time for *vendemmia*. The Wilkinsons met them: Frieda looked very buxom, Lawrence very sick. Though thrilled to be home, he complained that "Italy had no life in it." He was, the Wilkinsons reported, "very irritable" with Frieda, and she "dreadfully sharp" with him. He even impugned the Brewsters, who (he charged) had spent their capital, saved nothing, then aimed to live in grand style. They lacked frugality, proportion, good sense. Lawrence's irritation denied benevolent feelings for anyone. "I'm disgusted with everything," he told Brett. This year, he said, "has been a bad one." In such an angry, agitated state, he was about to begin the final version of *Lady Chatterley's Lover.* He could hardly have guessed the outcry that would follow its publication.

Lawrence wrote the book in only six weeks, from 26 November 1927 to 8 January 1928. His handwriting, now large and loose, forecasts the change. The final version is more rigid and damning in its denunciations of the world but more sympathetic to Connie and the gamekeeper (he is now called Mellors) and their urgent need to be healed. In short, Lawrence now makes illness more central, widens the class divide, endows Mellors with intellect and bitter experience, and introduces a fresh layer of contempt.

What makes Lawrence's book famous is not the story of adultery, or even its attacks on capitalism, but his audacious renderings of female sexual experience. What makes it so pungent is not the characters' crossing of class barriers but Lawrence's hostility to his society. He skirts the smear of pornography by making the book's sexual encounters into a vital source of life, when all around the characters—at Clifford's estate, Wragby; in the mining village, Tevershall; in England as a whole—forms of death threaten to smother the flame of connection that Connie and Mellors kindle.

Above all, the novel prizes tenderness and compassion. They are the only avenues to health. Now the opening chapters show how insensitive are rich, privileged people: Clifford's egotism is more pronounced and his bullying, especially of his private nurse, Mrs. Bolton, more subtle. But Lawrence does more. He adds to the final version a new character named Michaelis, who illustrates the kind of cad whom Connie, in her loneliness, chooses as a lover, and although she likes him, the narrator mocks his cheap appeal: "You couldn't go off at the same time as a man, could you?" Michaelis sneers, wanting his own "after-humming" of male pleasure. His attack, at a moment of emotional surrender, devastates Connie. She had expected understanding, not contempt.

Unlike Clifford and Michaelis, Mellors is substantial and intriguing. He is also complex. His experiences reflect those of Lawrence's difficult early life, while his mature views reveal Lawrence's brash, vinegary voice. Mellors has been disappointed by the social and personal collapse he has borne, mostly alone. Having escaped from the working class—and become, like Angelo Ravagli, a lieutenant in the army—Mellors is stronger and wiser than the insecure Parkin of the two earlier versions. Stiffly in control of his feelings, he is now a man's man—vigorously heterosexual, intolerant of authority, and self-educated. He is also "quite the gentleman." Many observers thought the same of Lawrence.

Mellors has also transcended the values of every class, subjecting each to a scathing critique. Achsah Brewster reports that Lawrence denied belonging "to any class of society." No class certified integrity of being. No class protected both sensitivity and passion. Even Lawrence rethought the prejudices of his characters and, for instance, repositioned Mrs. Bolton's tale of Mellors's wife, Bertha Coutts, and (in the final version) gave it to Mellors, who knows at first hand his wife's common vulgarity. He remembers that she has made him a victim. Her manipulative egotism resembles Michaelis's. Hence, both Connie and Mellors have been damaged by the same modern "disease." Everywhere the novel mistrusts what any class can offer.

Beyond the boundaries of class, the gamekeeper boldly educates Connie into sexual experience, as Otto Gross had educated Frieda in 1907. The keeper offers Connie a more confident sexuality than any she has known. Lawrence masterfully divides restorative impulses from deathly sensations. Michaelis's orgasm, for instance, is quick and selfish, a form of masturbation, whereas Mellors, sensing that Connie is unsatisfied, pauses briefly, then begins once more "the unspeakable motion [. . .] swirling deeper and deeper," until she reaches an intensity that, in her unconscious cries, connects her to a higher power. Her body is the tiny temple of the universe. The unspeakable motion is the rite of connection. The orgasm, cleansing and purifying, is the resurrection.

If Connie achieves an orgasm that awakens her whole self in rapturous fulfillment, Mellors achieves a different kind of orgasm, rooted so deep in his soul that it becomes, Lawrence says, "fathomless." As I explain elsewhere, Mellors achieves a state of transcendence without words to define it. It remains a divine male mystery.

Stage after stage, Mellors takes Connie from daylight intercourse to nighttime experimentation, across the full range of his male sexuality. He initiates; she responds. He guides; she learns. But the ultimate scene, of anal intercourse, worried even Lawrence. His word choice becomes abstract and indirect, describing a night when, once she "let him have his way," he "stripped her to the very last, and made a different woman of her." Even Lawrence, struggling to dignify passion, observed boundaries. Mellors can freely use the word *fuck*, but Lawrence would not describe the sensations of anal intercourse, with its mix of pain and pleasure. He preferred filters like "burning the soul to tinder" or "[she] thought she was dying." He preferred them because anal intercourse was probably outside his range. Writing in 1931, Frieda corrected Murry's contention, insisting that Lawrence "never had any kind of queer sexual relations with me, as you had with Brett for instance (she told us, wrote it to him) *Never –* " There is no reason to doubt Frieda.

In the final version many of Lawrence's additions yield, like a poisoned barb, a new register of contempt. It arises from his simmering bitterness and chagrin. Contempt is the currency of those, like Lawrence, who have abandoned love. Michaelis is called a "Dublin mongrel," Clifford is "like an idiot," and Connie's sister Hilda labels men "nasty, selfish little horrors." This is the language of insult and attack, part of the new "kick" that Lawrence wanted to launch. It's not that he loses his direction by choosing embittered characters but that his need to reform society is so intense that it sometimes obscures the novel's underlying compassion. That was the risk of rewriting the novel while he was very ill.

A different problem arose in the novel's ending. By protecting the two lovers from the hard shell of social decay, Lawrence needed to test their attachment to each other and bring them into the future. At the end Connie goes to her sister in Scotland, Mellors to a farm. With her large inheritance of thirty thousand pounds, Connie may buy Mellors a farm—she hasn't yet—so that he can work. He has only a small army pension. Though pregnant and apart from her baby's father, Connie has rejected an upper-middle-class system without yet knowing how to replace it. Money provides options, as it does everywhere.

Lawrence, despite his great courage, *was not sure* if an unhappy person should leave a marriage in order to find love, or should honor a commitment and remain married. *Lady Chatterley's Lover* has it both ways: Connie leaves Wragby, but Clifford, occupying his estate, enjoys his own sexual stimulation—kissing Mrs. Bolton's breasts. But this fantasy begs the question of which behavior is moral. If one considers only Connie's fulfillment, she is right to go. But if she and Mellors do not live together—they may not—then Connie's fulfillment is temporary. She may need to raise her child alone. Still, Mellors's commitment to Connie is impressive. His final letter illustrates his own persistent courage: "We fucked a flame into being," he concludes. The flame—the fusion of male and female—will endure. All boundaries fall away from the deepest inner connection between a man and a woman. It links humanity to the cosmos, and love to eternity.

In its final version the novel stands surprisingly close to Lawrence's life. The married woman leaves her sick husband, as Frieda considered doing. The sick husband finds an alternate form of sexuality, as Lawrence attempted with Brett, managing, like Clifford, just some kisses. The gamekeeper, who evolves from the militaristic Parkin/Ravagli to the brave iconoclast Mellors/Lawrence, allows Lawrence to explore both sides of his personal dilemma. Clifford maintains control of his money (as Lawrence did the profits from his novel, soon to be published); Mellors, wanting a divorce from his lurid wife, Bertha, works as a hired laborer, earning sums like those Lawrence earned for his short newspaper pieces. In fact, the novel's sex scenes were so shocking, the contemptuous tone so unfamiliar, the class struggle so intense, the marriages so fraught with discord, that Lawrence was long able to disguise his and Frieda's life story of 1926 and 1927, even as he struggled to understand the conflicting claims of love within the limits constructed by society. At the end Connie and the keeper hope to be married and to have a family.

A complex publication saga lay ahead. In 1928 the demands placed on a writer like Lawrence were a huge professional burden. He needed to locate multiple typists, edit a typescript, order sales slips, design and advertise the book, correct proofs, sign and number copies of the published book—and groom Pino Orioli to be his private publisher. The six months that followed—from the novel's completion in January 1928 to its publication in June—are among the most stimulating and rewarding of Lawrence's short life.

Each step toward publication led him into new territory of risk. Despite Frieda's concerns, he had already invested money in the highly speculative American stock market (he had, though ashamed to do so, sent a check for four thousand dollars to Bonbright & Company, an investment firm in New York); now he needed to invest money in a novel whose sexual content, certain to be judged obscene, would preclude copyright protection. He would then risk pirated copies coming onto the market. Worse, he had no professional experience in design, production, marketing, and distribution. Yet he was unusually confident. He was also feisty. For a man as sick as Lawrence—at Christmas, Frieda thought him "very weak"—he took amazing risks. "I am determined to [publish] it," he told Orioli—and then "fling it in the face of the world."

Lawrence had good reason to finish the manuscript quickly. He and Frieda had accepted Aldous and Maria Huxley's invitation to Les Diablerets, Switzerland, for a winter holiday, from 19 January to 7 March 1928. In the snowy Alps, Lawrence, staying mostly indoors, arranged to secure a typescript of his novel. Catherine Carswell and her friends helped, as did Maria Huxley, who typed the last half. By 5 March he at last possessed a corrected typescript in triplicate: one copy for Orioli's printer in Florence, one for Martin Secker in London, and another for Alfred Knopf in New York. (In a move that surprised everyone, he expurgated the "commercial" copies for Secker and Knopf.) Then, despite his good spirits, came a sudden burst of unshielded anger.

Returning in March from their skiing holiday, the Lawrences arrived at the train station in Florence. The Wilkinsons met them, listened to venomous tales about the Huxleys, watched the Mirenda's peasants toss spring flowers into their car, and, one week later, heard Lawrence say—apparently in Frieda's hearing—that if he were making a will, he would insist on a clause: "Not a penny if [Frieda] marries again! Not a penny!" If Lawrence made a will with such a provision, thereby excluding Angelo Ravagli from touching his assets, it did not survive. A month later Frieda had her covert revenge as the gap in the marriage widened. Like Connie to the keeper, Frieda had been writing to Ravagli, perhaps encouraging him. While Lawrence was busy correcting his proofs, which were scattered with printers' error, Frieda wrote her mother a disenchanted letter that has (amazingly) survived. It is a letter expressing a wife's need to resist sacrifice:

> Aber... so wie ich reisen möchte wird L. krank – Heute geht's ihm nicht so ganz, aber eh der Schnee schmilzt ist es besser hier wie in der Schweiz ... aber mit aller inneren Macht mach ich mich langsam freier, ich halt's nicht aus immer nur diese Krankheit zu leben – und mich selbst immer nur zu opfern – so versteh ich das Leben nicht.
>
> But... just when I want to travel, Lawrence gets ill – Today he's not so very well, but... with every bit of inward strength I make myself slowly freer, I can't bear always just living this illness – and always *just* sacrificing myself – that's not what I understand by life.

To be free of sacrifice is to be free of the burden of a husband's illness. As the bright days of spring fell under the shadow of Lawrence's declining health, Frieda confronted the cost of sacrifice and duty and, in response, imagined her life outside the limits of the Villa Mirenda.

For Lawrence, other matters were more urgent than Frieda's suspicious disloyalty. On 9 March he and Orioli met in Florence, then carried the corrected typescript to the old-fashioned printshop, the Tipografia Giuntina, where the typesetters worked by hand. If they had spoken English, they might have perused the 423 corrected pages of *Lady Chatterley's Lover* and hesitated. But they didn't. In fact, the book, printed on creamy, hand-rolled Italian paper, required only three months in production before Orioli began to mail copies to people who had sent him orders. The great shock came a few months later, in July, when the United States Customs began to block the book's entry into America and when, soon afterward, British booksellers, having read it, canceled their orders. "Damn the Americans – damn and damn them," Lawrence wrote in panic.

CHAPTER 20

Where Should We Live?

In the feverish excitement of publishing *Lady Chatterley's Lover,* Frieda seldom participated. Her unpublished letters rarely mention Lawrence's intense work on the novel. It was solely his accomplishment, his victory. Recognizing how subtly biographical the novel had become, Lawrence is not likely to have shown her the manuscript. She had other concerns that occupied her. Still, she played her part. She cooked lunches of pigeon and broad beans, went for long walks with Lawrence to see the violets and poppies, prepared tea, modeled an arm or a leg when Lawrence (as a respite from writing) worked at large oil paintings, went shopping with her servant, Giulia, for local delicacies. And in the evenings she sewed or embroidered. The Tuscan spring made her, she said, feel "blissfully happy." She mildly endorsed Lawrence's grand publishing experiment, but the couple had grown so far apart that she did not suggest revisions, correct his proofs, fetch them from Florence as they appeared, or help with his many business letters. The unique publishing thrill was his. Even he barely understood the splash he would make outside mainstream publishing. The risk to his reputation he bore valiantly.

Rushed into action, Lawrence needed a careful, clever distribution strategy. The various authorities he had hoped to flout as long ago as 1915, when they had attacked *The Rainbow,* had not disappeared. They were watching. In the United States the nineteenth-century Comstock Laws had made it illegal to mail obscene books and provided a minimum penalty of six months at hard labor. But now, backed by his own money, Lawrence could distribute *Lady Chatterley* outside the range of commercial publishers and, he hoped, circumvent the authorities. Still, he acknowledged, the novel "will set me apart even more definitely than I am already."

Pressed into service, the typesetters in Florence printed fifteen hundred order forms that Lawrence could send to friends (who might interest other friends), and six hundred more that Pino Orioli could send to booksellers. The novel's price was a steep £2, or $10, for a signed and numbered copy (roughly £100, or $150, today). By 1 April, Orioli, who had agreed to a commission of 10 percent of the novel's proceeds, brought Lawrence the first proofs. They revealed a spattering of strange errors, and Frieda later remembered the book's thousands and thousands of mistakes. Worse followed. The Giuntina, a small shop, had only enough type to set up half the novel. The workmen had to stop and print one thousand copies on expensive paper and two hundred on cheap stock (later sold as a second edition), then set up the novel's second half in May and June. But Lawrence had seldom been more excited. "It's rather fun doing it," he told Koteliansky. Because Lawrence was already famous, orders flooded in—five hundred from England alone. He knew then that he could sell his Florence edition. He did not, however, know when customs agents might intercept a parcel and glance through his book.

In June he felt confident enough in Orioli's supervision to leave the Villa Mirenda for the Swiss Alps, where he hoped the cool air might rescue his damaged lungs. The Brewsters had just arrived for a visit, unaware of his decline. When they saw Lawrence dressed so neatly in white flannels and blue coat yet looking so pale and emaciated, they suddenly realized, Achsah wrote, "that he was very ill." Earl found him much weaker. The Brewsters, knowing that time was short, agreed to join the Lawrences on their long journey north. It was the kind of venture they all liked: singing "revival" hymns in the train, exploring the quaint shops, reading the long menus in French.

But at a rustic hotel in France, the manager knocked at Earl's door—Lawrence had coughed all night, a local law banned tuberculars, they must leave. They were shocked, then infuriated. Eventually, the Lawrences went higher, to Gsteig bei Gstaad in Switzerland, at four thousand feet, where Lawrence gasped going uphill but, nonetheless, rented a cottage in the mountains, a mile from the village. He hoped the change would "make a new man of me"—though nothing could do that, despite Frieda's assertions that "he is getting stronger" and that "the fighting does his soul good." The amiable Brewsters stayed below, in a hotel, coming every day to tea, sometimes sitting on the grass and singing songs like "Goddesses Three." Lawrence drank Ovaltine and other concoctions, put hot clay on his chest, and, on his walks, admired the delicate pink crocuses. When the leaves turned in October, the Lawrences went to visit Frieda's mother in Baden-Baden, staying in a rambling hotel near the town. For entertainment they attended outdoor concerts, saw plays in German, and played cards. Always, Lawrence looked eagerly for updates on his novel.

His publishing escapade had already begun. All summer Pino Orioli, Lawrence's intrepid ally, had been sending news about *Lady Chatterley's Lover*. Lawrence's personal copy arrived in Switzerland on 28 June. Orioli cautiously began to distribute the book. From Florence he mailed two hundred copies to England in late June, while Lawrence, though fussing with anxiety, offered a guiding hand: "I think you might send three or four copies every day to America." Though Orioli did so, he gambled on their delivery. Eventually, he sent about two hundred, followed by copies to English people who would not "talk" about the book. Lawrence did not hear from America until August, when an acolyte named Maria Cristina Chambers wrote to him that her New York friends had received their copies. Where were hers? Her anxiety to read the book, she claimed, exceeded "any other anxiety." Lawrence had earlier confided to Kotelianksy, "I don't think there's any risk [of prosecution] – at least not yet." No clear alarms had sounded. While supervising Orioli—always by mail—he also wrote letters touting the novel and began keeping immaculate records (as would a publisher) of the book's costs, receipts, and purchasers. Now an entrepreneur, he hoped for a substantial return on his investment. He would thereby escape any threat of poverty.

Despite his precautions, problems emerged. Although Orioli confirmed that copies to England "have been delivered without any trouble," London booksellers like William Jackson and Stevens & Brown, having scrutinized the novel for themselves, began to refuse their copies—more than one hundred—that had been delivered by post. "Damn them all," Lawrence cursed. He therefore asked his London friends Koteliansky and Enid Hilton to rescue those copies and deliver them individually to buyers—or to hide them and keep quiet. He soon reported that over five hundred had been sold. Unabashed, Frieda bragged to a skeptic, "[It's] a triumph, so there!" He had flung the novel in the public's face—and his reputation into the gutter.

Alas, the United States Customs, carefully enforcing the Comstock Law of 1873 (which banned any "obscene, lewd, or lascivious book"), confiscated most copies sent to America. "I shall send no more to America," Lawrence declared early in September. He had been defeated there. Now he faced a new worry. Pirates might pounce on his tender novel and launch their own editions, paying him nothing. He had not secured a copyright. The risk rose after 1 September, when Herbert J. Seligmann, an ardent admirer, published a review in the *New York Sun* that called the novel "magnificent beyond praise." Few agreed. Some readers, Lawrence acknowledged, hurled "insults and impudence" at the book. They were outraged at its explicit forays into sex acts.

Meanwhile, Lawrence fought bravely for his health. Whereas the Mirenda's dampness had weakened him, he imagined that the Swiss mountains would "harden" his lungs. They did not. After a while he felt worse. His "tormenting cough" had never let up. "I'm so sick of not being well," he confided to Koteliansky. Desperate, he and Frieda decided to try a tonic of sea air. They accepted an invitation from their friends Richard Aldington and Arabella Yorke, who had recently distributed copies of *Lady Chatterley's Lover* from their country cottage in England. Joined by Aldington's longtime paramour, Brigit Patmore, the group spent the month of 15 October to 17 November 1928 on the private French island of Port-Cros, where umbrella pines covered the steep slopes and where, on cool evenings, Aldington built bonfires in the open chimneys of their dwelling. Lawrence admitted that he was a "disagreeable" companion. Aldington, working on a novel called *Death of a Hero*, thought him "bad-tempered, satirical, sharp," and portrayed him as Mr. Bobbe, a dangerous snipe. What Aldington disliked, Brigit found entertaining. Lawrence would imitate Earl Brewster's mournful singing or tell a story about a Sinhalese servant who slithered up behind the mild Achsah and whispered, "If spider bite *lady*, lady die," and so terrify Achsah. Despite touches of malice, Lawrence relished making his listeners laugh.

By this time no one pretended to ignore Lawrence's decline. Even during afternoon swimming expeditions, he could not be left alone. Alarmed, Aldington would listen all night to his dreadful hollow cough. Almost as bad, Aldington began paying nightly visits to both Arabella and Brigit, infuriating Lawrence, who was enduring disloyalty in his own triangle. Worse, Frieda caught the flu in Italy, possibly from Ravagli, and gave it to Lawrence, who spent two days hemorrhaging. "I should like it here," he told Koteliansky with brutal irony, "if I had shaken off this cold." When he was better, he lashed out—not at Frieda, who kept quiet, but at the press clippings that arrived by mail boat. One called *Lady Chatterley's Lover* "the foulest book in English literature." Enraged, throwing branch after branch onto the fire around which his island friends had gathered, Lawrence seemed mesmerized by the hot, towering flames. In symbolic disgust he incinerated his enemies—and his wife's paramour—and turned them all to ash.

Failing fast, Lawrence did not know what to do or where to go. "I feel there's nowhere to go, in Europe," he told Brett, and to another friend he wrote, "My health has been very bad." Every cure had eluded him. He had tried mountains, sea, working hard (for six weeks, at the Mirenda), hardly working (in Germany), being with people, being alone. All provided temporary improvement, then a rapid relapse. Frieda accommodated his indecision, partly because she did not know what to do for him and partly because she was courting a romantic option beyond her marriage. The little journeys she took by herself—to Alassio, Florence, and elsewhere—allowed her to rendezvous with Ravagli, who made himself available. Her stamina and sunny disposition always prevailed.

After conquering the month-long rigors of Port-Cros, Lawrence needed a gentler, more hospitable place where his friends, new and old, could also stay. A hotel seemed best. Surprisingly, he turned his compass away from the place he had loved the most. "I do *not* want to stay in Italy this winter," he announced. He does not explain that Italy was Ravagli territory—the place Frieda preferred. He would not condone her affair. Their alternative was France. That is where they went.

In the sunny village of Bandol, ten miles from Toulon, they found the Hotel Beau Rivage, small, comfortable, and inexpensive, whose owner, Madame Douillet, impressed them. It cost only forty francs a day, with good local food. Here they spent the winter of 1928–29. In the mornings Lawrence wrote prickly essays and short poems and, on good days, revised the typescript of a novel by Mollie Skinner, a woman he had befriended in Australia.

After Christmas, Frieda reported that Lawrence had become "quietly contented." At last they had a lot of money. Although Lawrence never forgot his early poverty and still sometimes scrimped, he sent money to his sisters for trips, frequently bought gifts for his friends, and paid for visitors' meals. On 29 March 1929 he reckoned his profits from *Lady Chatterley's Lover* at £1,240 (about $100,000 today), which, at the Beau Rivage, could have supported him and Frieda for years.

His declining energy now dictated not only where he lived but what he wrote. For London newspapers like the *Evening News,* he had discovered that he could—in a couple of hours—toss off short articles on contemporary mores. The best is "Insouciance," a gallant plea to live not with abstractions like Bolshevism and Fascism but "through our instincts and our intuitions." They connect us to what is best in life—the glassiness of a lake, the sulkiness of a mountain, the sweaty perfume of haymakers. He also tossed off flat, barbed lyrics he called "pansies" and "nettles," one of which ("What does she want?") shows a frightened, impotent narrator resisting aggressive women:

> What does she want, volcanic Venus, as she goes fuming round?
> What does she want?
> She says she wants a lover, but don't you believe her.
> . . . .
> How are we going to appease her, maiden and mother
>   now a volcano of rage?
> I tell you, the penis won't do it.
> She bites him in the neck and passes on.

In a chatty tone, as if talking to a visitor, he impales sexually powerful women who, rejecting satisfaction, move from lover to lover. In the last line the bitten object is ambiguous: a bitten *lover* is less disturbing than a bitten *penis;* the latter would suggest Lawrence's fear of castration by a woman unwilling to be appeased. Gone is the manly capacity to offer

D. H. Lawrence, c. 1929, photo possibly taken by Lady Ottoline Morrell
(© National Portrait Gallery, London)

sexual satisfaction; its failure might bring death. Either way, these skunky late poetic blossoms yield a flavor all their own. Lawrence explores the caverns of his chagrin and discovers there not insight but spite.

The chilly winter days passed slowly. What helped were the youthful friends—a succession of them—who came to the Beau Rivage in Bandol. They stimulated and entertained the Lawrences. Some came as disciples, others to collect the fruit, now overripe, of Lawrence's experience. These young men were like the sons Lawrence had never had. They were the counterparts of Frieda's children.

The first to arrive in Bandol, in November 1928, was a quiet, sensitive writer named Rhys Davies. He had recently published a novel called *The Withered Root* and found the Lawrences amiable and direct, she laughing and generous, he subtly malicious. After a three-course lunch at the hotel, Lawrence—usually too tired to walk—spent the day lazily watching the boats from his hotel balcony or sitting by the water, recounting for Davies the events of his childhood. In the evening the trio congregated in Frieda's room for more talk. Frieda curbed Lawrence's barbed tongue. He would criticize her excesses—too many cakes, cigarettes, false assumptions—and earn a quick, stinging rebuke. Their differences harmonized into a counterpoint of bright and bitter feelings that showed less coherence now. They were well-worn companions, less charming and more chafing now.

P. R. Stephensen, a tall, athletic, manly Australian, a graduate of Oxford, was the second to arrive. He pleased Lawrence by fearlessly advocating freedom of speech. Hoping to publish unconventional books, Stephensen wanted Lawrence to authorize a limited, unexpurgated edition of the oil paintings—twenty-four in all—that he had completed during the *Lady Chatterley* years; they had hung, bold and imposing, on the walls of the Mirenda. They were mostly homages, in oil, to the human body. The little-known *Fire-Dance*, for example, completed a few months earlier, poses two nude men circling red flames against pillars of straight phallic pines. It is full of erotic energy.

Lawrence, yielding to Stephensen, wrote a vigorous essay to introduce and defend his courageous paintings. As in "Insouciance," he admires those who—like Paul Cézanne—can capture not just the apple but the "appleyness" of the fruit, by seeing it from the front *and* from all around.

Rhys Davies, c. 1940, photo by Howard Coster
(© National Portrait Gallery, London)

That is what Lawrence had aimed to do in painting—to combine intuition, instinct, and mind. "My beliefs I test on my body," he says, "on my intuitional consciousness." Stephensen, printing Lawrence's keen defense of his work, rapidly sold his edition of 550 copies. Lawrence earned a hefty five hundred pounds. Just twenty years earlier, in Croydon, he had earned ninety-five pounds for a whole year of teaching.

Coming to Bandol for a winter holiday was Brewster Ghiselin, age twenty-five, a handsome American studying at Oxford. The third young man to arrive, he came to Lawrence for inspiration and guidance. In January he and Lawrence discussed beaches, ranches, the working class, and poetry; perused the local market in the church square; watched the fishermen struggle with their nets; and occasionally strolled together among the pinewoods above Bandol. "He rarely preferred to be alone," Ghiselin observed, but created around him an easy, tolerant atmosphere in which others could appreciate, without condescension, his amusing tales of human absurdity. "His quick attention accented every scene and event."

Like others who came, these young men enlivened the Lawrences' conversation, roused their spirits, buffered their irritations. They savored Lawrence's wisdom, visited his past journeys, and elicited Frieda's irresistible laughter, buoyancy, and favorite anecdotes about her husband.

Months before the Lawrences were ready to leave Bandol, however, Lawrence got bad news. Pirates had surreptitiously prepared two photographed editions of *Lady Chatterley's Lover*. Using a process called photolithography, pirates placed pages of the novel on a sheet of metal or glass, exposed it to ultraviolet light, then washed the sheet with solvents that left behind only the printed words. They were then etched to produce a printing plate. Pirates worked covertly in basements or, after business hours, in shops. The costs of manufacturing were therefore low—and profits high.

Lawrence, hugely upset, asked the Huxleys to verify the bad news. Writing from Paris on 11 December 1928, Maria described a signed copy of *Lady Chatterley,* looking "very like the real one," which she had seen in a bookshop in rue de Castiglione. "[B]ut the dirtiest to come – [the price was] 5000 frs!! [or $200]." It was twenty times more costly than Lawrence's original. Enraged and forced now to confront the sobering truth that the pirates had outmaneuvered him, Lawrence felt too ill to take decisive action. Although he realized in December that he "must really try" to publish a cheap paperback edition, he waited till March 1929 to make his move. By then, determined but feeble, he had only a year to live.

CHAPTER 21

The Heroic Fight

In that decisive final year, Lawrence would challenge, as long as possible, the death sentence that crept closer. "What a game life is!" he wrote in December 1928, calculating the risks that every move required. To see life as a game allowed him to dodge the warnings about his health, to foil Frieda's desire to live in Italy, and to outwit the pirates sneaking editions of *Lady Chatterley's Lover* onto the market. The game was not yet so much with death as with the fires still smoldering inside him, burning rapidly. "I have to struggle so hard to keep [true to] what I am," he wrote to Stephensen, the Australian who had reproduced his paintings, mostly of nude men and women. Though sometimes suffocating in despair, Lawrence would not yield the game without a final, heroic fight.

While Frieda went to Germany, Lawrence went to tend one of the fires. He arrived in Paris on 11 March 1929, accompanied by the young novelist Rhys Davies. Before leaving Bandol, Lawrence had bought a new gray suit, shirt, shoes, gloves, and hat. He would, Frieda imagined, make a dashing figure in Paris as he pursued publishers for his novel. For a month he and Davies stayed at the Hotel de Versailles; they were joined by Frieda. To save Lawrence from braving the strong March winds, she organized grand picnics in her hotel room. Venturing out, she brought back French wine, vegetable salads, cheese, apples, and batons of fresh bread—all of which supplied a festive feast.

On many days Lawrence had too little energy to hunt for a publisher who would prepare an edition of his novel cheap enough to beat the pirates, but finally he and Davies located Edward W. Titus, a middle-aged American bookseller who edited a magazine called *This Quarter*. Titus agreed to supervise a cheap Paris edition, and Lawrence agreed to write a foreword, which later became "A Propos of *Lady Chatterley's Lover*," defending the novel as a "healthy" book that aimed to harmonize mind with body. In a passage in his manuscript, he proclaimed that "we should judge all things first by feeling," adjusting them to reason "afterwards." It was his and Frieda's strongest intuition. They always honored it.

> civilisation have taught us to separate the word from the deed, the thought from the act or the physical reaction. We now know that the act does not necessarily follow on the thought. In fact, thought and action, word and deed are two separate forms of consciousness, two separate lives which we lead. We need, very sincerely, to keep a connection. But while we think we do not act, and while we act we do not think. The great necessity is that we should act according to our thoughts, and think according to our acts. But while we are in thought we cannot really act, and while we are in action we cannot really think. The two conditions, of thought and action, are mutually exclusive. Yet they should be related in harmony.
>
> And this is the real point of this book. I want men and women to be able to think sex-fully, completely, honestly, and cleanly. Even if we can't *act* sexually to our complete satisfaction, let us at least think sexually, complete and clean. All this talk of young girls and virginity like a blank white sheet on which nothing is written, is pure nonsense. A young girl, and a young boy is a tormented tangle, a seething

D. H. Lawrence, page 7, manuscript of "My Skirmish with Jolly Roger" (1929), later expanded into *A Propos of "Lady Chatterley's Lover"* (Courtesy of Special Collections Research Center, Southern Illinois University Carbondale)

Edward Titus soon printed three thousand copies of the novel, to be sold at sixty francs each—as compared to the five thousand francs a bookseller had quoted Maria Huxley—then reprinted the novel many times, selling cheap copies all over Europe. Lawrence had shrewdly demanded half the profits; within a year Titus had paid him more than forty thousand francs (at that time about fifteen hundred dollars; today about twenty-five thousand dollars). Still, even as Lawrence had achieved his goal, the noise and dirt of Paris repulsed him. "These big cities take away my real will to live," he lamented. He needed the warmth and peace of the Mediterranean Sea.

Lady Chatterley's Lover proved to be far more popular than Lawrence had ever anticipated. It had opened new doors to sexual inquiry and asked readers "to *think* sex, fully, completely, honestly, and cleanly" (see preceding page). Then Lawrence realized that he could do more. Apart from the Paris edition, he could prepare a fully expurgated copy for a public edition. He had earlier considered the prospect. Although such a text could be sold all over England and America, he hesitated: "I'm of two minds about it." Could he (he wondered) trim the book into a different shape? As late as July, he thought he would "try once more." But Edward Titus, for one, strongly opposed it on aesthetic grounds and judged it "a great débâcle of principle to expurgate." Before long, Lawrence's bookseller friend Charles Lahr, working with P. R. Stephensen as editor, hired a printer named Graves to produce a third edition in his London basement, reset from Lawrence's own Florence edition. Though he approved it in spirit, Lawrence was dead when the secret third edition was published. However, only a carefully expurgated edition, published without risk of prosecution, could secure for Lawrence the book's copyright. That did not happen until 1932, when Martin Secker issued an edition 10 percent shorter than the original.

Lawrence, following his intuition, moved south. Going from France to Spain (avoiding Italy), he spent two months on the balmy Spanish island of Mallorca, 120 miles from Barcelona, and stayed in the Hotel Príncipe Alfonso while he awaited the big London show of his paintings, which he had endorsed. At the elegant Warren Gallery, Dorothy Warren, whom he had met years earlier, opened her show of twenty-five of his paintings, mostly oils, on 4 July 1929. Stirred by newspaper reports, people came by the thousands. *Contadini,* a portrait of a peasant named Pietro who worked on the Mirenda estate, was especially admired for its blend of shadow and light falling on the man's torso.

Although Lawrence imagined that Dorothy would be "afraid of the police," neither of them expected the raid that followed the next afternoon, when inspectors removed thirteen of Lawrence's paintings, all those with pubic hair, and charged the Warren Gallery with obscenity. For months the paintings were sequestered in police custody, at serious risk of being destroyed. Lawrence relished the assault on London's bourgeois viewers, but he hated the threatened destruction of his creative work. He wrote to Dorothy: "There is something sacred to me about my pictures. [. . .] No, at all costs or any cost, I don't want my pictures burnt." The seized paintings were ultimately saved, but some of Lawrence's smoldering fight was cooling: he stopped painting for good. These assaults on his frail ego did not go unnoticed. Frieda, too, was alarmed: "I fear this medieval-burning-of pictures attitude has gone to his very marrow – It grieves me bitterly for him."

Many other things also upset Lawrence—pirates, publishers, obscenity laws, disloyal people, impudent women, illness, doctors. Visiting Germany again, in the summer of 1929, he did allow specialists in Munich to examine him. It was too late for medicine to help, and treatments were, at best, experimental. Nevertheless, he was his own best doctor: getting stronger, feeling better, hardening himself. He lived at the edge of hope.

But the odds in his game were rapidly changing. Now a shell of himself, he could hardly walk without pausing for breath. "He is so, so frail!" Frieda confided to Dorothy Warren. Earlier, Aldous Huxley had noticed how, sapped of energy, "he just sits and does nothing." Yet during that final autumn, he managed to write *Apocalypse,* a book that eloquently resurrects a pagan vision of the world. It helps readers collect their fragmented spirits and become part of a vibrant cosmos whose center is the sun.

In September, when he returned to Bandol on the Mediterranean coast, he rested one week at the Beau Rivage and once again found it a "pleasant little hotel by the sea." But when Frieda insisted on having a house, he agreed to rent the modern, three-bedroom Villa Beau Soleil. It offered big balcony windows and superb views. The Lawrences remained there for four months, until he got much worse. "I lost a lot of strength in Germany," he told Frieda's sister Else; gone was his cheerfulness about himself and others. A fresh fury infected him, and he now spoke of his friends with raw intolerance. Frieda commiserated as best she could, and as she told his sister Emily in December, she tried to be cheerful. But in January he acknowledged, "I hardly go out at all." Still, he clung to the desperate hope that America might offer a remedy. "I believe New Mexico would cure me again," he told an acquaintance.

Sometimes the past troubled him. One day he said to Frieda, "Why, oh why, did we quarrel so much?" Typically, she offered no sugar tablet but replied, "Such as we were, violent creatures, how could we help it?" No blame, no apology, no insight—just a calm acceptance of human nature. With the onset of winter, she realized she could do little to help him or alleviate his suffering. Lawrence had to return to the elements—the stars, sea, flowers—in his own way. The final journey was his.

At last Lawrence listened to British specialists like Dr. Andrew Morland, who urged him to go to the French sanatorium at Vence to get well. The rest, the good food, the sanitary precautions—all would help. "I am perfectly sure," his friend Koteliansky urged, "that if you followed Dr. Morland's advice you would get well in a very short time. [. . .] I wish you could overcome your objections and for a while do what Morland advises." On 6 February 1930 Lawrence yielded and prepared himself to enter the Ad Astra Sanatorium. "It is difficult for him [. . .] He is so *weak*," Frieda told her sister Else.

Bravely, Lawrence put all his papers in order, destroying many in the process. He decided against making a will. Two months earlier Frieda, acknowledging that Lawrence was now "*very* frail," had written to Brett in the blunt mode she preferred, "What's between him and me is *there*, if he and I have other relationships, it's all to the good." That is a blithe, incautious dismissal of a serious fracture in the Lawrences' relationship: Lawrence felt far more chagrin at her disloyalty than she allowed. His pride rebelled against being churlish and confessing his hurt. Guessing how she felt, however, Lawrence made no provision for settling his estate. The fight he had waged in his writings was the only fight that mattered. His possessions and accumulated money did not much matter, or he would have given Aldous or Maria—the most responsible of his close friends—instructions about his will. He could not have fathomed the ensuing complications for his heirs.

His last poems, wrenching in their finality, chart his progress toward a self, solitary and small, whose only consolation is closure: "Only in sheer oblivion are we with God." Dying is unpredictably slow. In "Difficult Death" he writes:

> It is not easy to die, O it is not easy
> to die the death.
> For death comes when he will,
> not when we will him.

In a famous poem he asks a favorite flower, a blue Bavarian gentian, to light his way—as he goes alone—into whatever lies ahead:

> Reach me a gentian, give me a torch!
> let me guide myself with the blue, forked torch of this flower
> down the darker and darker stair [. . .]
> to the sightless realm where darkness is awake upon the dark.

Now darkness comes "awake." When sight disappears, failing, along with other organs, another world may open to embrace his essence. Like a torch going out, he prepares for death by tolerating the pain of each breath, yielding his body with grace, and awaiting the lengthening nights. Later, Frieda wrote, "How decently he let go, slowly even of me."

At the Ad Astra he was given a large room, balcony, bathroom, and a Swiss nurse. In those final days Lawrence could sit out on his balcony and enjoy the view of mimosa in bloom, wanting, he said, "to be thoroughly cheered up somehow." The doctors ordered X-rays and gave him injections, but as he confided to Maria, "Of course they can do nothing for me." He lost his appetite and could barely walk. On 14 February Frieda wrote, with anguish, that "he can't even write and is unhappy." Though feeling miserable, he told his sisters not to travel to Vence. Instead, Frieda visited him each day, rousing his spirits, but she plainly saw the unexpressed horror in his eyes.

Of all opponents Death is the most daunting. In a sense Lawrence defied even Death. His courage never failed him as he lapsed slowly toward

Oblivion, the last wonder!
when we have trusted ourselves entirely
to the unknown.

He had long felt his life slipping away from him. Yet he wanted not to die in a place full of desperate people but "at home." Abruptly, on 1 March, Frieda took him away from the sanatorium. A taxi drove him to the nearby Villa Robermond which she had rented. The next day, as the end approached, he bravely relied on others. Aldous efficiently made the arrangements, Maria held Lawrence in her arms, Frieda read to him, Barbara Weekley prepared meals. Aldous wrote to his brother, "The heart had begun to go [. . .] and he seemed to have hardly any lungs left to breathe with." Lawrence suffered distressingly. Soon his pain was so great that, in a final flicker of awareness, he pleaded for morphine. A doctor came and administered the powerful drug. Lawrence grew calm, and at ten thirty that night, when his breathing faded like a boat gliding out of sight, he died peacefully.

Frieda had never seen him so undaunted. Two days later his body, placed in an oak coffin, was motored to the hillside cemetery above Vence. Along with Frieda, her daughter Barbara, and the Huxleys, both Edward Titus and Robert Nichols—as well as Achsah Brewster and Ida Rauh—joined them. Lawrence's sisters, though keenly disappointed, could not arrive in time. "It was all beautiful and dignified," Frieda told them, "because there were only people there who loved him deeply." After the mourners, without a ceremony, quietly said goodbye to Lawrence, they put masses of mimosa on his coffin, covering it before the long shovels of dirt filled in the grave. All around, birds sang.

Shortly after he died, Frieda recalled how exalted she felt after his difficult, heroic fight had ended: "His death [*she told his agent Nancy Pearn*] was so splendid, so bravely he fought right to the last, he knew quite well about himself, and then he asked for morphine, I think he knew it was the end, then he lay down and said: 'I am better now' and soon breathed his last, slow breaths – Dead, he looked fulfilled and splendid, all the suffering gone – I am so full of admiration for his unconquerable spirit that my grief has no bitterness or misery in it – He has left me all his love and all his love for the world – "

What Lawrence left behind was a gift to Frieda. Misunderstood and maligned, his unselfish love needed, she knew, to be secured for the future. The world must appreciate the purity and brilliance of his search for a particular kind of manhood, one showing both strength and vulnerability. Even if he left behind no written will, she felt confident that he had given her the inner fidelity that would sustain her always and the love that would inspire her to build him a shrine in New Mexico. She had lived with Lawrence for so long that she knew what he expected without instruction. There were dozens of unpublished manuscripts that, by default, he had entrusted to her. She faced now immense responsibility—and also a mission. To E. M. Forster she wrote that Lawrence "gives me his strength." Now there was no limit to her love for Lawrence.

She needed time to assess what Lawrence had meant to the world. His generosity of spirit would shape her energies and renew her purpose. She wrote confidently to Murry: "I *am* Lawrence to a great extent – I have it all right inside me like a flame that could not be extinguished. I love the earth, because his bones are in it – I love everything *more* since he is dead – I know that death is a change [and] only a dissolution into the elements, and I like the elements better because he is of them now – He gave me even death – ." Inspired with fresh understanding, she believed that she could embody his very spirit. She would transform his death not into acceptance or triumph but into a love of the earth's elements that would enable her to act, going forward, on Lawrence's behalf and to secure his essence for posterity. She would go to America and find Lawrence "at the ranch – in the life we made there." He would wish to be at the ranch again.

Slowly reenergized, she would also require someone to help her. She had not yet learned to be efficient and professional nor to school herself in contract negotiation. She had hoped that Murry would be available. He was not. He was writing his own book on Lawrence and had angered her with his partisan, dismissive views. Her daughter Barbara, though often at her side, was too emotionally unstable to assist her. Frieda would have to turn to someone she could trust, someone who was disciplined and unsentimental, someone who might help her honor Lawrence in the years ahead. This person would need to leave behind both a career and a family. Would he?

CHAPTER 22

The Lost Will

A few months after Lawrence's death, the demands and pressures on Frieda multiplied—just when, she told Murry, "I would like to adjust myself, to find myself, and know what I want." There was no time for that. She realized that Lawrence's life meant more to her than she had imagined. "Dead or alive he is the realest thing to me," she wrote after the funeral. She busied herself for Lawrence's sake. To adorn his grave on a hill above Vence, she ordered a local stone mason to create a pebble mosaic of a phoenix; with Aldous Huxley she planned the publication of Lawrence's many letters; and in Florence she prodded Pino Orioli to publish Lawrence's manuscripts of *Apocalypse* and *Last Poems*.

She acknowledged, however, that Lawrence had apparently made no will. Nor had she callously insisted that he do so. In April 1930 she explained to Edward Titus what would happen if no will could be found among his papers: "1000 £s for me, pictures [and] Mss mine, but copyrights after my death go to the [Lawrence] family – but during my lifetime *all* the interest is mine." For a while that arrangement seemed satisfactory. The assets would be shared. Lawrence's published and unpublished works would generate abundant royalties, and Frieda might have hundreds of manuscripts to sell. She could probably live well.

Gradually, however, Frieda changed her mind. She believed that without money she could not adequately serve and protect Lawrence. Confronted with what she imagined was an impending crisis, she resolved to save Lawrence from one man's greed: George Lawrence, his older brother. He was a man practically unknown to Frieda, but he determined her future course of action.

Money had always been Lawrence's domain. Like his mother, he managed all things well; in his later years he was frugal but also very generous. The fact that he had made all financial decisions complicated Frieda's life. Lacking his sure hand, she appeared insecure and disorganized. The Huxleys' friend Robert Nichols described her—when Lawrence died—as "stupid" and "unpractical." She had never wanted to put practicality ahead of spontaneous living and never wanted to let a duty compromise an impulse of goodwill. There she was clear. In this respect she, like Lawrence, followed her inner lights. "I go entirely by my instinct," she declared. Still, she had made many financial commitments—to Lawrence's last expenses, to the cost of Barbara's continuing medical treatments, and to her own anticipated travel in Europe and then to America, where she wanted to take Lawrence's remains.

Luckily, John Middleton Murry, who had arrived at Frieda's side after Lawrence's death—partly to sample the wonders of a widow's love—remembered that in 1914 Lawrence had made a will that Murry had witnessed. But where was it now? Had Lawrence intentionally destroyed it, along with a lot of his other papers, before he departed, with anguished resignation, for the Ad Astra Sanatorium? No one knew.

While Frieda tried to weigh her financial commitments and to confront the vexing problem of the will, she got a series of emotional shocks: Lawrence's friends—including Mabel Dodge Luhan, Dorothy Brett, Murry, and Catherine Carswell—began to compose their memoirs of him and to share occasional drafts with Frieda. Brett criticized Frieda (as she always did) and seemed unfair, but Mabel wrote a confessional memoir, called *Lorenzo in Taos* (1932), which portrayed the Lawrences as she saw them. "Frieda would not let things slide. I mean between them," Mabel wrote. "Frieda would sting him in a tender place [. . .] and start him flaming. [. . .] He would almost dance with rage before her where she sat solid and composed." Mabel's caricatures—showing Frieda as crass and shallow, Lawrence as giggly and insecure—would have inspired surprise and disgust. They revealed Mabel as an antagonist.

Murry's book, *D. H. Lawrence, Son of Woman* (1931), infuriated Frieda more than the others. "Your book was awful for me! [. . .] Your rancour against [Lawrence] does not allow you to see him *whole,* to see his genius purely, such as it was." Frieda wanted to keep his wholeness intact for herself and not to allow the spite or animosity or antagonism of others to falsify her marriage to him. "You made a fairy-tale out of our life," she added, "but a sordid, personal one! [. . .] And in such bad slimy taste!" She suspected that Murry had written the book only "to make money." It seemed tawdry and cheap. It was a slur.

Appalled by these three biographical accounts, Frieda realized how Brett, Mabel, and Murry had damaged and distorted Lawrence's essence and twisted him into a cartoon. They had trampled on the sacred ground of her bond with Lawrence. She would now forcefully reject anything that trivialized his genius. Swiftly, bravely, impulsively, she froze her memories of her husband into a romance of love and loyalty. Searching inside herself, she redefined her marriage to Lawrence as a pure smelting of temperaments, out of which grew a love that enhanced their capacity to be alive and gave them the freedom to complete what the other partner had not provided.

The truth—as always—was much more complex. Beset by so much tumult, Frieda could see nothing except the way Lawrence "grows bigger and clearer for me." She would live for that. Thus simplified, her vision of Lawrence would give her the compass she had lost. That compass pointed to America.

In March, Frieda had already decided, she told Brewster Ghiselin, "to bring him to the ranch, with a real Indian funeral and make it a lovely place for him." She knew for certain what Lawrence would have wanted—eternal rest. But the ranch was thousands of miles away. She had also hoped that her daughter Barbara, who was especially fond of Lawrence, would accompany her to Taos; but Barbara had suffered a nervous breakdown and in November 1930 went to England to recuperate—on the very day that Frieda went to be with her beloved mother in Germany. Just as Frieda arrived from France, her mother died. She was unable to say goodbye.

"Fate is cruel to me this year," she told Edward Titus on 5 December. Now, with setbacks in all directions, she needed someone to sustain her. If she were to build Lawrence a shrine at the ranch, she could live in

America for six months at a time (the period a U.S. visa allowed). Even at the Ad Astra Sanatorium, Lawrence had pined for the ranch as his spiritual home; and now, to honor his wish, she would go and prepare a place for his final burial. But the ranch, though it offered emotional security and few expenses, had one disadvantage: it was too lonely and remote for a widow. She would require a companion. Having once, in 1914, described the Weekley family as "eine ruppige Bande" (a rough bunch) and "untergeordnet" (inferior), she had now revised her priorities and preferred a man different from the husbands she had married.

Frieda had not forgotten Angelo Ravagli. Now a captain in the Italian Bersaglieri, he had met her, on and off, for almost five years, providing erotic satisfactions that Lawrence could not. Transferred to Pieve di Teco in April, he was at last stationed near his home in Savona. But the pull of his family was not strong enough to hold him. Like Otto Gross, he was a conqueror of women. His son, Stefano, interviewed later, said that after Lawrence's death, "Frieda was in great trouble. She was very disorganized, and she needed someone who could help her manage the Lawrence estate." The opportunity of going to America, the privilege of assisting with a great man's affairs, and the thrill of obliging a woman flush with money all swayed Ravagli. He was an opportunist. Frieda would give him a monthly allowance for his help and pay his wife the monthly army check she had always received. These were new costs to nibble at the profits of Lawrence's writing. Frieda's relationship with Ravagli, however, involved more than a business arrangement. He was a partner with limited influence. His peculiar status—he was more than a gigolo but less than a husband—made him feel insecure, without any moral authority. He often put on airs to boost the respect he thought he lacked. In fact, most who met him liked him.

Spring comes late to the mountains above Taos, New Mexico. In May 1931, when Frieda and Ravagli stepped off the SS *Conte Grande* in New York City, they were in no hurry. Ensconced in the Prince George Hotel, they ambled along the city's noisy streets and, in time, met with Lawrence's American agents and with Benjamin Stern, the lawyer who helped Frieda buy back copyrights to Lawrence's early works. But the Depression plagued America. Many fortunes had plummeted. Maria Cristina Chambers, one of Lawrence's friends, wrote from New York in

March, "Four of my dearest friends have [recently] killed themselves." The Depression was not a time to be without money. Boarding a train, Frieda and Ravagli went on to Taos, arriving on 2 June. They were now a couple, full of bravado.

They bought Tony Luhan's deluxe Buick LaSalle for eight hundred dollars and hurried up to the Kiowa Ranch, which Brett had readied for them. There Frieda could inaugurate the simple life again, start a garden, and bring back her beloved animals. Yet Brett, loyal only to Lawrence, blared her contempt of Frieda and Ravagli to all who would listen. In her own romance of the past, Lawrence had, by force of character, poured his purity into Frieda and stabilized her. Brett, alarmed but upstaged by the happy new couple, even believed that she was more truly Lawrence's widow than Frieda. She resented Frieda's power to resurrect herself. Confused by all that was happening and especially by her own emotions, Frieda believed that Ravagli "makes me forget my life with Lawrence, that life of otherness." It is not that she lacked appreciation for her past life but that, in order to live vitally, she had outgrown her need for the framework of marriage.

Mabel Luhan, more worldly than Brett, embraced the new couple. Invited in July to a grand celebration at the ranch, Mabel found Frieda wildly happy with the tables of food, the festive setting, and the strings of lights on a Venetian theme. Couples danced to a gramophone on the freshly raked lawn. "Angelino," Mabel wrote, "is a marvelous dancer—moving tenderly and gravely through the most subtle patterns of the modern step. There is something of the noble child about him and a beauty of cheerful health. We all like him." He was animated and amusing. In his heart Ravagli was a simple Roman soldier. He was physical, practical, and full of stamina. He did not deny his appetites, especially for women, and at Frieda's party he had reached under the table for Mabel's hand. He appeared to be honest and open but was also cunning, beguiling, and amoral. He was neither analytical nor introspective, nor was he a reader of books. He was an excellent handyman. Even Brett, caustic now, acknowledged that Frieda was happier with Ravagli than she had been with Lawrence. "I do like," Frieda acknowledged, "his gentleness and warmth." She allowed him space to be himself, even if it cost her the approval of some of Lawrence's friends.

At the ranch the summer weeks filled with sudden storms, repairs to the buildings, and visitors who came to see for themselves how the ranch had changed. The LaSalle made trips to Taos easy, though money for supplies was limited. Yet as the autumn approached, Frieda recognized that she and Ravagli, if they returned to the ranch, would need to build a bigger, warmer house. She would need money for that too. "I get into a panic of being without money," she wrote to Philip Morrell. As the walls in Lawrence's story "The Rocking-Horse Winner" had warned, "There *must* be more money."

The path to more money led back to Europe. On 16 November 1931 Frieda and Ravagli, having closed the ranch for the winter, left for New York City. Ravagli had been recalled by the Italian army and, when he returned dutifully to his Bersaglieri regiment, was sent to Imperia, a town in northwestern Italy. Frieda shuttled between England, Italy, and France—at home in none. She and Ravagli remained in Europe for eighteen months, Frieda often in London, where she proudly presented herself as Lawrence's widow, capably nurturing his rising reputation. She had lunch or tea with old friends such as Ottoline Morrell, Dorothy Warren, the Brewsters, and Koteliansky; she attended rehearsals of Lawrence's play *David* at the Old Vic Theater; and she visited her three grown children. She also met with Lawrence's young literary agent, Laurence Pollinger, to conduct business. Pollinger efficiently interpreted contracts for Frieda, sought broadcast opportunities, and pursued foreign rights, all of which lay beyond her competence. Daunted by these new opportunities, she relied on Pollinger's professional guidance. Especially important was the contract for the 1932 publication of Lawrence's letters, edited by Aldous Huxley and published by Heinemann in London and Viking in New York. This collection of letters presented Lawrence's vibrant immediacy as no other document had. Frieda was delighted.

She knew, however, that her future greatly depended on how Lawrence's estate would be settled. In 1930 she and George Lawrence, Lawrence's oldest brother, had been named co-administrators; but she detested him, partly because she (and Lawrence) had never trusted him and partly because, as she wrote to Lawrence's sister Ada, "You know how Lawrence would have hated his money to go to George." Lawrence, in fact, had not seen his brother for fifteen years. George had left school at age fifteen, briefly entered the army, married, and become critical of Lawrence's novels. Frieda believed that she, as his devoted wife, must guard Lawrence's money along with his legacy. Unfortunately, her hatred of George and his apparent greed alienated her from Lawrence's family, even from Ada, Lawrence's beloved sister. Months before the will was settled, a French visitor named Emile Delavenay, spending a weekend with Ada in August 1932, recorded "Ada's intense hatred of Frieda."

Proud and independent, Ada had acquired much of Lawrence's fierce integrity. To Ada he had often made unflattering comments about Frieda and her past. Ada remembered them. In a forceful letter composed three months later, Ada wrote scathingly to Frieda, accusing her of commonness and disloyalty: "Remember! I know a little too much about you [for you] to try this devoted wife stunt on me. [. . .] I could fill a book with the things he told me. [. . .] After living so long with Bert I had hoped you might have absorbed a little of his integrity and honesty of purpose, but apparently you don't know [their] meaning. [. . .] This is the end of our relationship – if you write I shall burn the letter unopened."

Ada, firmly protective of her brother's memory, wanted her Eastwood "Bert" to be a temple of purity to which family and friends could make a pilgrimage. She had hoped to build a family museum in Eastwood. Frieda, however, wanted to be financially secure before leaving for America to enshrine Lawrence's spirit there. She acknowledged the expense of supporting Ravagli's family in Italy, though for now she kept the Ravaglis a secret. Ada—had she known—would not have been charitable. Their goals conflicted. Ada believed in fairness to family (acquiring the copyrights after Frieda's death), whereas Frieda believed in her right to let the courts decide. On 11 November would come the long-awaited decision.

Despite the prospect of a costly lawsuit, Frieda had, early in 1932, hired an excellent barrister, Charles D. Medley, to present her case in court. More than anything, he needed evidence of a will. Before Frieda had left for America in 1931, she had asked Murry, "Would you say [something] about a will in case George [Lawrence] claims Mss?" (Murry had recalled that he and Lawrence had made nearly identical wills, witnessed—in Lawrence's case—by Murry and Katherine.) Imagining what a lawyer might require, Frieda had asked him, "Have you *your* will with L[awrence]'s and my signature?" Fortunately, she remembered it from 1914. It was the silver key to her future security.

Returning to England in October, her six-month American visa having expired, she realized that a costly legal battle was imminent. No matter the cost, she was determined to crush George's claims on the estate. Much earlier, in November 1930, she had warned Lawrence's sister Emily that "your brother wanted me to have everything, he told me so, and he and I knew nothing about the law. He thought as I did [. . .] that everything goes automatically to the wife." He would be wounded to know "what a difficult position" she now encountered. (Nevertheless, Lawrence had chosen not to make a will in his last days.)

Frieda went forward, cautious but confident. "Medley is sure [of the case], I can see," she told Murry. While all parties waited for a court date, compromise still seemed possible. Lawrence's family, of course, wanted the copyrights after Frieda's death. "They could have them," Frieda acknowledged, "but it's the *freedom* to act as I like, that I want – I must be independent." Frieda may appear ungenerous, but she believed, with Lawrence, that George deserved nothing, and she knew that under George's direction, Lawrence's legacy might be compromised if she died prematurely. Only she would be able to protect Lawrence from foolish incompetence.

Once a November court date was set, Medley decided to gather depositions from those who knew Lawrence well. He chose Pino Orioli and Norman Douglas, both living in Florence. Frieda remembered what Douglas had said and in October wrote to Murry: "The curious thing is, that it was really *Douglas's* evidence, whose visit [to the Villa Mirenda] as you know caught Lawrence in a mood of intense resentment against his family, where I believe Lawrence *sensed,* what was coming from them – when Ada had just written: let me have Mss and pictures to make a Lawrence 'museum' for the family – He was so furious, it was such bad taste on Ada's part – Then he raved against the family – " That Lawrence, when irritated, could be outspoken and ungracious is not a surprise. Yet no one believed that George Lawrence, having never visited his brother or showed him any fraternal respect, should have a share of the estate. Still, the family felt entitled to part of what might be lucrative assets, for they had often cared for Lawrence when he was ill and had shown him special fondness. But they did not realize the depths of Frieda's growing antagonism.

After many irritating delays, the elderly judge, Lord Merrivale, aged seventy-six, heard the case on 3 November 1932. He heard Frieda tearfully describe Lawrence's last wishes, weighed Murry's declaration that Lawrence had made a will in 1914, and pondered the disquieting depositions from Orioli and Douglas. When the verdict was read, all were surprised.

CHAPTER 23

Taos, Ravagli, and the Manuscripts

Judge Merrivale gave the whole estate to Frieda, less five hundred pounds each to George and Emily. Ada, feeling grievously injured, wanted nothing. "She will live on her hatred now," Frieda reflected, but she was also disappointed that the relationship, once so warm, had ended in hostility. Frieda heralded the judge's decision as "a triumph for Lawrence and our life together." She was grateful that she had never urged Lawrence to worry about her financial needs. "[T]o the last," she reminded Laurence Pollinger, "he could never doubt my integrity of feeling for *him,* in which 'money' and 'safety' had no part." She could now work on Lawrence's behalf: to give him peace at the ranch, to stabilize his copyrights, to control his unpublished work, to locate his manuscripts (some of which had disappeared), and to recall in writing the years of their shared life. Although she relished the press coverage that the court's decision inspired, she later regretted that her bitter feelings had turned her forever against Lawrence's Eastwood family. She never saw them again.

Aware of the freedom and the opportunities that America offered, she went to Savona to visit Angelo Ravagli and to organize their departure for New Mexico. She disliked Europe, which seemed to her close friend Aldous Huxley to show now an "awful sense of invisible [...] hate, envy, anger crawling about." She was eager to tie up loose threads. "I'm so busy doing a thousand things," she wrote to Knud Merrild, still living in Los Angeles, "[that] my life seems full to bursting." Once Frieda decided to move to America, in 1933, she set about consolidating her position as Lawrence's widow. In New Mexico she would pursue a plan for Lawrence's body, still lying in the cemetery at Vence; she hoped to build a larger house on her ranch; and she especially treasured Lawrence's handwritten manuscripts—at least 175 in her possession. They were her capital. Earlier, Lawrence himself had commented on their value. He told Brett, in 1929, that the two complete manuscripts of *The Plumed Serpent* are "worth the whole ranch." Frieda anticipated that a research university might buy them all and keep the collection intact. The manuscripts would offer students an exceptional opportunity to study a writer's composing and revising processes.

Suffering various crises since Lawrence's death, Frieda needed—more than anything—stability. She had weathered the challenges of the will, helped her daughter recover her health, encouraged the publication of Lawrence's books, bought Ravagli out of the Italian army, and tested the waters of Taos to see if they would permit a widow and a married man to move freely in their midst. She knew there would be gossip in Taos, but she ignored it—"nothing [is] hidden anywhere," she remarked to Mabel. Only at the Kiowa Ranch, however, could she fully capture her memories of Lawrence. He had given her the standards that would enable her to live fully and well. "His absolute integrity," she told Mabel, "means everything to me – He counterbalances the weight of this awful humanity."

Arriving at the ranch in April 1933, Frieda and Ravagli began to construct a new house a few yards below the cabin that Lawrence had helped to rebuild. Made of logs, the new house had a large kitchen, living area, two bedrooms, a bath (and by 1936 a big room to hold Lawrence's paintings). Challenged and energized, Ravagli acted as his own contractor and, like Lawrence, hired local labor to reduce costs. Frieda worked too, "*so hard, my hands are already quite rough.*" In August, Frieda allowed that she had spent only five hundred pounds (at that time twenty-five hundred dollars) to build the house. While Ravagli supervised all aspects of construction, Frieda cooked, gardened, washed clothes, fed the lambs, and made butter from the rich milk of her Jersey cow, Anita. As she had done for years, she sewed and read in the evenings.

Now she could honor her commitments to Lawrence. Knowing that he would want her to write about their life together, she began working on a memoir. A lot could be omitted, especially the nasty exchanges that others had recounted. To guide her, she had only her personal memories and some letters, no firm daily anchor such as the journal that the Wilkinsons had kept in Florence or the diaries of John Middleton Murry. Yet she went forward in her own way. Moved to compose lyrical vignettes of their shared life, she portrayed Lawrence with a directness and authority that only she could have mustered. Their supreme happiness figures most prominently. She avoids the difficult, exasperating episodes in order to secure Lawrence for posterity. That is what a faithful widow should, she knew, have done. She had also fixed his meaning for herself. He was a hero and a figure of salvation in a world that had fought against him.

When she finished her memoir, she asked Walter Goodwin, owner of the Rydal Press in Santa Fe, to publish it in a fine limited edition of one thousand signed copies. He issued it in June 1934 as *Not I, But the Wind*. Serving as Frieda's assistant, Ravagli sent out circulars to advertise the book, which sold steadily. In October the Viking Press in New York published a slightly shorter trade edition, and in England her friend Alexander Frere-Reeves issued the British edition for Heinemann. Many admirers wrote her letters. The book was a small triumph. She never wrote another.

As the Taos winter of 1934 approached, Frieda welcomed a visitor who had known Lawrence well. He was Knud Merrild, who arrived at the Kiowa Ranch on 4 December with his wife, Else, whom he had married in 1926. In a newly discovered letter, he tells his friend Kai Götzsche, with whom he had spent the winter of 1922–23 in a cabin near the Lawrences, that Frieda had scarcely changed in the intervening decade: "Frieda is to me exactly the same as for 11 years ago – if possible even more full of life, spiritual as well as bodily life flows in and out of her, and fills the whole place with life so it seems that Lawrence is still here, only gone for a trip somewhere." To this warm appreciation, Merrild adds a curious detail. Living in the Del Monte cabin that he and Götzsche had once shared is "a young Italian writer and his wife." They were the Lucianis, low-life swindlers whom Lawrence, were he alive, would have avoided.

Frieda and Ravagli soon faced a shocking difficulty. Always gregarious and charming, Ravagli had befriended Nicholas Luciani, who—with his wife—had concocted a nasty caper. With money borrowed from Frieda, regaled now as a rich widow, he would (he said) buy California grapes, open a winery, and make a lot of money. Ever generous and willing to please Ravagli, Frieda lent Luciani eleven hundred dollars—more than she had paid for the deluxe Buick LaSalle. But Luciani outwitted her.

Suddenly the local sheriff drove to the Kiowa Ranch and knocked at the door. He accused Ravagli of participating in a scheme, hatched by the Lucianis, to solicit women for sex. Nor was Frieda spared. She was accused of stealing a purse that Luciani's wife, posing as Frieda's cook, had "planted" in the new log house. She was caught in a trap.

Terrified that he would face rapid deportation, Ravagli fled in the LaSalle to another state. Frieda, equally alarmed, quickly followed him, driven by the faithful Merrild, who had been visiting her for ten days. She met Ravagli in Alamosa, Colorado, ninety miles away, in mid-December. They drove on, about twelve hundred miles, to New Orleans and, after locating a ship, sailed to Buenos Aires, where they lived with Ravagli's sister and brother in dreary poverty. But they had escaped an arrest! They did not return to the ranch till spring, when the Lucianis had disappeared. The ship had taken them to safety.

Chastened, Frieda and Ravagli returned to the ranch freshly aware of the need for careful judgment. The episode of the Lucianis warned Frieda about Ravagli's caprices. He lacked Lawrence's discernment. But the Buenos Aires interlude had also renewed the couple's appreciation of New Mexico's openness and stark beauty—what Lawrence had also loved. Frieda wrote to Ottoline Morrell on 6 April 1934, "I am so longing for the ranch again – after all, my life is there – if I had Lawrence there, I would have everything." In the blazing spring sunshine of 1934, Frieda and Ravagli worked all day at the ranch. They planted the vegetable garden, made flower beds around the house, set out fruit trees, mended fences, and rode the horses. She most enjoyed, she told Laurence Pollinger, "looking after things here at the ranch, like my life with Lawrence was." She had never abandoned Lawrence's spirit. "I have had such a lovely summer here at the ranch," she wrote in August. "People and work and sunshine." In the ten years since 1924, her life had changed; better financed now, she could at last memorialize what was most important.

That was the sacred shrine for Lawrence's remains and a plan for getting them to America.

She therefore sent Ravagli to Lawrence's grave in Vence, France, on 5 December 1934. Assisted by friends, he eventually got permission to disinter Lawrence's body, take it to Marseille for cremation, and in April 1935 (having spent time with his young family in Italy) sail from Villefranche on the *Conte di Savoia* and bring Frieda a box of what he claimed were the precious ashes. "I am glad [Lawrence] is no longer at Vence," she told Pollinger. At last Lawrence might have eternal peace.

Frieda did not, however, know that Lawrence's Taos admirers, roused by their own ideas of loyalty, were concocting a caper that would gravely wound her. Mabel Luhan, now more manipulative than ever, gathered a few friends who determined that Lawrence's sacred ashes belonged not to Frieda but to the world. Nothing could have enraged Frieda more than a covert attempt to steal part of her life with Lawrence. When Brett unexpectedly joined forces with Mabel—and (worse) when Frieda's daughter Barbara and her husband, Stuart Barr, visitors to the ranch, swelled Mabel's camp of antagonists—Frieda was appalled. She wrote to her sister Else, "Mabel and Brett told [Barbara] chilling stories about me." The stories were lies. Frieda always remembered the standards of openness and honesty that Lawrence had taught her. She felt viciously betrayed. "I was so shocked and angry," she wrote, remembering how she had stood at Lawrence's small, ugly grave in Vence, "telling myself: here lies all that I could really call my own in this life, because he gave himself to me, body and soul." After his death, her loyalty burned with a different flame. She was left now with his soul.

Flanked by Ravagli, Frieda then made a bold decision: she would mix the ashes with mortar and pour the concoction into the altar of the little chapel that she and Ravagli, some months earlier, in 1934, had begun building on the hillside above the ranch. There Lawrence would be safe for all time. On 15 September 1935 she proudly organized a ceremony around a huge bonfire to consecrate the ashes. Three Indians sang plaintive songs. It was a sacred time in a sacred space, abounding with homage to Lawrence's greatness. Mabel's entourage did not attend.

The D. H. Lawrence Chapel, in progress, 1934–35
(Courtesy of Bibliophilia Books)

The D. H. Lawrence Chapel, completed, 1998 (Lynn K. Talbot)

Frieda may have foiled her enemies, but she had not reckoned the extent of her financial costs. The Depression had altered Americans' feelings of security. Everywhere, owners defaulted on their mortgages; jobs were lost; books sold slowly. In London, Martin Secker's publishing business, like Seltzer's in America, failed. Although Frieda and Ravagli lived cheaply at the ranch by doing all their own work, the harsh New Mexico winters forced them to journey to a warmer place—to Los Angeles. There, although the sun shone splendidly, the high-flying film studios had inflated all costs.

Frieda had wisely held back her greatest prize: Lawrence's manuscripts. They were immaculately handwritten with a fountain pen, often without correction. She could, she imagined, sell them if she needed money. While wintering in Los Angeles, she met a German art dealer named Galka Scheyer, who led her, on 25 March 1936, to an enterprising young bookseller on La Cienega Boulevard. This man, in his early thirties, specialized in manuscripts. His name was Jacob "Jake" Zeitlin. Poor but ambitious, he was thrilled that Frieda would ask him to try to sell the precious manuscripts in her possession. When he finally saw the collection, he found it overwhelming. "It is really a magnificent thing," he wrote.

His shop assistant was a brilliant young man in his twenties named Lawrence Clark Powell, who, when he met Frieda and Ravagli on 1 April 1936, immediately recorded his impressions: "I liked her immensely. We talked a good deal in the shop and then at lunch. Her voice is German and hoarse, her face is weathered, fine. She is alive and hearty and warm-hearted. [. . .] Her Italian bersaglieri [. . .] is short, husky, curiously boyish, shy. [Fifty years later Powell added:] He was volatile, genial, a very companionable guy. But I spotted him. He was a wolf, really—a satyr. He screwed anything he could." Larry Powell believed that Frieda tolerated Ravagli's lust for other women because he made few demands and, as a skilled handyman, performed whatever services she required. He was strong and rugged—a carpenter, painter, potter, plumber.

On that same day in April, Jake Zeitlin had already invited a rich client, the English novelist Hugh Walpole, to peruse Lawrence's complete manuscript of *The Rainbow,* priced at the astounding price of twenty-five hundred dollars. For prospective buyers, Jake asked Larry Powell to prepare a full description of all the manuscripts. He began work a full year later, in the vault of the Security National Bank, giving details about 118 of Lawrence's works, then eventually asking a friend named Ward Ritchie to publish the descriptive catalog as a paperbound book, along with a secret list of tentative prices.

Why was Powell's work delayed for so long? The answer is that Frieda had meanwhile met someone who proposed a bigger, more important project than a catalog. It was what she knew she could not accomplish on her own or with Ravagli's help. It was a full-scale biography of Lawrence. Frieda therefore left California and went back to the ranch to welcome an energetic young couple from Harvard University. Loving the unspoiled Taos Valley, they stayed with her for ten days. They, too, were fascinated by the manuscripts and recognized their immense value. Their names were Harry K. "Dan" Wells and his wife, Jeanette "Jenny" Hill.

Talented and outgoing, the Wellses came from moneyed families, had gone to the best American schools, and, in order to gather material for their proposed biography, had spent a whole year, 1935–36, traveling by bicycle all over Europe. They impressed everyone with their knowledge, enthusiasm, and cash. They had already met those who had been close to Lawrence—Frieda's sister Else, Lawrence's sister Ada, Jessie Chambers, Bertrand Russell, and Pino Orioli—and bought Lawrence's letters and manuscripts wherever they could. They even coaxed Orioli into selling many documents housed in a trunk that he had stored for the Lawrences when they left Florence. In the 1930s everyone, even faithful stewards, needed money.

The Wellses also visited John Middleton Murry at his farm in England, where he was experimenting with a cooperative venture in land management. Frieda soon repeated, with dismay, what Dan Wells had told her—that Murry thought Lawrence should have kept on writing about the English Midlands. The conversation that Frieda reported inspired a vigorous riposte from Murry: "Why do you take things on hearsay? [. . .] I have never in my life said anything of the kind; and if young Mr Wells extracts that meaning from anything I have written, then all I can say is that he is very stupid." For a decade afterward, Frieda and Murry exchanged no more letters—till 1946, when another world war had ended.

The Wellses, having returned to America, carefully guarded their extensive cache of Lawrence material. Coming to the famous Taos ranch, they were ecstatic. Arriving in August 1936, they found Frieda dressed in a plaid Bavarian costume and found Ravagli proud of what he said he was tending: "vegetables, flours, corn, oats, cows, horses, cats, lambs, [and] good milk." Equally delighted, Frieda greeted the couple with gusto. "It's like being in another world," Jenny wrote. The Wellses loved Taos so much that, for twenty-five hundred dollars, they bought sixty acres nearby. When Dan Wells discovered how many manuscripts Frieda possessed, he was eager for Harvard University to purchase them so that he could have complete access for his proposed biography. (Unfortunately, it was never written.) To that end he arranged for Jake Zeitlin to ship the manuscripts for display in Harvard's Treasure Room and for Frieda to give a talk in December on Lawrence's poetry. "I am thrilled," she told Jake. For two happy months Frieda and Ravagli lived with the Wellses. Jenny was amazed at how open their relationship had become, Frieda unruffled when Ravagli took young women to dances. "They seemed," Jenny said, "to be able to enjoy each other's company without being possessive."

To persuade Harvard University to purchase all the manuscripts, Frieda and Jake finally agreed on a special price. It was twenty-five thousand dollars—about half their appraised value. Jake urged Frieda to keep the collection intact and preserve its coherence. He was impressed that so many manuscripts had survived. Amazingly, Harvard stalled for a time, then declined the offer. Lawrence's work was still too bold, too tainted, the *Lady Chatterley* scandal still too fresh. The library's director, Robert P. Blake, wrote to Jake that "our rather limited resources" could not accommodate the cost.

Blake's decision would have profound consequences for Lawrence's manuscripts. They would be dispersed—a few lost, some given away (for instance, *St. Mawr* went to Aldous Huxley), but many went to private collections long off limits to scholars. In May 1937 Dan Wells, having lost his enthusiasm for biography, arranged for Harvard to return the Lawrence collection to Jake. Afterward, paid one hundred dollars, Larry Powell spent the whole month of June on his (delayed) descriptive catalog of the manuscripts. "I [had been] planning to write a book on Lawrence," he recalled. But in the depths of the Depression, when a loaf of bread or a quart of milk cost a nickel, there were few buyers of books. No one knew when the Depression would end.

Though well-off by Taos standards, Frieda was nonetheless worried about money. She had bought a new car in 1936, had invited the Huxleys to spend the summer of 1937 on her ranch (they required a new bathroom in the original cabin), and wanted to oblige Ravagli's wish to build a swimming pool. Then came a different temptation, not from Ravagli or a shyster like Nicholas Luciani but from an Austrian neighbor who tentatively offered to sell her his ranch near Taos. She wanted to buy it but hesitated, worried that she could not afford it. More worries followed. Jake Zeitlin had bad news: his business had not flourished, and he faced possible bankruptcy. He wanted to protect Lawrence's manuscripts (still mostly unsold) and returned them to Frieda. It was a low-water mark.

Frieda was saddened, but she had emerged from disaster before—when, in 1932, George Lawrence had shaped her determination to protect her rightful inheritance. He had changed the direction of her life. Five years later, at the height of the Depression, another man—an unusual manuscript collector with a keen eye for value—came along. He possessed a fortune. With the power of his money, he could change lives. But he was a peculiar man. Whenever possible, he avoided salesmen of any sort. After he discovered that he could negotiate directly with Frieda, they were elated.

CHAPTER 24

The Challenge of Texas

In the United States economic conditions in the late 1930s steadily worsened. Needing money, Dorothy Brett had offered to sell Jake Zeitlin one hundred of her handwritten Lawrence letters (rare collector's items) for thirty-five dollars each. He could not find a buyer. (She eventually got a mere seven hundred dollars from the University of Cincinnati.) Frieda gradually realized that she would have to reduce her expenses or enlarge her income. She remembered the financial hardships that she and Lawrence had endured during the war. She had recently spent two thousand dollars to retrieve the American copyrights of most of Lawrence's books, and although in 1938 Random House would agree to reprint the Thomas Seltzer titles of the 1920s, her royalty payments were delayed.

In an act of serendipity, Jake Zeitlin had introduced Frieda to an eccentric manuscript collector named Thomas Edward "Ed" Hanley (1894–1969). He had always loved books. His father owned lucrative gas wells and a brick factory in the town of Bradford, Pennsylvania, and had sent his son to Harvard. A bachelor, now aged forty-four, Hanley had met Frieda and eagerly began to buy "direct" the manuscripts of Lawrence's essays, short stories, and novels. Eventually, he bought at least sixty—about half of those that had been offered for sale. He became Frieda's golden hen. "It *would* have been a mistake to sell to Harvard - " she reminded Jake in 1937. Now, if a big expense arose, she gathered an egg from Hanley's nest. He made regular purchases for twenty years, allowing Frieda to go on doing what she had done for years—to publicize

Lawrence, to live quietly, and to develop her talent for friendship. After 1933 neither she nor Angelo Ravagli worked for anyone but themselves. Ed Hanley gave them freedom.

Then came voices from the past. Aldous and Maria Huxley arrived to spend the summer months with Frieda and Ravagli. Disillusioned by the worsening political conditions in Spain, Italy, and Germany, the Huxleys had left Europe forever. Driving across America, with Maria at the wheel of their Ford, they arrived at the ranch on 1 June 1937. Aldous; their son, Matthew; and their friend Gerald Heard were passengers. At once, all four pitched in to help Ravagli build a bathroom (and a drain field) in the small Lawrence cabin. When I interviewed Matthew in 1987, he remembered Frieda well: "She was a marvelously outgoing, warm, loving woman. And Angelino was [. . .] very protective of her, defending her against the outside world." Writing to a friend, Maria explained that Aldous was now able, at the ranch, to work again; she celebrated the unsurpassed views of the desert below and praised Frieda's generosity. But she was amazed at the primitive life that Frieda had embraced. Worse, Frieda allowed visitors casual, easy access to her: "Frieda is continually visited out of the blue by vague friends or strangers [who] want to see Mrs D. H. Lawrence." Frieda allowed them access because she was generous and wanted to keep Lawrence alive for others. Maria refused: "I firmly say Aldous is working." A European at heart, Maria found America an alien, unconquerable country; Frieda found it bracing and beautiful. Maria minded all the hard work, the scrubbing and sweeping, the lifting and loading, that ranch life required; Frieda didn't bother if the work didn't get done. She left it for another day. She was busy enjoying her freedom.

As autumn approached, Frieda was now fifty-eight. She had to reconsider the harsh winters at the ranch. They were long, snowy, and brutally cold. She remembered their ferocity from the 1922–23 winter that she and Lawrence had spent at nearby Del Monte Ranch. The roads were often washed out by flooding or blocked by snow; as she grew older, the simple life had grown more daunting—wood to be cut and stacked, supplies far away, no maid to assist her. She had considered moving off the mountain to the Taos plateau.

When Edward von Maltzahn came and urged her to buy his sprawling ranch of three hundred acres, located only a few miles from Taos, she decided to act. He and his wife, Hanni, had tired of America's economic downturn and wanted to return to Austria. Partly as an act of friendship for someone she admired, she agreed to the purchase, paying him forty-five hundred dollars in cash. His fine ranch offered grassy plains in one direction, bold mountains in another, and the ancient Indian Pueblo in still another. Near the main road sat a solid adobe house. She called it the "Lower Ranch" and stayed there, off and on, for the rest of her life. "I am in my new place," she told Merrild on 3 March 1938, "and love it very much." Ravagli groused because, having two places to manage, he had more work; but he would be able to pursue more easily his new avocation, pottery, which he had learned when he visited Italy in the winter of 1937–38. He believed he was an artist, too, not just a ranch hand. He wanted to build his own kiln, earn his own money, and be independent. Before leaving for Hollywood in October 1940, Frieda told the Merrilds that "Angie has done some nice pottery." He made vases, bowls, cups, and tiles.

Angelo Ravagli, ceramic tile of D. H. Lawrence's phoenix, c. 1940 (Lynn K. Talbot)

Whatever Ravagli earned could never compete with Ed Hanley's cash. For a group of three manuscripts, including the expurgated typescript of *Lady Chatterley's Lover,* Hanley agreed to pay Frieda nineteen hundred dollars in ten monthly installments, beginning in January 1938; then three thousand dollars more, in installments, for seven additional manuscripts. Staggering sums they were—forty-nine hundred dollars combined—more than the cost of the sprawling three hundred-acre Lower Ranch. Paying in installments was not Hanley's only eccentricity. Big and square-shouldered, taciturn and dull, he came to Los Angeles each winter, looked at items Jake Zeitlin had for sale, then reserved what he wanted until he was ready to buy. Jake explained: "I would have to be patient and listen to him every day. [. . .] He would take a small, cheap room at the Hollywood Roosevelt Hotel. [. . .] He said he'd rather spend his money on books. And no matter where you went to dinner, all he wanted was a hamburger or a steak and a glass of milk." On Saturdays what excited Hanley more than Lawrence's manuscripts was the circus and its clowns, acrobats, and showgirls. His marriage to an Egyptian belly dancer named Tullah Innes surprised all who knew him. Today he is remembered for his acumen in choosing manuscripts for his collection. As late as 1956 (when Frieda died), he was sending her regular checks. He had endowed her life in America.

To escape the harsh winters, Mabel Luhan, and sometimes Brett, left Taos. Frieda was also tempted and, using Hanley's checks, went from 1937 to 1941 (and occasionally thereafter) to the mild climate of Southern California. Frieda remembered that in 1923 Lawrence had gone to Los Angeles by himself and (like Ed Hanley) had loved the circus and its performers. Lawrence had liked the city "on the outside." Now Ravagli liked it too. He and Frieda stayed in a sequence of furnished Hollywood apartments costing about a hundred dollars a month.

The city provided more than a mild climate. "Hollywood is really cosmopolitan," Frieda wrote. It offered good restaurants, easy walks, and access to a new and glamorous set of friends introduced by the Huxleys. When Aldous began his lucrative work as a screenwriter in Hollywood, he and Maria met directors, writers, actors, even scientists. In 1938, after Ravagli returned from Italy, where he had visited his family, he drove Frieda to Hollywood for Occidental College's production of *David,* the play that Lawrence had written at the ranch. There they visited the Huxleys and, during this visit and one the following winter, met many of the Huxleys' friends, among them Grace and Edwin Hubble. He was a gifted astronomer who studied galaxies, she a cultured graduate of Stanford University. Meeting Frieda at the Huxleys' apartment in 1938, Grace found her handsome and powerful, like the women "who followed their fighting men through the ancient forests of Europe." Seated on the sofa, she was "a broad-shouldered, deep-chested, shapeless bulk in a burgundy-red chiffon dress, and long strings of beads, and grey stockings. [. . .] Her blue eyes danced or looked straight through one, and she laughed a great deal."

Like other friends, Grace admired Frieda's aristocratic bearing. (Lawrence had once smiled and said, "[S]he thinks herself very aristocratic"). Now she was more mellow and serene but still striking. All noticed her laughter; the abrasive intensity of the Lawrence years had faded. Frieda relished meeting others such as Charlie Chaplin and his wife, Paulette Goddard. Performing wickedly funny imitations of Hollywood stars, Chaplin delighted Frieda; Paulette graciously entertained. A young writer named Dudley Nichols took Frieda to see director John Ford filming *The Long Voyage Home.* Affable and creative, Nichols became especially close to Frieda. "To me," she wrote, "you are almost a symbol of the best in America." He read Lawrence with special sensitivity and admired her willingness to preserve the ranch. She appreciated the kindness and warmth of these new friends.

But Frieda also had a mission—to promote Lawrence. She found a publisher, the *Virginia Quarterly Review,* for two early plays and an unpublished story discovered in London. In Hollywood she approached William Dieterle, a German director, hoping that he would film *The Plumed Serpent* in Mexico, from a script that she and a writer named John Beckett had crafted. In 1940 she sold the film rights to *Lady Chatterley's Lover* and implored Aldous Huxley, Zoë Akins, and Christopher Isherwood to work on the script; sadly, these highly paid writers were too busy. Hollywood had consumed them. When Isherwood visited Frieda in April 1940, he found her lively and interesting but "already an old woman," hawking "hopelessly undramatic" material. Undeterred by rejection, Frieda marched loyally on. Her enthusiasm for Lawrence's work was contagious, but her ignorance of the rapid technological changes in the film industry hampered her efforts. She had abundant energy but little expertise.

In 1943 she was lucky. She met a man in Santa Fe named Willard Hougland, who helped her publish, in America, a daring manuscript that she had long held back. "I wouldn't have had the guts to [try to] publish it," she told him. He interested the Dial Press in New York in the first version of *Lady Chatterley's Lover,* which Dial issued in April 1944. Frieda wrote to Dudley Nichols, "I always loved it best." The original print run of 17,500 copies quickly sold out after an American vice squad, headed by John S. Sumner, charged the book with obscenity. His charge, which garnered free publicity for the book, was upheld by a New York magistrate in May, but that decision was reversed in November. Legally, the book could then be distributed in the mail. Writing in the *Nation,* Diana Trilling compared this version to the third, found it "more economical, more visual, and wittier," but believed that it "distorted Lawrence's sexual message and therefore had to be discarded."

While Frieda had met with success in 1944, the war years of 1941–45 were especially difficult for her and Ravagli. A German and an Italian living in a country at war with their native lands, they were cautious, uneasy, and sometimes fearful. "In the last war I suffered tortures," she admitted to Witter Bynner. Though Ravagli often listened to the radio for news, he tried not to think about the war and his family—and kept busy. He wrote to Frieda's nephew Friedel Jaffé in 1941: "Is not use to talk about of what it goes on. It makes you sad only. The life must go on." His oldest son was fighting for the Italians in Libya.

Frieda remembered all too well living in Cornwall when England was at war with Germany and when she, speaking with an accent, was regarded as a suspicious alien. "I am so very sick of war and more war. It makes me so angry," she told Richard Aldington, who, like the Huxleys, had come to America. He advised her to go quietly about her life, finding solace in her domestic round of activities. When the British government blocked royalties and dividends for all expatriates, she and Ravagli became more frugal. She had done so before. "[W]e need so little, with the chickens and cows and no rent to pay," Frieda acknowledged. It helped that Ravagli was industrious. Mostly, they sequestered themselves at the

Angelo Ravagli, Frieda Lawrence, and Johnie Griffin, c. 1946 (Arthur J. Bachrach)

Lower Ranch from March 1942 to December 1944 and found pleasure in meals at Taos restaurants and long visits from friends. "Life seems to have become very elemental," she told Friedel in 1943. By now she was also a chain-smoker, never far from a pack of Camels.

In time, even the Lower Ranch, despite Ravagli's many improvements, offered little relief from the wind and snow gusting from the mountains nearby. Storms were frequent. In Taos, Frieda met an attractive widow named Johnie Griffin. Originally from Philadelphia, she owned Texas oil wells that had made her almost as rich as Ed Hanley. She liked Frieda and Ravagli and offered them the use of her fine winter house near Brownsville, Texas, twelve hundred miles south of Taos. Beginning in December 1944, they stayed there for several months at a time. Ravagli (and sometimes Frieda) could fish in the port channel, and Frieda now had time to herself. She could cut flowers from the yard, savor the scent of orange blossoms, watch for wild quail in the fields nearby, and welcome days of peace to help her forget the horrors of war. As she wrote to Dudley Nichols in 1945, "One can only try and hang on to the best in oneself."

That sentence may encode a guarded response to Ravagli's flirtations, one of which threatened the domestic stability that Frieda now cherished. Two months after she wrote to Nichols, in the summer of 1945, she wrote candidly to her nephew Friedel, whose friend Otto Frohnknecht had just visited Taos: "He will have told you about Angelino's love affair – I dont let it disturb me – Angelino has made it possible for me, to live the way I want to live – all these years – We have seen a lot together, but if he wants to leave me, then that is that – " He had begun an affair with Dorothy Horgan, a woman who migrated every summer from New York City to Taos. Her daughter, Barbara, remembers that her mother was not deeply involved with Ravagli and gradually let the affair cool into friendship. A year later, in August 1946, Frieda thanked Mrs. Horgan for a "box of [birthday] chocolates" and much later, in 1954, for lovely shoes at Christmas. Surely amused by these gifts, Frieda could afford a long view of fidelity. In 1926 Lawrence had been distressed by Frieda's "love affair"; now, by contrast, she refused to let a similar affair disturb her. She had accepted Ravagli's frequent dalliances as the price of his companionship.

Two years later, after a final sojourn in Hollywood, Frieda began to remember the simple life she had spent on the sparkling Mediterranean and the lakes of Italy. Long afternoon drives around the Gulf of Mexico, near Brownsville, had revealed secluded hamlets and beaches warmed by the winter sun. In January 1947 she and Ravagli, driving south to Brownsville, came to a waterfront settlement a few miles from Port Isabel, Texas. It seemed, Frieda told Knud Merrild, like a European fishing village, the kind she knew so well. There she bought a flat seaside lot with a small house. From its windows she could see the fishermen's boats crawling along the channel, the bright-winged gulls diving for food, and the quacking ducks drifting across the sky. They contributed to the serenity she found in Port Isabel. "It keeps on being fun here," she told Brett. Later, in 1954, she wrote to John Middleton Murry:

> We are on the Laguna Madre, with pelicans and herons and gulls and ducks and wild geese. Sometimes I get up before dawn (it's warm) and there are fireflies and they mistake my cigarette for another firefly and come and investigate. And then the first birds in the bushes begin their chirping and the gulls screech and fly around in long swoops, the last

stars fade and the pink of the dawn spreads over the water. Later on, the fishermen come in their sailing boats and draw in their nets. They throw out the small fish and then there is such a commotion and fuss around them of all the seabirds diving for those fish – You would enjoy all this "otherness."

This celebration of "otherness" is one that Lawrence could have written. The place that Frieda had bought, though it needed landscaping and many repairs, would provide the place of her retirement. With Ravagli she was settling into comfortable routines and modest luxury. The coast of Texas gave her peace.

CHAPTER 25

Last Years

Frieda's last years offered surprising symmetry. Her move south from the Taos Mountains to Port Isabel on the water resembled the moves that, earlier, she and Lawrence had made—to Lake Garda in 1912, to Taormina in 1920, to Lake Chapala in 1923, to Spotorno in 1925, and to Bandol in 1928. In those exceptional places, they had loved the bright sunlight, the unspoiled walks, the restful daily rhythms, and the rugged fishermen managing their boats and nets. Frieda had always felt "moored" by Lawrence, her mother, and, at times, her three children. Now all of that had changed. She had severed her ties to Lawrence's extended family; her mother and husband were long dead; and she rarely saw her children—or those of Angelo Ravagli. Though affectionate and hardworking, he had not met some of her emotional needs. But she had adapted. To create the familial support she wanted, Frieda gathered a group of close friends, many of them unmarried, who turned to her as to the sun—for warmth, generosity, and understanding. Frieda spent her last years replacing the families she had left in Europe.

These friends (and occasionally relatives) conferred the homage she still enjoyed as Mrs. Lawrence. Near her Lower Ranch, Frieda had given Brett two acres of land; William Goyen, a writer, took two acres to build a small adobe house; and Willard Johnson, who had followed the Lawrences to Mexico, inquired about *his* two acres. Frieda soon had a distinguished neighborhood. She could now, in peace, go fishing with Brett and, she told Murry, sit "in the lovely places with the aspens and firs, by the mountain streams." They offered security.

In January 1947, traveling south to Port Isabel for the winter, Frieda learned that her vibrant younger sister, Johanna Krug, penniless after her property in Austria had been confiscated, could visit her in America for a few months. Frieda was jubilant. Johanna, a widow since 1944, was ready to leave war-torn Europe and the massive rebuilding that had begun. At the side of Frieda's small waterfront house, Ravagli built Johanna a large bedroom full of sunlit windows. Lawrence's financial legacy had made possible this sweet reunion of sisters. Since 1912 Lawrence had supported Frieda, making sure—even when they separated in 1923—that she had sufficient income to avoid penury. "Don't stint yourself for anything," he had assured her then. Their separation had not imposed on her the pain of financial catastrophe.

Some of her relatives could not, however, come to America, not even for a long-awaited wedding. Nor could Ravagli's. In Taos, Frieda married Angelo Ravagli on Halloween 1950, partly to be sure that he could inherit half of her estate (which he did) and partly to be sure that he could return from Italy without passport difficulties. He had long (and often) feared that he might be deported. When he went again to visit his family in April 1952, Frieda recognized that she could now afford a round-trip plane ticket from New York to London (it cost $711). Even better, she realized that her young friend Miranda Masocco of Santa Fe could accompany her. They departed on 6 June, after the writer Carl Van Vechten gave them a grand dinner party.

In 1999 I interviewed Miranda. She remembered that in dressing for the flight, Frieda wore "a Mexican blouse, a full Mexican skirt, ballet slippers, and a little Mexican beanie." Over her shoulder she had thrown a huge ham for her son, Montague. Silver necklaces and bracelets, festooned with turquoise, jangled with her every step. In motion she was a bejeweled icon of the American Southwest. Much heavier now, she cut a striking figure. She didn't mind that her fellow airplane passengers, who dressed spiffily in those days, found her oddly independent. She was still Mrs. D. H. Lawrence! In London she stayed with Montague and his wife, Vera; met her grandchildren; then moved to the Kingsley Hotel to see friends like Martin Secker, John Middleton Murry, Alexander Frere-Reeves, and her trusted agent Laurence Pollinger, who managed the Lawrence Estate and was then searching for a director to film *Lady Chatterley's Lover*. Her last trip to Europe had been a success.

During the 1950s, whether in Taos or in Port Isabel, Frieda spent her days doing what she liked—writing letters after breakfast; straightening the house; watering her flowers; making jellies or pickles in season; going to Taos's La Doña Luz restaurant for a hearty lunch with Rebecca James, Earl Stroh, or Helene Wurlitzer; reading or napping or shopping in the afternoons; preparing pasta and salad for supper; and in the evenings watching the new phenomenon, black-and-white television. She rarely listened to music. It was the daily round of many retired couples, with one difference: Frieda could anticipate a stream of letters and visits from admirers of Lawrence. She had never tired of hearing what drew readers, especially young people, to his work. His significance still grew.

Lawrence's work surged in popularity. Paul Morel's struggle to escape the working class and Ursula Brangwen's journey to find sexual freedom resonated with readers. After the war ended, in 1945, millions of American veterans migrated to college campuses; in Britain socialist measures had encouraged the working classes to educate themselves. Alive to these huge social changes, a publisher named Allen Lane, head of Penguin Books, gambled that classic volumes, attractively printed, would sell well at modest prices. In 1950 he published ten of Lawrence's novels. They were a huge success.

Lawrence's reputation as a serious writer expanded with the publication of two books—Richard Aldington's 1950 *Portrait of a Genius, But . . .*, an excellent biography of Lawrence based on close personal observation, and Witter Bynner's waspish memoir, which appeared a year later, called *Journey with Genius*. These two books illustrated aspects of Lawrence that Frieda had largely forgotten. "At long last I have read [your] book," she wrote to Aldington. "It was a strange experience – I forgot that it was about Lawrence [. . .] and about me, [I seemed] like another person. Many things, [such] as our wills clashing, I had not really grasped." She acknowledged that "though he bullied me, I also felt free to be myself." That freedom was the gift that Otto Gross had given her in

1907. As the years passed, her maturity had helped her protect her female identity and integrity. But she was quickly becoming part of a legend. Legends generate half-truths fashioned by others.

Later a New York publisher took on a bolder project. Barney Rosset of Grove Press, despite the strong objections of the Lawrence Estate (which claimed the copyright), decided to publish the unexpurgated Florence edition of *Lady Chatterley's Lover* that Lawrence himself had supervised. The full unexpurgated text had never been copyrighted. Rosset wrote to Frieda in 1956 and secured her permission. But he delayed publishing his edition till 1959. In June of that year the Supreme Court decided the case of *Kingsley Pictures v. Regents,* a dispute over a French film adaptation of *Lady Chatterley's Lover* that had been banned in New York State. The reason? The film showed adultery in a favorable light. The Court's decision in favor of *Kingsley* (nine to zero) narrowed the definition of obscenity in the United States. The Grove Press edition, which followed, was heralded by critics but was also regarded as too explicit, its message too preachy, its symbols too obvious. (Alfred Kazin, however, admired the book's "rushing, swift, extraordinarily keen language" aiming to register ecstatic sensation.)

The Post Office Department quickly seized copies of Rosset's book, then judged it unfit to be mailed. In the court case that ensued, Rosset won. Judge Fred van Pelt Bryan ruled that the book was not obscene (it did not violate community standards) and was therefore mailable. The barrage of publicity created a huge public demand. A year later in England, in 1960, Penguin Books, standing firmly behind the integrity of Lawrence's novel, challenged British obscenity laws and eventually faced a jury, which rendered a welcome verdict of not guilty. Still today, on a wall at the London literary agency of Pollinger Limited, hang framed copies of two royalty statements that Penguin Books issued to the Lawrence Estate. They show that sales of *Lady Chatterley's Lover* from 10 November 1960 to 30 June 1961 totaled 3,226,556 copies. The novel's financial rewards, though they came after Frieda's death, were stupendous.

A few years earlier, before sales of Lawrence's books had exploded, Frieda met a striking, sophisticated couple who, when shown the handwritten manuscripts of *Lady Chatterley's Lover,* which Frieda had long held back, were astonished. They had never seen anything so seductive. Frieda met the wife first, a sculptress named Amalia de Schulthess, whom Jake Zeitlin described as one of the most beautiful women of her generation. In 1941 she and her husband, Hans, had immigrated to America from Switzerland, where, as the scion of an aristocratic banking family, he was accustomed to having his way in all matters. When Amalia brought Hans to visit Frieda in 1954, Frieda liked the homage he paid her. "Frieda *liked* good-looking young men—she liked their adulation," Amalia remembered when I interviewed her in 1989.

When Hans paged slowly through the three *Lady Chatterley* manuscripts—Frieda's greatest treasure—he admired them immensely. Determined to have them, he at once offered her $10,000 ($100,000 today), more than double what she had paid Edward von Maltzahn for the Lower Ranch of three hundred acres. The offer was astounding. Frieda had not wanted to part with the manuscripts—she loved touching them and remembering the majestic Villa Mirenda where they had been written—but she also wanted the flamboyant de Schulthesses to have them.

Frieda parted with the manuscripts just months after a rising American institution had approached her. It wanted to buy her whole Lawrence collection. Under the creative leadership of Harry Ransom, Dean of Arts and Sciences, the University of Texas at Austin had agreed to build a humanities research center that would house one of the world's great collections of modern literary manuscripts. Ransom had come to the English Department in 1934, had risen through the academic ranks, and was, when he met Frieda in 1954, soon to become provost (in 1957), then chancellor (in 1961). Earlier the Texas state legislature had given the university two million acres of West Texas land, on which, in 1923, a well, named Santa Rita No. 1, gushed oil—and then millions and millions of dollars. Dean Ransom wanted funding for his research center. The legislature agreed, in 1953, and eventually enabled him to purchase huge collections of manuscripts and books. Frieda and Ravagli were invited to a reception in her honor in November 1954, but a few months later she complained that "[T]here at Austin it was all so vague." One observer wrote that Ransom exuded spellbinding charm but "never really committed himself" to the specifics that troubled smaller minds. Yet Frieda was intrigued by Ransom's vision. Such a center would honor Lawrence, protect his work, be state funded, and be part of an impressive campus. She did not think she would "live so very much longer."

There was one problem—Angelo Ravagli. Having no sentimental attachment to this trove of manuscripts in Frieda's possession and feeling always uneasy about money, he insisted that Dean Ransom sign a sales agreement; but, while furiously buying everything in sight, in New York and London, Ransom casually ignored Frieda's new husband: "Angelino got worked up and wrote more harshly than he ever meant to. [...] You see Angelino wants to be businesslike and American!" Frieda explained to Warren Roberts on 30 November 1954. A draft of a letter that Ravagli sent to Ransom on 24 November demands a document that would "legally bind both parties" and requires the "approval by the President and the Regents of the University." Without it, Ravagli insisted they must "call the deal off." And so, responding to the man's arrogance, Ransom did. Like Hans de Schulthess, he was accustomed to having his way. It was therefore the second time—Harvard was the first—that a rich American university missed an opportunity to purchase Lawrence's manuscripts. When, in 1965, the University of Texas did finally acquire the *Lady Chatterley* manuscripts, the price had shot up from ten thousand to fifty thousand dollars (half a million dollars today). Lawrence would have been grimly amazed.

Frieda's disappointment in the University of Texas did not last long. Her love of new friends was seldom affected by matters of money. Among the last of her new friends was a handsome, crewcut television producer named Louis Gibbons. When I interviewed him in 1994, he remembered that he especially liked Taos, which he found serene and quaint; he loved Lawrence's work, so vibrant and rich; and he responded enthusiastically to Frieda, whose eyes, he said, were "a deep vivid blue, and full of young, blue, flashing fire." When he visited the Lower Ranch in 1952, she wore a yellow dress with flowers and, over it, a red apron, also with flowers, trimmed in blue; then she showed him, room by room, dozens of Lawrence's paintings. Later, invited to lunch in December 1954, he and his partner, Thomas Young, drove from Dallas, Texas, to Port Isabel to sample Frieda's hearty bean soup, green salad, chopped venison (it was a little tough), ice cream, and strawberries. They later drove to nearby

Padre Island, where Frieda, beckoning them to follow, kicked off her moccasins and ran into the warm, shallow waves of the Gulf of Mexico. At age seventy-five she found the smallest pleasure an adventure; her delight in shared experience was inexhaustible. A few weeks later she wrote to Gibbons, "We have had springlike weather and gone to Padre Island a lot." It was a winter paradise.

But the sun was setting on her and her friends. In 1955 Maria Huxley, to whom she and Lawrence had felt especially close, died of cancer. To Grace Hubble, whose husband, Edwin, had died two years earlier, Frieda wrote that Aldous had come to visit her "and has accepted his great loss." He was at peace. She added that "Maria is so alive to me as people one has loved are! We who have loved and were loved are lucky!"

The following summer, of 1955, was her last. Dignitaries came from the University of New Mexico to accept the Lawrence Ranch as a gift. It would offer a retreat for faculty and students. She had also made her will, keeping all the money "in the family," she told her son, Monty. "It's been a lively summer," she added, "almost too much for an old woman, I don't have time to get old." In April 1956 a virus sickened Frieda, and she was hospitalized in Santa Fe, New Mexico. Although warned about her health, she and Ravagli returned, after a few days, to Taos and their normal life. On 8 August, already compromised by diabetes and the effects of heavy smoking, Frieda's health collapsed. At 11:00 p.m. that night she suffered a severe stroke, which paralyzed her right side and robbed her of speech. On 11 August—it was her seventy-seventh birthday—she died at home, surrounded by friends. Louis Gibbons arrived from Dallas two days later, just in time for the viewing of Frieda's body at a Taos funeral home and for the simple graveside service at the Lawrence Chapel. He stood with Angelo Ravagli, who would live twenty years more, mostly in Italy. As Frieda's coffin was lowered in place, William Goyen read his manly tribute to Frieda. It began, "We remember her for her rare gift of life."

CHAPTER 26

At the Close

For D. H. Lawrence, one of the great writers of the twentieth century, marriage was the central human relationship, as it was for Frieda—and as it was, though in different ways, for contemporaries like the Joyces, the Woolfs, and the Fitzgeralds. The struggles that both ennobled and diminished the Lawrences create a portrait of affection and commitment enmeshed with distance and betrayal. The Lawrences' contribution to a modern sensibility is their understanding of this difficult balance of affection and anger, of love mixed with loss, of desire diminished to disrespect. With some success, they turned passion into affection inside the limits of love.

Together, Lawrence and Frieda were a couple who sought independence at a high cost. That cost demanded frequent negotiation. They bargained, often nonverbally, to preserve a relationship that, by 1927, had hit the wall of suppressed anger. Lawrence gradually felt aggrieved, Frieda disenchanted. They tacitly agreed to accept the deterioration of sensibility without the emotional wreckage of divorce.

Across the years Lawrence and Frieda worked hard to sustain their love. In 1917–18 she "fought the homosexuality" out of him. In 1923 she refused to return to Mexico to help him purchase and operate a banana farm. In 1927, when he was very sick, she grudgingly nursed him while feeling entitled to another man's ardent attentions. In 1928, without notice to his wife, Lawrence created a vitriolic portrait of Bertha (Frieda) in *Lady Chatterley's Lover;* Bertha has abused her husband and run off with other men. In this way Lawrence fought Frieda in a passive-aggressive response that she could not prevent. There is no evidence that she tried to alter the passages that impugned that part of her character. (Her handwriting appears nowhere in the manuscript of the novel.) In short, Lawrence had the last word.

It is not, therefore, possible to call their marriage exemplary or complete. Their bouts of dissension were too disturbing and intense, and their complex antagonisms too unguarded, to provide a model of companionship. "[W]e must'nt be too much on top of each other," Frieda had warned Mabel Luhan in 1922, and Lawrence had added, "[W]e are much too quarrelsome" to live in a small space. Theirs was a relationship whose essentials they thrashed out in order to discover which parts were genuine.

For the Lawrences what was genuine was not the conventional notion of respect or deference or accommodation; it was the discovery that jealousy and possessiveness and friction complemented love and fidelity. In the spaces between them, the Lawrences tried valiantly to decode the varied impulses that energized them. That required awareness of the emotional rhythms of assertion and submission, and of attraction and repulsion. Not without difficulty, they listened to their spontaneous inner voices, and in this conflicted space, they joined forces against the drift of their culture toward what Lawrence later called "counterfeit" emotion, that is, emotion arising not from relationships but from external stimuli such as (today) films and digital messages.

Lawrence strongly criticized his culture—its shallowness and triviality—but after his death Frieda slowly reconciled herself to it, partly because she mostly ignored its norms. She chose friends, such as Mabel, Brett, and Louis Gibbons, who often lived outside convention. That is what money from Lawrence's books and manuscripts had made possible: it had freed her to develop her gift for friendship outside the binding structures of work. She had managed her assets well, including money from Ed Hanley and Hans de Schulthess. After her death, her estate was valued at $200,000 (nearly two million dollars today). Her fear, in 1932, of having no money had vanished.

The Lawrences made many demands on others, partly to probe for the human truths that others had found, partly to clarify their respective natures. Both recognized the need to open spaces around them that were big enough to express their inner selves and to cherish what was, in each of them, unique—Frieda's gusto and bravery, Lawrence's insight and creative power. If Lawrence used Frieda to help him clarify his beliefs in spontaneity and sexual discovery, she used him to refine her belief in individual freedom, in defending her value as a woman, and in embracing the rhythms of natural life. One of those rhythms was sexual. Frieda confided to Murry in 1931, "[S]ex happened between us and we were staggered, overwhelmed." In the early years of their marriage, they unsheathed their innermost selves and, without fear, exposed their vulnerability: and each, Lawrence said, was reborn into and out of the other. It was a consummation of their entire selves. If Lawrence saw Frieda as his road into the Unconscious, where perplexing truths about the self could be found, Frieda saw Lawrence as helping her shape her immense vitality—not into proud submission to her husband (as did Achsah Brewster or Maria Huxley), nor into unchecked domination (as did Ottoline Morrell or Mabel Luhan), but into a full understanding of her unique female virility.

Both Lawrence and Frieda located the core elements that defined them. Frieda understood life "purely through *feel*," she said. Remaining a strong soldier all her life, she nonetheless possessed the gift of female compassion and empathy, which she bestowed on friends who sustained her before and after Lawrence's death. She rarely spoke of the men, like Otto Gross or Ernest Weekley, who had disappointed her. "One has to forget an awful lot!" she told Murry in 1955. She refused to let disappointment shape her future.

By contrast, Lawrence—more vulnerable and sensitive—gradually relocated love to a place where its disappointments would matter less. He grew weary of the betrayals, however subtle, of men like Garnett, Murry, Hocking, Seltzer, Magnus, Douglas, and the Danes. In his later years he lost his appetite not for camaraderie, which he always sought, but for the sustained richness of an unbroken commitment from men such as Koteliansky and Brewster. Even Frieda acknowledged that "Lawrence *never* loved Aldous and Aldous *never* him." That richness of full commitment to another person Lawrence never found with a man. Instead, he accepted chagrin as the consequence of his life's experiences. It accounts for Mellors's tirades in *Lady Chatterley's Lover* and for the bitterness of the late poems and essays.

What remains is a victory of exploration. The Lawrences' achievement, across the years, lies partly in how they defined the margin between monogamy and adultery. It is, of course, a crucial space in every marriage. The Lawrences repeatedly tested the width of that space, always returning—somewhat chastened—to each other. Frieda defined the space broadly, Lawrence narrowly. For Frieda sex was a cherished gift to be given expression; for Lawrence it was a sacred gift, an act of religious ecstasy, providing potential access to the divine. He therefore gave marriage greater primacy than did Frieda, even as he recognized its fragility. In 1946 Frieda acknowledged to Murry: "Lawrence's and my love, when it came off, was an immense joy in everything, every potato peeled, every sunset, everything that happened, big or little, *was* a gift received from life and each other – I dont think anybody realises the quality our relationship had – " Their realization of reciprocal love, when it succeeded, was an achievement they celebrated. It was uniquely human.

In *A Propos of "Lady Chatterley's Lover,"* in 1929, Lawrence celebrated "the instinct of fidelity in both man and woman. [. . .] The instinct of fidelity is perhaps the deepest instinct in the great complex we call sex." Yet fidelity is not the same as harmony. The Lawrences' achievement lies also in their struggle to sort out a conflict of values that was never resolved. Lawrence's unfulfilled longings—some of them sexual—turned into a biting disappointment, which he blamed for his illnesses; Frieda's dissatisfaction vented itself in a covert affair with Angelo Ravagli, whose duplicity she cavalierly dismissed. In short, the Lawrences' maturity eventually allowed them to discover a complex friendship, without emotional displays or sexual connections, which was at once enabling and disabling but which fostered many days of contentment. However much their love was marred by neglect or disloyalty, the Lawrences believed that they enabled each other to understand the core of their being. If they only partly succeeded, that is because deep pockets of egotism blocked them from completing themselves. They reached across the male-female divide, blended their impulses of assertion and dependence, but never fully met. What developed instead was the sharp crosscut of temperaments that formed layers of mutual antagonism, affection, stimulation, and peace.

To see Lawrence and Frieda as completely as we see the Woolfs or the Joyces requires us to admit the erosion of their commitment to marriage. Their slow loss of emotional coherence after 1925 meant that Frieda would, after his death, need to engage in *recovering* Lawrence. As soon as he died, she mounted a strong commitment to his memory that she could pursue for the rest of her life. She made the marriage whole again. Her love grew simpler and purer the longer Lawrence was dead. Although her respect and affection for Angelo Ravagli, her third husband, cannot be doubted, it did not rival her passion for Lawrence.

There is, finally, another reason for rediscovering the essence of the Lawrence legend. It is that the Lawrences interpreted the tensions of modern life as few have done. They fought against greed, loneliness, and mechanization. They early recognized the virtues of simple agrarian life and its daily rhythms. Their assault on false values created a template that others might follow. Inviting risk, the Lawrences reevaluated the nature of friendship, redefined the meaning of purity, and tested the limits of love. In so doing, they found that at the far side of risk lay meaning, significance, and—often—moments of intense revelation. These moments measure their achievement.

Acknowledgments

I waited fifty years to decide on the final shape of this biography. I wanted, finally, to communicate all that I understood about the Lawrences' lives and what they might mean to readers today. This endeavor required the assistance of many others, especially my wife and youngest son. My wife, Lynn K. Talbot, has shared her collection of two thousand letters (mostly unpublished) that Frieda Lawrence wrote. She has translated letters written in German, deciphered redacted passages, answered complex questions of history and culture, traveled with me in the Lawrences' footsteps, discovered new photographs, and assisted in many other ways. She also read the manuscript more than once. So did my son, Andrew Talbot Squires. When just a boy, Andrew guided us from Florence, Italy, to the Villa Mirenda, taking us along a narrow country road that led from the tiny bus stop in Vingone (where he got directions), up a hill and down again, in July heat, to one of the Lawrences' favorite homes. Years later, he offered much advice, read the present manuscript with a lawyer's eye for discrepancies and infelicities, and fixed problems with technology.

The responses of professionals also contributed much to the book. I was fortunate to have manuscript reports from the Louisiana State University Press which helped me to present the book more clearly. Keith Cushman, a scholar possessing unsurpassed knowledge of Lawrence, offered exceptionally good suggestions on the manuscript. I thank him for fifty years of friendship. Later, my colleague Paul Sorrentino provided incisive comments. His wisdom has been a gift.

Members of my family have long supported my research and offered me unstinting kindnesses. I am pleased to acknowledge Kelly M. and Jennifer Squires, Cameron and Socorro Squires, Katherine M. Squires, Judith S. Sconyers and Peter Finne, Nancy Ellen Squires and Wayne Speight, Craig F. Talbot, Helen C. West, Glenn F. and Irene Windell, and Sylvia Jean Wright.

Over several decades many others have assisted me with suggestions, comments, new materials, friendship, and inspiration. I thank Tim Bates, John P. Broderick, Thomas B. Brumback, Janet Byrne, Hilbert H. Campbell, Joseph Caruso, Albert DeFazio, Ellen Dunlap, Arthur M. Eastman, John P. Elia, Michael Fainter, Lawrence B. Gamache, Jay Gertzman, Louis Gibbons, Anita I. Haney, Andrew Harrison, Cathy Henderson, Ann and Paul Hlusko, Earl G. Ingersoll, Dennis Jackson, Russel Kacher, Jonathan Long, John W. Long, Keith Madsen, Robert Manson Myers, Louis I. Middleman, James N. O'Neill, George A. Panichas, Gerald J. Pollinger, Richard W. Probst, F. Warren Roberts, Carolyn and Donald Rude, Cornelia Rumpf-Worthen, Taha Ashayer Soltani, Bertha Spangler, Jack Stewart, Alison G. Sulloway, Elmer Turman, Lindeth Vasey, Frank R. Vass, Jenny Wells Vincent, Clayland H. Waite, Judith Woodruff, John Worthen, and Louise Wright. David A. Hogge generously read the final proofs.

Lesley Pollinger and Katy Loffman, representing the Estates of D. H. Lawrence and Frieda Lawrence Ravagli, have been faithful trustees as well as good friends. I thank them for permission to quote from many unpublished documents. The holders of manuscripts and photographs have also given permission to reproduce documents in their possession.

At the LSU Press, I have been capably served, especially by James W. Long, who has expertly guided the manuscript through its early stages; others who made admirable contributions include Catherine L. Kadair, managing editor; Barbara Neely Bourgoyne, designer; Sunny Rosen, publicity; Elizabeth Gratch, copyeditor; and Jessica Freeman, indexer.

Notes

Quotations in the text are cited here by page reference, followed by end words of the quotation, then their source (published or unpublished), date, and provenance. Some letters, identified as "unpublished letters," have been partially published in three earlier books on which I worked, abbreviated as *Love and Loyalty, DHL's MSS,* and *Living at the Edge.* Letters from the Alexander Turnbull Library are previously unpublished.

ABBREVIATIONS

AvR	Anna von Richthofen (Frieda's mother)
Chávez	Fray Angélico Chávez History Library, Santa Fe, New Mexico
DHL	D. H. Lawrence
DHL Letters	*The Letters of D. H. Lawrence,* 8 vols., various editors (Cambridge: Cambridge University Press, 1979–2000). Volume and page number follow each citation.
DHL's MSS	Michael Squires, ed., *D. H. Lawrence's Manuscripts: The Correspondence of Frieda Lawrence, Jake Zeitlin and Others* (London: Macmillan, 1991)
FL	Frieda Lawrence
HRC	Harry Ransom Center, University of Texas at Austin
JMM	John Middleton Murry
Leo Baeck	Leo Baeck Institute, Center for Jewish History, New York City
Living at the Edge	Michael Squires and Lynn K. Talbot, *Living at the Edge: A Biography of D. H. Lawrence and Frieda von Richthofen* (Madison: University of Wisconsin Press, 2002)
Love and Loyalty	Michael Squires, *D. H. Lawrence and Frieda: A Portrait of Love and Loyalty* (London: André Deutsch, 2008)

233

sütterlin	Letters written in *sütterlin,* an old-fashioned German script that Frieda learned at school; transcribed and translated by John Worthen and Cornelia Rumpf-Worthen. These ninety-three letters, largely unpublished, are held at HRC.
Turnbull	Alexander Turnbull Library, Wellington, New Zealand

INTRODUCTION

1 "male dove": unpublished letter, FL to Edgar Jaffe, c. 8 Feb. 1914, HRC, in *Love and Loyalty,* 4.

2 **conception of women:** Ann Hathaway's life is imagined in Germaine Greer's excellent *Shakespeare's Wife* (London: Bloomsbury, 2007).
"not a meeting": *DHL Letters,* I:402-3, [15 and 16 May 1912], to FL.

3 "struggling on": *DHL Letters,* VIII:7, 30 Aug. 1913, to JMM.
"whole again": unpublished letter, FL to JMM, [18 Aug. 1930], Turnbull.

4 "what I think": FL to Ottoline Morrell, [2 Aug. 1915], in Mark Kinkead-Weekes, *D. H. Lawrence: Triumph to Exile, 1912-1922* (Cambridge: Cambridge University Press, 1996), 240.
"wildly" at a German ball: unpublished letter, FL to Else von Richthofen, 10 Feb. 1897, Tufts University.
"Hello, Darling": Edward Nehls, comp., *D. H. Lawrence: A Composite Biography* (Madison: University of Wisconsin Press, 1957), 1:255-56; hereafter cited as Nehls, *A Composite Biography.*
"manly men": Mabel Dodge Luhan, *Lorenzo in Taos* (New York: Knopf, 1932), 83.
"show with men": unpublished letter, FL to JMM, [Jan. 1931], Turnbull.

5 "have a look in": unpublished letter, FL to JMM, [Jan. 1931], Turnbull.
"to a goose": unpublished letter, FL to JMM, 19 Sept. 1936, Turnbull. Similarly, T. S. Eliot claimed that if he had followed family expectations and married Emily Hale, he would have become not a poet but a mediocre philosophy teacher.

6 "quite differently": unpublished letter, FL to Max Shames, 16 Mar. 1949, HRC.
"made accessible": unpublished letter, FL to JMM, 6 Apr. [1931], Turnbull.

8 "dose of morphia": *DHL Letters,* I:404, [16 May 1912], to FL.

1. THE END OF LONELINESS

11 "a lifetime": *DHL Letters,* I:384, 17 Apr. 1912, to Edward Garnett.

12 "and ourselves": Frieda Lawrence, *Not I, But the Wind* (New York: Viking, 1934), 7.
"are right": *DHL Letters,* I:403-4, [15 and 16 May 1912], to FL.

13 "beforehand, never": *DHL Letters,* I:414, 2 June 1912, to Sallie Hopkin.
"both crazy": *DHL Letters,* I:421, 3 July 1912, to Edward Garnett.
"filthy hound": *DHL Letters,* I:484, 5 Dec. 1912, to David Garnett.
"for them": unpublished letter, FL to Else Jaffe, [2 Nov. 1912], in *sütterlin,* HRC.
"each other": *DHL Letters,* I:420, 3 July 1912, to Edward Garnett.

14 "Walter [. . .] the house": D. H. Lawrence, *Sons and Lovers,* ed. Helen and Carl Baron (Cambridge: Cambridge University Press, 1992), 51-52.

"almost torture": Ibid., 210.
"despise himself": Ibid., 216.
"All the [...] the stars": Ibid., 398.
15 "he whimpered": Ibid., 464.
"is love": *DHL Letters,* I:440, 19 Aug. 1912, to Sallie Hopkin.
16 "things around": *DHL Letters,* I:503, 17 Jan. 1913, to Ernest Collings.
17 "spite of this": "Bei Hennef," in D. H. Lawrence, *Look! We Have Come Through!* Intro. by Frieda Lawrence, Foreword by Warren Roberts (Austin: HRC, University of Texas Press, 1971), 25–26. Although this poem originally appeared in *Love Poems* (1916), Lawrence placed it in the *Look!* cycle for the collected edition of his poetry (1928).
"We have [...] indescribably beautiful!": unpublished letter, FL to AvR, [15?] Sept. 1912, sütterlin 31.

2. ENGLAND AND GERMANY

19 "In the morning [...] my face": D. H. Lawrence, "The Lemon Gardens," *Twilight in Italy* (London: Duckworth, 1916), 48.
"flowers bloom": FL, *Not I, But the Wind,* 43.
"it's her": *DHL Letters,* I:462, 15 Oct. 1912, to Edward Garnett.
20 "like life": *DHL Letters,* I:477, 19 Nov. 1912, to Edward Garnett.
"so plucky [...] you down": *DHL Letters,* I:479, 19 Nov. 1912, to Edward Garnett.
"with laughter": FL, *Not I, But the Wind,* 44.
22 "to eat": Dorothy Brett, *Lawrence and Brett, A Friendship* (Philadelphia: Lippincott, 1933), 279.
"perfect beasts": DHL to George Neville, n.d., in John Worthen, *D. H. Lawrence: The Early Years* (Cambridge: Cambridge University Press, 1991), 99.
"hard-working [...] than Mr. Lawrence": Ibid., 118–19.
23 "was exquisite": D. H. Lawrence, "The White Stocking," *The Prussian Officer and Other Stories,* ed. John Worthen (Cambridge: Cambridge University Press, 1983), 153. The quoted passage was revised in 1914.
"his studies": Jessie Chambers, *D. H. Lawrence: A Personal Record by E.T.* (London: Cape, 1936), 75.
24 "debasing struggle": *DHL Letters,* I:93, 16 Nov. 1908, to Louisa Burrows.
"put out [...] insect": D. H. Lawrence, *The White Peacock,* ed. Andrew Robertson (Cambridge: Cambridge University Press, 1987), 152, 324, 287.
"by fretting": D. H. Lawrence, *Lady Chatterley's Lover,* ed. Michael Squires (Cambridge: Cambridge University Press, 1993), 79.
25 "invincible spear": "Death-Paean of a Mother," *Guardian* (UK), 9 Nov. 1990.
"hard and bitter": *DHL Letters,* I:230, 17 Feb. 1911, to Ada Lawrence.
26 "be alone": *DHL Letters,* I:285, 12 July 1911, to Helen Corke.
"the rest": D. H. Lawrence, *The Trespasser,* ed. Elizabeth Mansfield (Cambridge: Cambridge University Press, 1982), 14.
"sensitive self": *DHL Letters,* I:353, 21 Jan. 1912, to Edward Garnett.
"but sorrow": *DHL Letters,* I:291, [19 July 1911], to Louisa Burrows.
"well suited": *DHL Letters,* I:361, 4 Feb. 1912, to Louisa Burrows.

27 "believed in me": quoted in Brett, *Lawrence and Brett*, 258.
28 "intellectual curiosity": quoted in Guenther Roth, "Edgar Jaffé and Else von Richthofen in the Mirror of Newly Found Letters," *Max Weber Studies* 10:2 (2010): 155.
"I am [...] with him": unpublished letter, FL to Else von Richthofen, n.d. [1898], *sütterlin* 5.
"never do it": unpublished letter in German, FL to Else von Richthofen, 1 July 1898, Tufts University.
29 "understand a lot": unpublished letter, in *sütterlin*, FL to Else Jaffé, [June 1907], Leo Baeck; translated by Helga Toepfer.
30 "gloomy millennia": Letter A, *The Otto Gross–Frieda Weekley Correspondence*, ed. John Turner et al., *D. H. Lawrence Review* 22 (1990): 165; emphasis removed.
"wonderland of love": Letter Q, summer 1907, *Gross-Weekley Correspondence*, 194.
31 "to church": Letter R, summer 1907, *Gross-Weekley Correspondence*, 194.
"my nature": unpublished letter, FL to JMM, [c. 7 July 1932], Turnbull.
"I am [...] your children": Else von Richthofen to FL, Sept. 1907, in Lynn K. Talbot, "From Old Germany to New Mexico: An Overview of Frieda Lawrence's Letters," *D. H. Lawrence Review* 37 (2012): 75.
32 "much as possible": Roth, "Edgar Jaffé and Else von Richthofen," 174.

3. ITALIAN PARADISE

33 "beyond belief": D. H. Lawrence, *Twilight in Italy and Other Essays*, ed. Paul Eggert (Cambridge: Cambridge University Press, 1994), 154.
"unthinkable [...] of love": unpublished letter, FL to Else von Richthofen, 2 Nov. 1912, *sütterlin* 32.
"the children": *DHL Letters*, I:521, 27 Feb. 1913, to David Garnett.
34 "committed adultery [...] habit!": *DHL Letters*, I:524, 5 Mar. 1913, to Arthur McLeod.
"against Frieda": *DHL Letters*, I:532, 25 Mar. 1913, to Ada Lawrence.
"difficult and unpleasant": *DHL Letters*, I:538, 5 Apr. 1913, to Ada Lawrence.
"Mrs Lawrence": *DHL Letters*, II:22, [14 June 1913], to Miss [Elizabeth] Whale.
36 "about me": Nehls, *A Composite Biography*, I:200.
"at first thinks": *DHL Letters*, II:49, 22 July 1913, to Arthur McLeod.
"wake me up": *DHL Letters*, VII:7, 30 Aug. 1913, to JMM.
"pure sunshine": *DHL Letters*, VII:10, 10 Oct. 1913, to JMM.
37 "quite unbelievable": unpublished letter, FL to Else von Richthofen, 30 Sept. 1913, *sütterlin* 37.
"one want?": Ibid.
"are uncharted": Virginia Woolf, *Jacob's Room* (1922; reprint, San Diego: Harcourt Brace, n.d.), 94.
"it is like": *DHL Letters*, II:82, 6 Oct. 1913, to Edward Garnett.
38 "I know": *DHL Letters*, II:125, 18 Dec. 1913, to William Hopkin.
"little place": unpublished letter, FL to Henry Savage, [19 Jan. 1914], Stanford University.
"is here": unpublished letter, FL to Edgar Jaffe, [c. 8 Feb. 1914], *sütterlin* 38.
"true nobility": *DHL Letters*, II:165, 22 Apr. 1913, to Edward Garnett.

39 "the great impersonal": *DHL Letters,* II:137, [19 Jan. 1914], to Henry Savage.
"of infinity": D. H. Lawrence, *The Rainbow,* ed. Mark Kinkead-Weekes (Cambridge: Cambridge University Press, 1989), 409.
"joint work [...] all life": *DHL Letters,* II:181, 2 June 1914, to Arthur McLeod.
"always poor": *DHL Letters,* II:174, [16 May 1914], to Edward Garnett.

40 "registrar's office": *DHL Letters,* II:196, 13 July 1914, to Sallie Hopkin.
"I met [...] you can": unpublished letter, in German, FL to AvR, 14 June 1914, Leo Baeck; my translation.

4. A HEART THAT'S BEEN SMASHED

41 "all unnaturalized [...] camps": *London Times,* 23 Oct. 1914, 4.

42 "very happy together": Edward Marsh, in Nehls, *A Composite Biography,* I:199, in *Living at the Edge,* 81.
"great passion": Ottoline Morrell to Bertrand Russell, in *DHL Letters,* II:253 n. 4, 30 Dec. 1914.
"German soldiers": quoted in Nehls, *A Composite Biography,* I:250-51. The excerpt is drawn from Compton Mackenzie's novel *The South Wind of Love* (1937); in 1953 he claimed that the novel's characterization of Lawrence and Frieda was "conversationally exact" (Nehls, *A Composite Biography,* I:570).
"colossal idiocy!": *DHL Letters,* II:212, 5 Sept. 1914, to James B. Pinker.

43 "in this world!": unpublished letter, FL to Ottoline Morrell, [c. 19 Mar. 1915], HRC.

44 "highly sexed": The observer is Leonard Woolf, quoted in *Downhill All the Way: An Autobiography of the Years, 1919-1939* (London: Hogarth Press, 1967), 102.
"a great lady": *DHL Letters,* II:281, [11 Feb. 1915], to Ottoline Morrell.
"When we [...] have been [...] what I think": FL to Ottoline Morrell, [2 Aug. 1915], in Mark Kinkead-Weekes, *D. H. Lawrence: Triumph to Exile, 1912-1922* (Cambridge: Cambridge University Press, 1996), 240. Text corrected from holograph manuscript.
"traitor to her": *DHL Letters,* II:462, 3 Dec. 1915, to Ottoline Morrell.
"her influence": FL, *Not I, But the Wind,* 82.

45 "I have [...] with him": unpublished letter, FL to Ottoline Morrell, Apr. 1915, HRC.
"into it": *DHL Letters,* II:256, 5 Jan. 1915, to Arthur McLeod.

46 "its shell": D. H. Lawrence, *The Rainbow,* ed. Mark Kinkead-Weekes (Cambridge: Cambridge University Press, 1989), 456.
"fascinating and horrible": Ibid., 346.
"the language": *DHL Letters,* II:428, 6 Nov. 1915, to S. S. Koteliansky.
"All the [...] terribly beautiful": DHL, *The Rainbow,* 220.

47 "scratch the door": *DHL Letters,* II:293, 24 Feb. 1915, to James B. Pinker.
"of the sky": *DHL Letters,* II:346, [25 May 1915], to Ottoline Morrell.
"state of dissolution": *DHL Letters,* II:347, 29 May 1915, to E. M. Forster.
"I love it": *DHL Letters,* II:261, [24 Jan. 1915], to S. S. Koteliansky.

48 "not himself": *DHL Letters,* II:294, 24 Feb. 1915, to Bertrand Russell.
the American edition: Benjamin Huebsch published an expurgated edition of *The Rainbow* in New York on 30 November 1915. The expurgations did not have Lawrence's approval.

"defiance of [...] exceptional strength": unsigned review in the *London Evening Standard,* reprinted in *D. H. Lawrence: The Critical Heritage,* ed. R. P. Draper (London: Routledge, 1970), 90.

"wind of war": James Douglas in the *London Star,* reprinted in Draper, *D. H. Lawrence,* 93–94.

"thousand fragments [...] often angry": *DHL Letters,* II:454, 28 Nov. 1915, to Cynthia Asquith.

"dank fog": *DHL Letters,* II:461, 3 Dec. 1915, to Ottoline Morrell.

5. A MAP OF PASSION

50 "I love it": *DHL Letters,* II:492, 31 Dec. 1915, to Catherine Carswell.
"about it": unpublished letter, FL to Ottoline Morrell, [9 Jan. 1916], HRC.
"for revenge": unpublished letter, FL to Ottoline Morrell, [17 Jan. 1916], HRC.

51 "wintry inflammation": *DHL Letters,* II:503, [11 Jan. 1916], to Catherine Carswell.
The doctor may also have whispered something else: John Worthen, however, believes that in 1916 Lawrence did not have tuberculosis; see Worthen, *D. H. Lawrence: The Life of an Outsider* (London: Allen Lane, 2005), 184.
"And I [...] is lost": D. H. Lawrence, "The Enkindled Spring," *Amores* (London: Duckworth, 1916). Later he revised the poem extensively.
"a great strain [...] unbearable": unpublished letter, FL to Ottoline Morrell, [9 Jan. 1916], HRC.
"to live one": unpublished letter, FL to Mark Gertler, [4 Mar. 1916], photostat, Harvard University.

52 "he has done": unpublished letter, FL to E. M. Forster, 11 July 1916, King's College Library, Cambridge.
"intellectual decomposition": *DHL Letters,* II:642, [c. 20 Aug. 1916], to Barbara Low.
"a brigand": *DHL Letters,* II:542, 17 Feb. 1916, to Katherine Mansfield and JMM.
"[write] bombs": *DHL Letters,* II:547, [19 Feb. 1916], to Bertrand Russell.

53 "'Isn't it [...] secret cruelty": D. H. Lawrence, *The First "Women in Love,"* ed. John Worthen and Lindeth Vasey (Cambridge: Cambridge University Press, 1998), 223.
"the whole world": Ibid., 220.
"physical being": Ibid., 247.
"thank God": *DHL Letters,* II:612, 30 May 1916, to E. M. Forster.
"publish publicly": *DHL Letters,* VIII:27, 23 Aug. 1917, to Esther Andrews.

54 "any clothes on": unpublished letter, FL to JMM, 30 Sept. 1955, Turnbull.
"with us": *DHL Letters,* II:604, [5 May 1916], to Ottoline Morrell.
"I see [...] nice ones": unpublished letter, FL to JMM, [Mar. (?) 1923], Turnbull.
"her and me": unpublished letter, FL to JMM, [1 Aug. 1932], Turnbull.
"never been loyal": unpublished letter, FL to Mark Gertler, [4 Mar. 1916], photostat, Harvard University.
"utterably unscrupulous": Virginia Woolf to Vanessa Bell, 11 Feb. 1917, quoted in *The Letters of Virginia Woolf,* ed. Nigel Nicolson (New York: Harcourt, 1975), I:278.

"free again [...] wonderful": Katherine Mansfield to S. S. Koteliansky, 3 July 1916, quoted in Kathleen Jones, *Katherine Mansfield: The Story-Teller* (Edinburgh University Press, 2010), 275. Jones attributes Mansfield's dissatisfaction partly to her illnesses, partly to the landscape, and partly to the Lawrences' frequent quarrels.

55 [Murry] "filth": *DHL Letters*, III:53, [15 Dec. 1916], to S. S. Koteliansky.
"loathing" for him: *DHL Letters*, III:83, 25 Jan. 1917, to Gordon Campbell.
"you were here": *DHL Letters*, III:127, 23 May 1917, to JMM.
"against me": *DHL Letters*, II:667, 15 Oct. 1916, FL to S. S. Koteliansky.
"inert matter": *The First "Women in Love,"* 441.

56 "the initiated": *DHL Letters*, III:180, [7 Nov. 1917], to Cecil Gray.
"religious mystery": *The First "Women in Love,"* 414.

57 "And [...] to him": unpublished letter, FL to JMM, [Jan. 1931], Turnbull. In 1956 Frieda told Murry, "I would have more sense now" (unpublished letter, FL to JMM, 28 Jan. 1956, Turnbull).
"a homosexual affair": Marianna Torgovnick, "Our D. H. Lawrence Moment," *Chronicle of Higher Education*, 4 May 2015, 62.

58 "evil face": *DHL Letters*, II:566, 6 Mar. 1916, to Dollie Radford.

6. CORNERED IN CORNWALL

59 "all about": *DHL Letters*, III:167, 12 Oct. 1917, to Cecil Gray.

60 "strange composition [...] of decay": D. H. Lawrence, "Edgar Allan Poe" (first version), in *Studies in Classic American Literature*, ed. Ezra Greenspan, Lindeth Vasey, and John Worthen (Cambridge: Cambridge University Press, 2003), 229–30.
"smart things": D. H. Lawrence, *Aaron's Rod*, ed. Mara Kalnins (Cambridge: Cambridge University Press, 1988), 164.
"cracked for ever": *DHL Letters*, III:329, [28 Feb. 1919], to S. S. Koteliansky.

61 "terrifying lust": D. H. Lawrence, "Tickets Please," *England, My England and Other Stories*, ed. Bruce Steele (Cambridge: Cambridge University Press, 1990), 44.
"travelling grasp": D. H. Lawrence, "The Blind Man," *England, My England and Other Stories*, ed. Bruce Steele (Cambridge: Cambridge University Press, 1990), 62.
"shell is broken": Ibid, 63. Bertie Reid is a sketch of Sir James Barrie, whose marriage to Mary Ansell (later Cannan) was apparently unconsummated. Lawrence imagines Barrie breaking his shell of reticence.
"old people": *DHL Letters*, III:222, 12 Mar. 1918, to William Hopkin.

62 "And I [...] sing again": Enid Hopkin Hilton, *More than One Life: A Nottinghamshire Childhood with D. H. Lawrence* (Dover, NH: Alan Sutton, 1993), 31–32.
"one big curse": unpublished letter, FL to William Hopkin, 30 Dec. 1918, Nottinghamshire Archives, quoted in *Living at the Edge*, 186.
"at margarine": *DHL Letters*, III:335, 10 Mar. 1919, to Beatrice Campbell.

63 "for us all": *DHL Letters*, III:347, 5 Apr. 1919, to Amy Lowell.
"self was not": Katherine Mansfield to Dorothy Brett, 27 Oct. 1918, in *The Letters of Katherine Mansfield*, ed. Vincent O'Sullivan (Oxford: Oxford University Press, 1987), II:129. Frieda, ill with the Spanish flu, did not accompany DHL on his visit to Katherine.

"a new country": *DHL Letters*, III:331, 2 Mar. 1919, to Harriet Monroe.
"its complications": *DHL Letters*, III:333, 6 Mar. 1919, to Cynthia Asquith.
"I believe": *DHL Letters*, III:337, [14 Mar. 1919], to S. S. Koteliansky.

64 "much married": According to Cecily Lambert, in Nehls, *A Composite Biography*, I:503.
65 "saying she [...] at D. H.": Ibid., I:504–5.

7. A FRESH START IN ITALY

66 "very hungry": FL to Cynthia Asquith, [1 July 1919], in *Frieda Lawrence: The Memoirs and Correspondence*, ed. E. W. Tedlock Jr. (New York: Knopf, 1964), 214, quoted from manuscript; hereafter cited as Tedlock, *Memoirs and Correspondence*.
67 "as possible": *DHL Letters*, III:367, 30 June 1919, to S. S. Koteliansky.
"for [my] health": *DHL Letters*, III:401, 30 Sept. 1919, to Benjamin Huebsch.
68 "his best": quoted in *Modern Fiction Studies* 24 (1978): 366.
"state of animosity": quoted in Nehls, *A Composite Biography*, I:507.
69 "sun and sea [...] line": *DHL Letters*, III:416, 17 Nov. 1919, to Rosalind Baynes.
"to live in": *DHL Letters*, III:420, [24 Nov. 1919], to Emily King.
"nice carelessness": *DHL Letters*, III:419, [24 Nov. 1919], to Catherine Carswell.
"a very sexual person": quoted in Louise E. Wright, "Talk about Real Men: Jack London's Correspondence with Maurice Magnus," *Journal of Popular Culture* 40 (2007): 367 (letter of 19 Nov. 1911).
70 "bisexual types": Maurice Magnus to Norman Douglas, 18 July 1920, quoted in Brenda Maddox, *D. H. Lawrence: The Story of a Marriage* (New York: Simon & Schuster, 1994), 269.
"We went [...] to me": FL, *Not I, But the Wind*, 98.
"and cheap": unpublished postcard, FL to Ada Lawrence Clarke, [9 Dec. 1919], University of Nottingham.
"go south": *DHL Letters*, III:424, [28 Nov. 1919], to Rosalind Baynes.
"the swindle": *DHL Letters*, III:435, 18 Dec. 1919, to Irene Whittley.
"extremely beautiful": *DHL Letters*, III:442, 4 Jan. 1920, to Catherine Carswell.
71 "lively and jolly": *DHL Letters*, III:446, 5 Jan. 1920, to Sallie Hopkin.
"We had [...] the Tarantella": FL to Violet Monk, 6 Jan. 1920, in Tedlock, *Memoirs and Correspondence*, 215–16.
"to look [...] selfconscious effort": *DHL Letters*, III:445, 4 Jan. 1920, to Catherine Carswell.
"in the world": *DHL Letters*, III:450, 9 Jan. 1921, to Sallie and William Hopkin.
72 "succulent herbage": *DHL Letters*, III:481, [8 Mar. 1920], to John Ellingham Brooks.
"wings of [his] soul": *DHL Letters*, III:522, [10 May 1920], to Compton Mackenzie.

8. INTOXICATED AND ALONE

73 "really lovely": *DHL Letters*, III:483, 9 Mar. 1920, to Amy Lowell.
"very much": unpublished postcard, FL to Margaret King, postmarked 27 Mar. 1920, University of Nottingham.
"better than Capri": *DHL Letters*, III:489, 20 Mar. 1920, to Fritz Krenkow.

74 "It is [...] north again": *DHL Letters*, III:510, 29 Apr. 1921, to S. S. Koteliansky.
"like a guest [...] Of life": D. H. Lawrence, *The Poems of D. H. Lawrence*, ed. Christopher Pollnitz (Cambridge: Cambridge University Press, 2013), I:303–5; hereafter cited as *DHL Poems*.
"end of August": *DHL Letters*, III:575, [22 July 1920], to Rosalind Baynes.
75 "I came [...] as this": D. H. Lawrence, *Memoir of Maurice Magnus*, ed. Keith Cushman (Santa Rosa, CA: Black Sparrow Press, 1987), 67.
"It has [...] about ripe": *DHL Letters*, III:581, 30 July 1920, to Hilda Brown.
76 "most people [...] to bed": Rosalind Thornycroft, *Time Which Spaces Us Apart* (Batscombe, Somerset: privately printed, 1991), 78–79.
"meet next": *DHL Letters*, III:609, [7 Oct. 1920], to Rosalind Baynes.
"incision [...] the centre": *DHL Poems*, I:231–37.
"black hole": Ibid., 304.
"A kiss [...] of loneliness": Ibid., 236.
77 "privacy ferociously": FL, *Not I, But the Wind*, 115. John Worthen believes that Frieda "found out" about the affair and was angry (*D. H. Lawrence: The Life of an Outsider*, 234).
"as if [...] and sightless": DHL, *Aaron's Rod*, 263.
78 "lifted-upness": *DHL Letters*, III:613, 18 Oct. 1920, to Robert Mountsier.
"like spring": FL to Irene and Percy Whittley, in *DHL Letters*, III:615, [23 Oct. 1920].
"quite near": unpublished letter, FL to Sally Hopkin, 10 Dec. 1920, Nottinghamshire Archive.
"an oyster shell": D. H. Lawrence, *Sea and Sardinia*, ed. Mara Kalnins (Cambridge: Cambridge University Press, 1997), 10.
"over parsnips": Ibid., 13.
"like pressed leaves": Ibid., 41.
"Suddenly [...] jeering insolence": Ibid., 24.
79 "wooden hearts": Ibid., 35.
"male life": Ibid., 129.
"das Glück": Benjamin Huebsch to DHL, in *DHL Letters*, IV:229 n. 2, 3 Mar. 1922.
"I am [...] of Europe": unpublished letter, FL to Robert Mountsier, 5 Feb. 1921, Northwestern University.
80 "I should [...] Thrasher's farm": *DHL Letters*, III:661, 5 Feb. 1921, to Robert Mountsier.
"Railroad and [...] Thrasher's Farm": unpublished account, "Moneys Received and Expended by Robert Mountsier, Acting as Agent for D. H. Lawrence, March 16 to April 26, 1921," Copley Library. By comparison, the *Dial* paid Lawrence thirty dollars to publish his poem "Snake."
"find my direction": *DHL Letters*, III:689, 22 Mar. 1921, to Robert Mountsier.
"go away": *DHL Letters*, III:676, 2 Mar. 1921, to S. S. Koteliansky.
"crisis for me": *DHL Letters*, III:693, [25 Mar. 1921], to Robert Mountsier.
"a trick": *DHL Letters*, III:678 n. 3, 3 Mar. 1921, to Robert Mountsier.
81 "my plan": *DHL Letters*, III:683, [15 Mar. 1921], to Mary Cannan.

9. CROSSING THE SEAS

82 "look back": *DHL Letters*, VIII:53, [23 Feb. 1922], to AvR.
"joining Frieda": *DHL Letters*, III:704, [22 Apr. 1921], to Catherine Carswell.

83 "tactful touch": Earl and Achsah Brewster, *D. H. Lawrence: Reminiscences and Correspondence* (London: Secker, 1934), 14.
"vice in her": unpublished letter, FL to Harwood Brewster Picard, 8 Mar. 1945 (in the possession of Keith Cushman).
"only Godhead": D. H. Lawrence, *Aaron's Rod,* ed. Mara Kalnins (Cambridge: Cambridge University Press, 1988), 296.

85 "eye of love": *DHL Letters*, III:734, 3 June 1921, to Evelyn Scott.
"shudder[s] . . . such love again": D. H. Lawrence, "The Captain's Doll," in *The Fox, The Captain's Doll, The Ladybird*, ed. Dieter Mehl (Cambridge: Cambridge University Press, 1992), 115.

86 "he answered": Ibid., 130.
"I want [. . .] but love": Ibid., 150–51.
"blissfully happy": *DHL Letters*, VIII:45, [25 Aug. 1921], to AvR.

87 "is heaven": *DHL Letters*, IV:92, [30 Sept. 1921], to Irene Whittley.
"own house": *DHL Letters*, IV:95, [8 Oct. 1921], to Robert Mountsier.
"early spring": *DHL Letters*, IV:80, 29 Aug. 1921, to Robert Mountsier.
"from the Pacific": *DHL Letters*, IV:95, 8 Oct. 1921, to Earl Brewster.
"angrier I become": *DHL Letters*, IV:98, 12 Oct. 1921, to Violet Monk.
"to Ceylon": *DHL Letters*, IV:110, 2 Nov. 1921, to Earl Brewster.
"There is [. . .] to go": *DHL Letters*, IV:125, 16 Nov. 1921, to Earl Brewster.

89 "We are [. . .] out here": unpublished letter, FL to Irene Whittley, [1 Oct. 1921], HRC.
"I am [. . .] the utmost": *DHL Letters*, IV:170–71, 18 Jan. 1922, to Earl Brewster.
"strong enough": FL to Mabel Dodge Luhan, 26 Jan. 1922, in *DHL Letters*, IV:181 n. 4.

10. FEVERS AND FORTUNE

91 "round the world": unpublished letter, FL to AvR, 20 May 1922, *sütterlin* 44.

92 "rather lovely really": *DHL Letters*, IV:208, 4 Mar. 1922, to Norman Douglas.
"I like [. . .] sharp sand": *DHL Letters*, IV:208, [7 Mar. 1922], to S. S. Kotcliansky.
"like a [. . .] pressure": *DHL Letters*, IV:213, 8 Mar. 1922, to Rosalind Baynes.

93 "if you walk a few yards": *DHL Letters*, IV:216, 24 Mar. 1922, to Emily King.
infected with malaria: David Ellis believes that Lawrence may have been infected in Sicily shortly before he sailed for Ceylon. See Ellis, *D. H. Lawrence: Dying Game 1922–1930* (Cambridge: Cambridge University Press, 1998), 611 n. 2.
"can't stand Ceylon": *DHL Letters*, IV:222, [3 Apr. 1922], to Anna Jenkins.
"dead off" Buddhism: *DHL Letters*, IV:218, 28 Mar. 1922, to Anna Jenkins.
to Buddha "hideous": *DHL Letters*, IV:221, 3 Apr. 1922, to Mary Cannan.
"all the time": *DHL Letters*, IV:225, [8 Apr. 1922], to Anna Jenkins.
"tropical fruits": *DHL Letters*, IV:224, [5 Apr. 1922], to Mary Cannan.
"from the world": *DHL Letters*, IV:245, 26 May 1922, to Robert Mountsier.
"Thirroul—Fur[nished] Cott[age]s to Let. Winter T[er]ms": quoted in Joseph Davis, *D. H. Lawrence at Thirroul* (Sydney: Collins, 1989), 32.
"The heavy [. . .] very comfortable": *DHL Letters*, IV:249, 30 May 1922, to AvR.

94 "Here we sit [...] every day [...] stay here": unpublished letter, FL to AvR, 22 June and 7 July 1922, *sütterlin* 45. Later, on 9 August, Frieda confirmed, "We've got to know absolutely no *educated* people here." FL to AvR, 9 Aug. 1922, HRC.
"a supreme truth": D. H. Lawrence, *Kangaroo,* ed. Bruce Steele (Cambridge: Cambridge University Press, 1994), 356.

95 "his dearest book – very striking": unpublished letter, FL to AvR, 7 July 1922, *sütterlin* 45.
"with men": unpublished letter, FL to JMM, [Jan. 1931], Turnbull.
"a glamour like magic": DHL, *Kangaroo,* 70.
"'Don't swank,' [...] he bitingly": Ibid., 69–70.
"into action": Ibid., 143.

96 "I've ever known": Ibid., 356.
A photograph taken at this time: photograph by William Forrester, Wollongong City Library, Australia.
"into the mountains": *DHL Letters,* VIII:55, [22 Aug. 1922], to AvR.
"important for us!": unpublished letter, FL to Else Jaffe, [31 July 1922], *sütterlin* 46.
"all the time": unpublished letter, FL to AvR, 9 Aug. 1922, *sütterlin* 47.
over four thousand dollars: The figure Thomas Seltzer quoted was $4,286.46 in his 1 February 1923 letter to DHL, in Jay A. Gertzman and Michael Squires, "New Letters from Thomas Seltzer and Robert Mountsier to D. H. Lawrence," *D. H. Lawrence Review* 28 (1999): 65.
"astonishingly famous": unpublished letter, FL to AvR, [c. 14 Sept. 1922], *sütterlin* 49.
a check for thirty dollars: D. H. Lawrence, check no. 5, Charleroi [PA] Savings & Trust Co., unpublished checkbook 1922–23 (Chávez). From this checking account, Lawrence sent his mother-in-law a further twenty-five dollars on 5 December 1922 (check no. 12) and the same amount on 3 February 1923 (check no. 15).

97 "latest fashion": unpublished letter, FL to AvR, [31 July 1922], *sütterlin* 46.
"a bit of quiet": *DHL Letters,* IV:293, 8 Sept. 1922, to Robert Mountsier.

11. MOUNTAINS IN AMERICA

99 "the pueblo": *DHL Letters,* IV:260, 9 June 1922, to Mabel Dodge Luhan.
"quite overwhelmed": *DHL Letters,* IV:294–95, [12 Sept. 1922], to Thomas Seltzer.
"she says": *DHL Letters,* IV:273, 3 July 1922, to Katharine Throssell.
"on the go": *DHL Letters,* IV:309, 25 Sept. 1922, to William Siebenhaar.
"It is [...] believe it": unpublished letter, FL to AvR, [c. 14 Sept. 1922], *sütterlin* 49.
"kind to me": *DHL Letters,* IV:306, [22 Sept. 1922], to Robert Mountsier.

100 "a little buffalo": *DHL Letters,* IV:352, 5 Dec. 1922, to AvR.
"happy here": unpublished letter, FL to AvR, [c. 9 Nov. 1922], *sütterlin* 50.
"heal Lawrence completely": unpublished letter, FL to AvR, [c. 14 Sept. 1922], *sütterlin* 49.
"live there": *DHL Letters,* IV:333, [31 Oct. 1922], to Elizabeth Freeman.
"Spanish with Sabino": unpublished letter, FL to AvR, [c. 9 Nov. 1922], *sütterlin* 50.

101 "embracing syphilitics": quoted in Armin Arnold, *D. H. Lawrence and America* (New York: Philosophical Library, 1959), 90.

"nothing spontaneous": D. H. Lawrence, *Studies in Classic American Literature* (Cambridge: Cambridge University Press, 2003), appendix V, "Whitman (1921–22)," 405.
"in my life": *DHL Letters*, IV:337, 7 Nov. 1922, to S. S. Koteliansky.

102 "very different [here]": *DHL Letters*, IV:349, 4 Dec. 1922, to S. S. Koteliansky.
"veal and pork as we want": FL to AvR, [8 Dec. 1922], in *DHL Letters*, IV:357; I cite the Worthens' translation (*sütterlin* 51).
"was so well!": unpublished letter, FL to AvR, 9 Jan. 1923, *sütterlin* 52.
"impudent" and "meddling": Gertzman and Squires, "New Letters from Thomas Seltzer and Robert Mountsier," 61.
"with me": Thomas Seltzer to DHL, in *DHL Letters*, IV 315n, 6 Sept. 1922.

103 "was helpful": Thomas Seltzer, letter of 3 Mar. 1923, in Gertzman and Squires, "New Letters from Thomas Seltzer and Robert Mountsier," 73.
"rid of him": *DHL Letters*, IV:377, 7 Feb. 1923, to Thomas Seltzer.
that "liar" Mabel: *DHL Letters*, IV:372, 24 Jan. 1923, to Elizabeth Freeman.
"did not believe in me": *DHL Letters*, IV:382, 10 Feb. 1923, to Thomas Seltzer.
"can't stand any more": *DHL Letters*, IV:378, 7 Feb. 1923, to Thomas Seltzer.
"far before love": *DHL Letters*, IV:368, 4 Jan. 1923, to Thomas Seltzer.
"I know I can love": FL to S. S. Koteliansky, 4 Dec. 1923, in Tedlock, *Memoirs and Correspondence*, 225.
"are really tiring": unpublished letter, FL to AvR, 2 Feb. 1923, *sütterlin* 53.
"It was rough": *DHL Letters*, VIII:75, 18 Mar. 1923, to Adele Seltzer.

104 "We might [...] come along": *DHL Letters*, IV:388, [16? Feb. 1923], to Willard Johnson.
Lawrence had invited five people: Merrild, Götzsche, Bynner, Johnson, and Mabel Luhan's friend Elizabeth Freeman.
"almost perfect" for tubercular types: T. Philip Terry, *Terry's Guide to Mexico*, rev. ed. (Boston: Houghton Mifflin, 1923), xxvi. DHL would have known that Katherine Mansfield, age thirty-four, had died of tuberculosis a few months earlier, on 9 January 1923.

12. THE MYSTERIES OF MEXICO

105 "country down there": Witter Bynner, *Journey with Genius: Recollections and Reflections concerning the D. H. Lawrences* (New York: John Day, 1951), 17.
"vile and degraded": FL to Adele Seltzer, 8 Apr. 1923, quoted in *D. H. Lawrence: Letters to Thomas and Adele Seltzer*, ed. Gerald M. Lacy (Santa Barbara, CA: Black Sparrow Press, 1976), 88.

106 "savage underneath": *DHL Letters*, IV:442, 9 May 1923, to Thomas Seltzer.
"we may settle": *DHL Letters*, IV:430, [21 Apr. 1923], to Kai Götzsche and Knud Merrild.
"TAKE EVENING TRAIN": *DHL Letters*, IV:435, [1 May 1923], to Frieda Lawrence.
"he ever did": FL to Adele Seltzer, 10 June 1923, in *DHL Letters*, IV:455.

107 "with nobody": D. H. Lawrence, *Quetzalcoatl: The Early Version of "The Plumed Serpent,"* ed. Louis L. Martz (Redding Ridge, CT: Black Swan, 1995), 31.
"Mysterious" and "not quite fathomable": Ibid., 20.
"wildness [was] undreamt of": unpublished letter, FL to AvR, [10 June 1923], *sütterlin* 57.

"above all love": DHL, *Quetzalcoatl*, 34.
"novel of mine": *DHL Letters,* IV:457, 15 June 1923, to Thomas Seltzer.
108 "spell [...] soul": DHL, *Quetzalcoatl*, 160.
"would die": Ibid., 300.
"great machines": Ibid., 304.
109 "I don't [...] to live in": *DHL Letters,* IV:458, 15 June 1923, to Thomas Seltzer.
"on this lake": *DHL Letters,* VIII:81, [22 June 1923], to Thomas Seltzer.
"desolate inside": *DHL Letters,* IV:473, [25?] July 1923, to Willard Johnson.
"she will sail [to England] on the 18th": *DHL Letters,* IV:478, 7 Aug. 1923, to S. S. Koteliansky; my emphasis.
"has changed": *DHL Letters,* IV:479, 7 Aug. 1923, to AvR.
"old ground": *DHL Letters,* IV:480, 7 Aug. 1923, to JMM.
110 "cheerful soul": *DHL Letters,* IV:483, 13 Aug. 1923, to JMM.
"manhood in them": *DHL Letters,* IV:463, [27 June 1923], to Knud Merrild.
"Norse gods": Adele Seltzer to Dorothy Hoskins, 7 Jan. 1923, in Lacy, *D. H. Lawrence,* 251; and in Adele Seltzer to her sisters, 16 Jan. 1923, in Lacy, *D. H. Lawrence,* 187.
"manage [a little banana farm]": *DHL Letters,* IV:459, [17 June 1923], to Kai Götzsche and Knud Merrild.
"make a life": *DHL Letters,* IV:470, 15 July 1923, to Kai Götzsche and Knud Merrild.
"among the mountains": *DHL Letters,* IV:481, 7 Aug. 1923, to Knud Merrild.
building a life together: see also FL to Kai Götzsche and Knud Merrild, [17 June 1923], *DHL Letters,* IV:459.
"I feel [...] wrote him so": FL to Adele Seltzer, [26?] Aug. 1923, in Lacy, *D. H. Lawrence,* 106.
111 "a circle of friends": DHL, *Quetzalcoatl*, 32.

13. HER SHIP GOES EAST

112 "a little while": Michael Squires and Lynn K. Talbot, "The Crisis of 1923: Five Newly Discovered Letters from D. H. Lawrence to Frieda," *Journal of D. H. Lawrence Studies* 3:1 (2012): 8–11.
"sail away from this world": *DHL Letters,* II:259, 18 Jan. 1915, to William Hopkin.
113 "The circus [...] life itself": Squires and Talbot, "The Crisis," 27.
"If I find [...] very much": Ibid., 13–15.
"looks at [...] an onlooker": *DHL Letters,* IV:507, [5 Oct. 1923], to Knud Merrild.
114 "difficult to live with": Knud Merrild, *With D. H. Lawrence in New Mexico: A Memoir of D. H. Lawrence* (1938; reprint, London: Routledge, 1964), 343.
"casual," without deep affection: Bynner, *Journey with Genius,* 194.
"It's time [...] very safe": *DHL Letters,* VIII:85, 22 Sept. 1923, DHL to FL. The story in the *Los Angeles Times* had appeared three days earlier (sec. A1).
"hidden somewhere": *DHL Letters,* VIII:85, 22 Sept. 1923, DHL to FL.
115 "must come back": *DHL Letters,* IV:513, 17 Oct. 1923, to Catherine Carswell.
"a visit": *DHL Letters,* IV:518, [20?] Oct. 1923, to Thomas Seltzer.
"alien": *DHL Letters,* IV:519, 22 Oct. 1923, to S. S. Koteliansky.

"important female": FL to Adele Seltzer, 2 Sept. 1923, in Lacy, *D. H. Lawrence*, 108.

"a ranch": *DHL Letters*, IV:513, 17 Oct. 1923, to Catherine Carswell.

Lawrence could have spared a few thousand dollars for it: In September 1923 DHL carried a balance of $590.90 in his Charleroi Trust account (Chávez). In 1922 he earned $4,250 in net income, and in June 1923 Seltzer paid him a further $4,306 (*DHL Letters*, IV:464), then another $1,000 on 15 August 1923 (*DHL Letters*, V:18 n. 4).

"I do hope [...] to it": unpublished letter, FL to Martin Secker, 8 Oct. 1923, HRC.

"emotion in others": Catherine Carswell, *The Savage Pilgrimage: A Narrative of D. H. Lawrence* (London: Chatto, 1932), 193.

"that Lawrence [...] than you": FL to Adele Seltzer, 2 Sept. 1923, in Lacy, *D. H. Lawrence*, 108.

117 "very tall [...] absolutely distinguished": unpublished letter, FL to AvR, [(22?) Sept. 1923], *sütterlin* 61.

"terribly attached [...] am here": unpublished letter, FL to AvR, 24 Dec. 1923, *sütterlin* 64.

"I had dreamed": unpublished letter, FL to AvR, [(9?) Jan. 1924], *sütterlin* 65.

Frieda and Murry may possibly have become lovers: Evidence for an affair is cited in Hignett, *Brett*, 138; evidence against it, in Worthen, *Outsider*, 297.

"very much": unpublished letter, FL to AvR, 5 Nov. 1923, *sütterlin* 62.

"I was [...] hurt child": unpublished letter, FL to JMM, [20 Apr. 1931], Turnbull.

"care much [for me]": Ibid.

118 "should not [...] in Mexico": FL, *Not I, But the Wind*, 144.

"Here I [...] me here": *DHL Letters*, IV:544, [17 Dec. 1923], to Idella Purnell.

"the greatness of Lawrence": Carswell, *A Savage Pilgrimage*, 209.

"no part or place": Ibid., 211.

"still and unresponsive": Ibid., 212.

"eschew emotions – they are a disease": *DHL Letters*, IV:581, 13 Feb. 1924, to JMM.

119 **pregnant with Murry's child:** For the evidence, see Hignett, *Brett*, 136.

"Taos is about the best place": *DHL Letters*, IV:539, 19 Nov. 1923, to Mabel Dodge Luhan.

"subtle, cunning homage": D. H. Lawrence, "The Border-Line," in *The Woman Who Rode Away and Other Stories*, ed. Dieter Mehl and Christa Jansohn (Cambridge: Cambridge University Press, 1995), 81.

"And dimly [...] own contentment": Ibid., 86.

120 "out of here": *DHL Letters*, IV:544, [17 Dec. 1923], to Thomas Seltzer.

he often put off writing important letters: In a biographical account of the Seltzers, Alexandra Lee Levin and Lawrence L. Levin explain that Thomas was "congenitally unable to do anything on time" (Lacy, *D. H. Lawrence*, 191).

"of Europe": *DHL Letters*, IV:600, 10 Mar. 1924, to JMM.

14. FRIEDA'S RUSTIC RANCH

121 "At the [...] bad year": *DHL Letters*, V:18, [16 Mar. 1924], to Catherine Carswell.

"as you can": Thomas Seltzer to DHL, in *DHL Letters*, VIII:89, 7 May 1924.

"there naturally": Thomas Seltzer to DHL, in *DHL Letters,* VIII:94, 8 May 1925.
"inexpressibly": *DHL Letters,* V:22, 4 Apr. 1924, to Mollie Skinner.
"depression": *DHL Letters,* V:26, 4 Apr. 1924, to Curtis Brown.

122 "growing lively again": *DHL Letters,* V:24, 4 Apr. 1924, to Martin Secker.
"grotesque [...] and English": Mabel Luhan, *Lorenzo in Taos* (New York: Knopf, 1932), 191.
"odd man out": Carswell, *A Savage Pilgrimage,* 200.

123 "fifty thousand dollars": unpublished letter, FL to AvR, [c. 15 July 1924], *sütterlin* 66. The claim of $50,000 is inflated. I would estimate that in 1924, when Frieda sold the manuscript of *Sons and Lovers* to Mabel, the Kiowa Ranch would have had a value of $2,500. That figure is based partly on what a collector named Thomas Hanley later paid Frieda for the complete manuscripts of *The Rainbow* ($3,500) and *Kangaroo* ($1,500). In addition, in 1937, during the Depression, Frieda's complete collection of Lawrence's manuscripts was offered to Harvard University for $25,000. See Michael Squires, *DHL's MSS,* 28 n. 7, 85–87.
"the world": *DHL Letters,* V:38, 2 May 1924, to Thomas Seltzer.

124 "great fun": *DHL Letters,* V:48, [26 May 1924], to Thomas Seltzer.
"simple and stylish": unpublished letter, FL to AvR, 8 Aug. 1924, *sütterlin* 67.
"Here, where [...] is America": *DHL Letters,* V:63, 28 June 1924, to AvR.

125 "pristine race": quoted in Knud Merrild, *With D. H. Lawrence in New Mexico: A Memoir of D. H. Lawrence* (1938; reprint, London: Routledge, 1964), 342.
"marvellous Indians": D. H. Lawrence, "The Woman Who Rode Away," in *The Woman Who Rode Away and Other Stories,* ed. Dieter Mehl and Christa Jansohn (Cambridge: Cambridge University Press, 1995), 42.
"badly hurt": *DHL Letters,* V:144, 5 Oct. 1924, to Clarence Thompson.
"steady suppressed growl": *DHL Letters,* V:126, 14 Sept. 1924, to Mabel Dodge Luhan.

126 "call them to you": Brett, *Lawrence and Brett,* 100.
"see the gods again": *DHL Letters,* V:77, 23 July 1924, to E. M. Forster.
"part of me": *DHL Letters,* V:135, 29 [Sept.] 1924, FL to AvR; my translation.
"Lawrence looks so good": FL to AvR, 29 [Sept.] 1924, in *DHL Letters,* V:135.
"has been [...] excellent": unpublished letter, FL to AvR, 8 Aug. 1924, *sütterlin* 67.

127 "cosmic beasts": D. H. Lawrence, "Mornings in Mexico," in *Mornings in Mexico and Etruscan Places* (1927; reprint, London: Heinemann, 1956), 65.
"in the Indians": unpublished letter, FL to Mabel Dodge Luhan, 3 July 1930, Yale University.
"There is [...] whole area": unpublished letter, FL to AvR, [15 Oct. 1924], *sütterlin* 69.

128 "her Ranch": *DHL Letters,* VIII:90, [14 Oct. 1924], to AvR.

15. MENACE AND MALARIA

129 "see the people": Brett, *Lawrence and Brett,* 160.
"these dying, apathetic Indians": unpublished letter, FL to AvR, [19 Feb. 1925], *sütterlin* 71.

130 "just right": *DHL Letters,* V:166, 15 Nov. 1924, to Emily King.
"never crumbled in an earthquake!": interview, Michael Squires with José Alvarez Padilla, 19 May 1995, Oaxaca, Mexico, in *Love and Loyalty,* 103.

131 **"mumbles unintelligibly"**: D. H. Lawrence, "Walk to Huayapa," *Mornings in Mexico*, intro. Michael Squires (reprint, London: Tauris Parke, 2009), 39–40.
"battered and shattered": *DHL Letters,* V:182, [7 Dec. 1924], to William Hawk.
"wasn't well down here": *DHL Letters,* V:211, 7 Feb. 1925, to William Hawk.

132 **"You, Frieda and I [...] in life"**: *DHL Letters,* V:192, [9 Jan. 1925], to Dorothy Brett.
"gall and wormwood": *DHL Letters,* V:182, [7 Dec. 1924], to Luis Quintanilla.
"soft repose [...] mystery": D. H. Lawrence, *The Plumed Serpent*, ed. L. D. Clark (Cambridge: Cambridge University Press, 1987), 81.
"to save her": Ibid., 103.

133 **"just a woman"**: Ibid., 325.
"the volcanic deeps": Ibid., 422.
"intimacy whatever": Ibid., 423.
"enormous cactus": unpublished letter, FL to AvR, 21 Jan. 1925, *sütterlin* 70.
"pulled him through": FL to Friedrich Jaffe, [(15?) Mar. 1925], in *DHL Letters,* VIII:92; my translation.
"bewitched by his Mexico": unpublished letter, FL to AvR, [19 Feb. 1925], *sütterlin* 71.

134 **"a perfect rag"**: *DHL Letters,* V:223, [11 Mar. 1925], to Idella Purnell.
"Mr. Lawrence": FL, *Not I, But the Wind*, 151.
"at El Paso": Brett, *Lawrence and Brett*, 232.
"immigration officials": FL, *Not I, But the Wind*, 151.
"The only gods are men": *The Plumed Serpent,* textual apparatus 427, line 9 (typescript reading).

135 **"feel better again"**: FL to Kathryn Herbig, 26 Apr. 1938, in *DHL's MSS,* 173–74.

16. THE ROUTE TO SPOTORNO

136 **"decidedly better [...] any more"**: unpublished letter, FL to AvR, 28 Apr. [1925], *sütterlin* 72.
"a fresh start": *DHL Letters,* V:172, 17 Nov. 1924, to Clarence Thompson.
"only half awake": *DHL Letters,* V:233, 6 Apr. 1925, to Ida Rauh.

137 **"himself out to them"**: unpublished letter, FL to AvR, [c. 22 Apr. 1925], *sütterlin* 73.
"hit her on the nose": Brett, *Lawrence and Brett*, 228.
"stronger than mine": FL to Dorothy Brett, 20 Feb. [1925], in "D. H. Lawrence and Frieda Lawrence: Letters to Dorothy Brett," ed. Peter L. Irvine and Anne Kiley, *D. H. Lawrence Review* 9 (1976): 41.
Scott Murray, who charged fifty dollars: An unpublished ledger shows checks from DHL to Scott Murray, numbered 65, 69, 75, and 76, totaling $49.75 (Chávez).
in Bavaria: Information about Friedel (in 1940 he changed his name to Frederick Jeffrey) can be found in the Christopher Jeffrey Collection, AR 25348 [2009], Leo Baeck. Friedel studied briefly (and unhappily) at St. John's College and Johns Hopkins University.

138 **"old relations"**: Thomas Seltzer to DHL, 2 July 1925, quoted in *DHL Letters,* VIII:95.
"last summer": *DHL Letters,* V:281, [17 July 1925], to Willard Johnson.
"very hot sun": *DHL Letters,* V:289, 24 Aug. 1925, to Catherine Carswell.
"less literary": *DHL Letters,* V:263, 10 June 1925, to George Conway.

"never yet beheld": D. H. Lawrence, "Reflections on the Death of a Porcupine," in *Reflections on the Death of a Porcupine and Other Essays*, ed. Michael Herbert (Cambridge: Cambridge University Press, 1988), 361.

139 "unending materialism": *DHL Letters*, V:294, 31 Aug. 1925, to Kyle Crichton.
"the hidden stuff": *DHL Letters*, V:308, [28 Sept. 1925], to Kyle Crichton.
"cold and [. . .] more money!": D. H. Lawrence, "The Rocking-Horse Winner," in *The Woman Who Rode Away and Other Stories*, ed. Dieter Mehl and Christa Jansohn (Cambridge: Cambridge University Press, 1995), 230.

140 "to the ground": Ibid., 235.
"feeling of hostility": Brett, *Lawrence and Brett*, 252.
"steamy hot": *DHL Letters*, V:302, [21 Sept. 1925], to Dorothy Brett.
"balance of $1,002 [. . .] $2,254": unpublished ledger kept by DHL, checks numbered 84 (21 Sept. 1925) and 88 (21 Mar. 1926), Chase National Bank of the City of New York (Chávez).

141 "And I between": FL to Dorothy Brett, [4 Nov. 1925], in Irvine and Kiley, "D. H. Lawrence and Frieda Lawrence," 55.
"girlish, hysterical voice": quoted in Nehls, *A Composite Biography*, III:10.
"pinched and small": Carswell, *The Savage Pilgrimage*, 227.
"look at them": *DHL Letters*, V:319, [17 Oct. 1925], to Catherine Carswell.
"I feel [. . .] no reason": FL to Dorothy Brett, [Nov. 1925], in Irvine and Kiley, "D. H. Lawrence and Frieda Lawrence," 57.

17. RAGE AND COMPASSION

142 "darkness of England": *DHL Letters*, V:337, [15 Nov. 1925], to Emily King.
"like the devil": *DHL Letters*, V:332, 4 Nov. 1925, to Dorothy Brett.
"Octavian Augustus": *DHL Letters*, V:42, 23 Nov. 1926, to Blanche Knopf.
"figs and nuts and pears": unpublished letter, FL to Emily King, [26 Nov. 1925], University of Nottingham.

143 "her will" . . . "one day": D. H. Lawrence, *The Virgin and the Gipsy and Other Stories*, ed. Michael Herbert, Bethan Jones, and Lindeth Vasey (Cambridge: Cambridge University Press, 2005), 37, 57, 65, 78.

144 "they like": unpublished letter, FL to JMM, 6 Apr. [1931], Turnbull.
"we drew and sang": unpublished letter, FL to AvR, [23 Dec. 1925], *sütterlin* 75.

145 "Don't you [. . .] false face": FL, *Not I, But the Wind*, 179.
"worse [. . .] keep still": *DHL Letters*, V:390, [11 Feb. 1926], to Dorothy Brett.
"I'm so [. . .] nice time": *DHL Letters*, V:401, 2 Mar. 1926, to Ada Clarke.
"really shattered": quoted in Nehls, *A Composite Biography*, III:22.

146 "Vengo a Capri": *DHL Letters*, V:400, 26 Feb. 1926, to Dorothy Brett.
"to death": Brett, *Lawrence and Brett*, 271.
"Women are [. . .] to others": Ibid., 278.
"for a time": Ibid., 272.

147 "I felt [. . .] It was hopeless": Quoted in *Living at the Edge*, 316–17, and, with revisions, in Hignett, *Brett*, 191–92.

"The greatest [...] what's happened": *DHL Letters*, V:408, [21 Mar. 1926], to Dorothy Brett.
"I find [...] many matters": *DHL Letters*, V:421, [22 Apr. 1926], to Earl Brewster.
148 "in its way": *DHL Letters*, V:447, 3 May 1926, to Margaret King.
150 "that villa": FL, *Not I, But the Wind*, 186.
"si estendeva per molte miglia": interview, Michael Squires with Alessandro Mirenda, 9 June 2001, *Love and Loyalty*, 119.

18. REVEALING THE SECRET

152 told her mother: unpublished letter, FL to AvR, [(28?) Apr. 1928], *sütterlin* 79.
"furniture": *DHL Letters*, V:448, 3 May 1926, to Ada Clarke.
"England seems [...] begin again": *DHL Letters*, V:514, 26 Aug. 1926, to Dorothy Brett.
"things literary": *DHL Letters*, V:516, [28 Aug. 1926], to S. S. Koteliansky.
"native Midlands": *DHL Letters*, V:521, 2 Sept. 1926, to S. S. Koteliansky.
153 "always lovely": *DHL Letters*, V:478, 23 June 1926, to Dorothy Brett.
"this year": *DHL Letters*, V:548, 2 Oct. 1926, to Gertrude Cooper.
"as we go": *DHL Letters*, V:549, 9 Oct. 1926, to Emily King.
"about the strike": *DHL Letters*, V:565, 28 Oct. 1926, to Ada Clarke.
"like an insanity": *DHL Letters*, V:552, [9 Oct. 1926], to Ada Clarke.
"The talk [...] let off steam": John Turner, ed., "D. H. Lawrence in the Wilkinson Diaries," *D. H. Lawrence Review* 30 (2002): 27–28; punctuation and paragraphing have been corrected; hereafter cited as "Wilkinson Diaries," with page number and date of diary entry.
154 "change the subject": Ibid., 29, 1 Nov. 1926.
"hated sex": D. H. Lawrence, *The First Lady Chatterley* (London: Heinemann, 1972), 314.
155 "She was [...] have to!": Ibid., 3–5.
"outwardly younger": unpublished letter, FL to JMM, 6 Apr. [1931], Turnbull.
"he was away": D. H. Lawrence, *John Thomas and Lady Jane* (London: Heinemann, 1972), 7.
156 "for painting": DHL, *The First Lady Chatterley*, 3.
"For the [...] great bells": Ibid., 35.
157 "English people": unpublished letter, FL to JMM, [6 June 1930], Turnbull.
158 "nice eyes:": *DHL Letters*, V:586, 24 Nov. 1926, to Dorothy Brett.
159 "any mischief": FL to Mabel Luhan, 30 Oct. 1926, in *DHL Letters*, V:568–69.
"the accompaniments": "Wilkinson Diaries," 35, 30 Jan. 1927.
"doing my novel": *DHL Letters*, V:629, 20 Jan. 1927, to Dorothy Brett.
"bottomless pools" of his imagination: *DHL Letters*, V:605, 19 Dec. 1926, to Dorothy Brett.
160 "medium build [...] military erectness": DHL, *John Thomas and Lady Jane*, 27.
"by death": Ibid., 100.
"her limbs": Ibid., 111.
"into hers": Ibid., 271.
"the mysterious [...] put perfectly": Ibid., 234.
"not bad, but beastly": *DHL Letters*, V:654, 11 Mar. 1927, to Nancy Pearn.
161 "very attractive": *DHL Letters*, VI:37, 14–15 Apr. 1927, to Mabel Dodge Luhan.

"know the gods [...] to them": D. H. Lawrence, *Sketches of Etruscan Places,* ed. Simonetta de Filippis (Cambridge: Cambridge University Press, 1992), 45, 9.

"I've had [...] sickening": *DHL Letters,* VIII:101–2, 4 May 1927, to Phyllis Whitworth.

19. THE THIRD VERSION IN FLORENCE

162 "doing much": *DHL Letters,* VI:67, 27 May 1927, to S. S. Koteliansky.

"all day": *DHL Letters,* VI:81, 11 June 1927, to Ada Clarke.

"knows him": "Wilkinson Diaries," 48, 18 July 1927.

163 "only more so": D. H. Lawrence, "Autobiographical Fragment," in "A New Edition of D. H. Lawrence's '[Autobiographical Fragment (A Dream of Life)],'" ed. Hiroshi Muto, *Journal of D. H. Lawrence Studies* (2018): 14. This text replaces the flawed text of the Cambridge edition.

"soon as possible": *DHL Letters,* VI:183, 10 Oct. 1927, to Max Mohr.

"My business [...] the ball-less": *DHL Letters,* VI:72, 28 May 1927, to Earl Brewster. Similarly, Frieda comments in a letter (c. 27 May 1927) to Phyllis Whitworth about the London production of Lawrence's play *David:* "But do go on fighting, *dont* give in, we have got to win!" Quoted in *DHL Letters,* VIII:104 n. 1, n.d., FL to Phyllis Whitworth.

"dauntless courage": *DHL Letters,* VI:73, 28 May 1927, to Mabel Dodge Luhan.

164 "Italy had [...] dreadfully sharp": "Wilkinson Diaries," 52, 19–20 Oct. 1927.

"I'm disgusted [...] bad one": *DHL Letters,* VI:212, 11 Nov. 1927, to Dorothy Brett.

165 "could you?": DHL, *Lady Chatterley's Lover,* 53.

"quite the gentleman": Ibid., 145.

"class of society": Earl and Achsah Brewster, *D. H. Lawrence: Reminiscences and Correspondence* (London: Secker, 1934), 276.

"deeper and deeper": DHL, *Lady Chatterley's Lover,* 134.

166 "As I explain elsewhere": Michael Squires, "D. H. Lawrence and Sexuality: Reassessing the Novels," *Journal of Homosexuality* 69 (2023), 1011–29, doi.org/10.1080/00918369.2021.2010436.

"let him [...] she was dying": DHL, *Lady Chatterley's Lover,* 246–47.

"Never – ": unpublished letter, FL to JMM, [Jan. 1931?], Turnbull.

"Dublin mongrel" [...] "like an idiot" [...] "little horrors": DHL, *Lady Chatterley's Lover,* 22, 110, 239.

167 "into being": Ibid., 301.

168 check for four thousand dollars to Bonbright & Company: D. H. Lawrence, check no. 96, 8 Sept. 1927, Chase National Bank (Chávez). Frieda, however, wrote to her mother, "We are both ashamed [of investing money in the American stock market], it is a bit vulgar to possess shares" (unpublished letter, FL to AvR, 28 Dec. 1927, HRC).

"very weak": unpublished letter, FL to AvR, 28 Dec. 1927, HRC.

"determined to [publish] it": *DHL Letters,* VI:289, 6 Feb. 1928, to Giuseppe Orioli.

"of the world": *DHL Letters,* VI:293, 12 Feb. 1928, to Dorothy Brett.

169 "Not a penny!": "Wilkinson Diaries," 61, 15 Mar. 1928.

"But [...] by life": unpublished letter, FL to AvR, [28? Apr. 1928], *sütterlin* 79. Worthen (*Outsider*, 375) offers his translation, which differs slightly from mine.

170 "and damn them": *DHL Letters*, VI:532, 30 Aug. 1928, to Giuseppe Orioli.

20. WHERE SHOULD WE LIVE?

171 "blissfully happy": FL to Witter Bynner, [9 Apr. 1928], in Tedlock, *Memoirs and Correspondence*, 229.

172 "I am already": *DHL Letters*, VI:332, 17 Mar. 1928, to Rolf Gardiner.
"The price was £2 or $10 for a signed and numbered copy": In 2023 copies of the original Florence edition, signed by Lawrence, were listed for sale at a median price of seven thousand dollars.
"thousands of mistakes": quoted in DHL, *Lady Chatterley's Lover*, xxviii n. 16.
"fun doing it": *DHL Letters*, VI:347, 31 Mar. 1928, to S. S. Koteliansky.
"was very ill": Achsah Brewster in Brewsters, *D. H. Lawrence*, 281.

173 "man of me": *DHL Letters*, VI:455 [9 July 1928], to Martin Secker.
"he is [...] soul good": FL to AvR, 1 Aug. 1928, in *DHL Letters*, VI:486–87.
"I think you [...] talk": *DHL Letters*, VI:448, [5 July 1928], to Giuseppe Orioli.
"other anxiety": Quoted in *DHL Letters*, VIII:108, 9 Aug. 1928, Maria Cristina Chambers to DHL.
"not yet": *DHL Letters*, VI:489, 4 Aug. 1928, to S. S. Koteliansky.
"any trouble": Giuseppe Orioli to Harold Mason, 17 Aug. 1928, in *DHL Letters*, VI:449–50 n. 3.
"Damn them all": *DHL Letters*, VI:481, 30 July 1928, to S. S. Koteliansky.

174 "so there!": FL to Richard Aldington, [31 July 1928], in *DHL Letters*, VI:485.
"no more to America": *DHL Letters*, VIII:115, 1 Sept. 1928, to Jacob Baker.
"magnificent beyond praise": cited in Michael Squires, *The Creation of "Lady Chatterley's Lover"* (Baltimore: Johns Hopkins University Press, 1983), 190.
"insults and impudence": *DHL Letters*, VI:491, 4 Aug. 1928, to Dorothy "Arabella" Yorke.
"tormenting cough": *DHL Letters*, VI:457, [11 July 1928], to Ada Clarke.
"not being well": *DHL Letters*, VI:458, 12 July 1928, to S. S. Koteliansky.
"disagreeable": *DHL Letters*, VI:596, [22 Oct. 1928], to Maria Huxley.
"satirical, sharp": Richard Aldington, in Nehls, *A Composite Biography*, III:253. In *Death of a Hero* (1929) Aldington portrays Lawrence, with surprising malice, as Mr. Bobbe, "a sandy-haired, narrow-chested little man with spiteful blue eyes and a malevolent class-hatred." Bobbe's "vanity and class-consciousness made him yearn for affairs with upper class women, although he was obviously a homosexual type. Admirable energy, [...] a sharp tongue and brutal frankness gave him power. He was a little snipe, but a dangerous one." Courtesy of Keith Cushman.
"lady die," and so terrify Achsah: Brigit Patmore, in Nehls, *A Composite Biography*, III:259.

175 "hollow cough": Richard Aldington, in ibid., III:253.
"I should [...] this cold": *DHL Letters*, VI:604, 31 Oct. 1928, to S. S. Koteliansky.
"foulest book in English literature": cited in Nehls, *A Composite Biography*, III:263.
"in Europe": *DHL Letters*, VII:25, 23 Nov. 1928, to Dorothy Brett.

"very bad": *DHL Letters,* VII:29, 24 Nov. 1928, to Carl Seelig.

"this winter": *DHL Letters,* VI:502, 12 Aug. 1928, to Bonamy Dobrée.

176 "is quietly contented": unpublished letter, FL to AvR, [29 Dec. 1928], HRC.

"profits from *Lady Chatterley's Lover*": For details, see Squires, *Creation of "Lady Chatterley's Lover,"* 221–23.

"our instincts and our intuitions": D. H. Lawrence, "Insouciance," in *Phoenix II: Uncollected, Unpublished, and Other Prose Works by D. H. Lawrence,* ed. Warren Roberts and Harry T. Moore (New York: Viking, 1959), 534.

"in the neck and passes on": D. H. Lawrence, "What does she want?" in D. H. Lawrence, *The Complete Poems,* ed. Vivian de Sola Pinto and F. Warren Roberts (New York: Viking, 1971), 539.

179 "my intuitional consciousness": quoted in Keith Sagar, *D. H. Lawrence's Paintings* (London: Chaucer Press, 2003), 121.

180 "rarely preferred to be alone": Brewster Ghiselin, in Nehls, *A Composite Biography,* III:293.

"to come – [the price was] 5000 frs!!": *DHL Letters,* VII:57, [11 Dec. 1928], to Maria Huxley.

"must really try": *DHL Letters,* VII:67, [16 Dec. 1928], to Laurence Pollinger.

21. THE HEROIC FIGHT

181 "What a game life is!": *DHL Letters,* VIII:111, 20 Dec. 1928, to the Wilkinsons.

"keep [true to] what I am": *DHL Letters,* VII:179, 15 Feb. 1929, to P. R. Stephensen.

182 a "healthy" book: D. H. Lawrence, *A Propos of "Lady Chatterley's Lover,"* in *Lady Chatterley's Lover,* ed. Michael Squires (Cambridge: Cambridge University Press, 1993), 307.

"afterwards": Ibid., textual apparatus 371, lines 45–47 (manuscript reading).

183 Titus had [. . .] 40,000 francs: D. H. Lawrence, unpublished memorandum, n.d. (Chávez).

"my real will to live": *DHL Letters,* VII:235, 3 Apr. 1929, to Ottoline Morrell.

"two minds about it": *DHL Letters,* VII:88, 23 Dec. 1928, to Charles Lahr.

"trim the book" into a different shape: *DHL Letters,* VII:144, 18 Jan. 1929, to Charles Lahr.

"try once more": *DHL Letters,* VII:368, 13 July 1929, to Laurence Pollinger.

"débâcle [. . .] to expurgate": *DHL Letters,* VII:392 n. 1; original typescript at the Copley Library.

the secret third edition: For details, see Craig Munro, "*Lady Chatterley* in London: The Secret Third Edition," in *D. H. Lawrence's "Lady": A New Look at "Lady Chatterley's Lover,"* ed. Michael Squires and Dennis Jackson (Athens: University of Georgia Press, 1985), 222–35.

184 "afraid of the police": *DHL Letters,* VII:214, [9 Mar. 1929], to Earl and Achsah Brewster.

"my pictures burnt": *DHL Letters,* VII:369, 14 July 1929, to Dorothy Warren.

"bitterly for him": unpublished letter, FL to Ottoline Morrell, [postmark 27 July 1929], HRC.

"so, so frail!": FL to Dorothy Warren, 23 July 1929, in Nehls, *A Composite Biography,* III:377.

"sits and does nothing": Sybille Bedford, *Aldous Huxley: A Biography* (1974; reprint, New York: Carroll & Graf, 1985), 215.

"by the sea": *DHL Letters,* VIII:111, 20 Dec. 1928, to the Wilkinsons.

185 "in Germany": *DHL Letters,* VII:509, 4 Oct. 1929, to Else Jaffé.

"go out at all": *DHL Letters,* VII:612, 3 Jan. 1930, to Edward Titus.

"cure me again": *DHL Letters,* VII:624, 21 Jan. 1930, to Maria Cristina Chambers.
"Why, oh why [...] we help it?": FL, *Not I, But the Wind,* 288.
Dr. Andrew Morland... French sanatorium at Vence to get well: Dr. Morland believed that Lawrence had suffered from tuberculosis "for a very long time—probably 10 or 15 years" (quoted in Nehls, *A Composite Biography,* III:424).
"I am [...] Morland advises": S. S. Koteliansky to DHL, 5 Feb. [1930], in Michael Squires and Lynn K. Talbot, "New Letters from S. S. Koteliansky and Charles Lahr to D. H. Lawrence," *Journal of D. H. Lawrence Studies* 1:3 (2008): 140–47 (letter on page 11).
"so weak": unpublished letter, FL to Else Jaffé, [5 Feb. 1930], HRC.
"very frail [...] to the good": FL to Dorothy Brett, [Nov. 1929], in Irvine and Kiley, "D. H. Lawrence and Frieda Lawrence," 98.

186 "with God": D. H. Lawrence, "Forget," *DHL Poems,* I:639.
"will him": D. H. Lawrence, "Difficult Death," ibid., 634.
"Reach me [...] the dark": "Bavarian Gentians," ibid., 610.
"even of me": unpublished letter, FL to JMM, [Jan. 1931], Turnbull.
"cheered up somehow" and "nothing for me": *DHL Letters,* VII:645–46, [12 Feb. 1930], to Maria Huxley.
"is unhappy": unpublished letter, FL to Mabel Dodge Luhan, [14 Feb. 1930], Yale University.

187 "to the unknown": D. H. Lawrence, "The Ship of Death [2]," *DHL Poems,* I:634.
"breathe with": Aldous Huxley to Julian Huxley, 3 Mar. 1930, in Keith Cushman, "D. H. Lawrence Bits," *DHLSNA Newsletter,* Mar. 2021.
"loved him deeply": unpublished letter, FL to Emily King and Ada Clark, 4 Mar. [1930], courtesy of Joan King.
"His death [...] the world": unpublished letter, FL to Nancy Pearn, 6 Mar. 1930, University of Nottingham; partially published in *DHL Letters,* VII:15.

188 "his strength": FL to E. M. Forster, [20 Mar. 1930], in *Selected Letters of E. M. Forster,* ed. Mary Lago and P. N. Furbank (Cambridge: Harvard University Press, 1985), 91 n. 1
"I am Lawrence [...] even death [...] we made there": unpublished letter, FL to JMM, [8 July 1930], Turnbull.

22. THE LOST WILL

190 "what I want": unpublished letter, FL to JMM, [8 July 1930], Turnbull.
"the realest thing to me": unpublished letter, FL to S. S. Koteliansky, [16 Apr. 1930], British Library.
"the interest is mine": FL to Edward Titus, [25 Apr. 1930], in *Frieda Lawrence and Her Circle,* ed. Harry T. Moore and Dale B. Montague (Basingstoke: Macmillan, 1981), 8.

191 "stupid" and "unpractical": Robert Nichols, as quoted in Bedford, *Aldous Huxley: A Biography* (1973; reprint, New York: Carroll & Graf, 1985), 226.
"by my instinct": unpublished letter, FL to Laurence Pollinger, 21 Jan. 1931, HRC.
Barbara's medical treatments: Frieda hinted, and Mabel Dodge Luhan later confirmed, that Barbara Weekley had contracted syphilis. Frieda wrote to Murry, "I *wont* write in words *what* Barby's awful disease *is.* If you *guess,* keep it to yourself, for God's sake." Unpublished letter, [18 Sept. 1931], Turnbull.

"Frieda would [...] solid and composed": Mabel Dodge Luhan, *Lorenzo in Taos* (New York: Knopf, 1932), 71–72.
"it was": unpublished letter, FL to JMM, [Jan. 1931?], Turnbull.

192 "You made [...] make money": unpublished letter, FL to JMM, Saturday [Jan. 1931?], Turnbull.
"clearer for me": FL to Witter Bynner, 23 July 1930, in Tedlock, *Memoirs and Correspondence,* 239.
"place for him": unpublished letter, FL to Brewster Ghiselin, [postmark 31 Mar. 1931].
"this year": FL to Edward Titus, 5 Dec. 1930, quoted in Moore and Montague, *Frieda Lawrence and Her Circle,* 24.

193 "*eine ruppige [...] untergeordnet*": unpublished letter, in German, FL to AvR, 14 July 1914, Leo Baeck.
"Frieda was [...] Lawrence estate": interview, Stefano Ravagli with Stefania Michelucci, Spotorno, Italy, 5 Sept. 1998, in *Living at the Edge,* 373.

194 "have [recently] killed themselves": unpublished letter, Maria Cristina Chambers to Giuseppe Orioli, 13 Mar. 1931, quoted by permission of Rosalind Wells.
"more truly [Lawrence's] widow than Frieda": Dorothy Brett to Alfred Stieglitz, [2 June 1931], Yale University, in *Living at the Edge,* 369.
"that life of otherness": FL to Mabel Dodge Luhan, [6 Aug. 1932], Yale University, in *Living at the Edge,* 371.
"Angelino [...] We all like him": Mabel Dodge Luhan to Una Jeffers, 3 June 1931, University of California at Berkeley, in *Living at the Edge,* 371.
"I do [...] and warmth": unpublished letter, FL to Dorothy Brett, [10 Feb. 1932], Yale University.

195 "without money": unpublished letter, FL to Philip Morrell, 19 Feb. 1931, HRC.
"to go to George": unpublished letter (copy), FL to Ada Clarke, [25 June 1930], British Library.

196 "hatred of Frieda": Emile Delavenay, "Sandals and Scholarship," *D. H. Lawrence Review* 9 (1976): 410.
"Remember! [...] letter unopened": unpublished letter, Ada (Lawrence) Clarke to FL, [c. 10 Nov. 1932], Turnbull.
"Would you [...] my signature?": unpublished letter, FL to JMM, [20 Apr. 1931], Turnbull.

197 "your brother [...] difficult position": unpublished letter, FL to Emily King, [1 Nov. 1930], courtesy of Joan King.
"I can see": unpublished letter, FL to JMM, [Mar. (?) 1932], Turnbull.
"must be independent": unpublished letter, FL to JMM, [4 Aug. 1932], Turnbull.
"against the family": unpublished letter, FL to Laurence Pollinger, [22 Oct. 1932], Turnbull.

23. TAOS, RAVAGLI, AND THE MANUSCRIPTS

199 "hatred now": unpublished letter, FL to JMM, [c. 15 Nov. 1932], Turnbull.
"life together": unpublished letter, FL to Laurence Pollinger, [7 Nov. 1932], HRC.
"had no part": unpublished letter, FL to Laurence Pollinger, [22 Oct. 1932], Turnbull.

"crawling about": Aldous Huxley to Naomi Mitchison, in Bedford, *Aldous Huxley*, 274.

"I'm so busy [...] to bursting": unpublished letter, FL to Knud Merrild, 20 Dec. 1932, HRC.

200 "the whole ranch": *DHL Letters*, VII:472, 9 Sept. 1929, to Dorothy Brett.

"nothing [...] awful humanity": unpublished letter, FL to Mabel Dodge Luhan, 2 Feb. 1934, Yale University.

"everything to me": Ibid.

"quite rough": unpublished letter, FL to Laurence Pollinger, 21 May 1933, HRC.

201 "Frieda is [...] his wife": Knud Merrild to Kai Götzsche, 7 Dec. 1933, in "Further Letters of D. H. Lawrence," *Journal of D. H. Lawrence Studies* 6 (2018): 8–9.

202 "have everything": unpublished letter, FL to Ottoline Morrell, 6 Apr. 1934, quoted in Houle Rare Books & Autographs, online listing.

"Lawrence was": unpublished letter, FL to Laurence Pollinger, [25 June 1934], HRC, in *Living at the Edge*, 177.

"I have [...] and sunshine": FL to Martha Gordon Crotch, [Aug. 1934], in Crotch, *Memories of Frieda Lawrence* (Edinburgh: Travara Press, 1975), 26.

203 "at Vence": unpublished letter, FL to Laurence Pollinger, 22 Apr. 1935, HRC.

"stories about me": unpublished letter, in German, FL to Else Jaffé, Dec. 1935, Leo Baeck; my translation.

"I was [...] and soul": FL to Mabel Dodge Luhan (unsent), [Aug. 1935], in Tedlock, *Memoirs and Correspondence*, 251.

206 "a magnificent thing": Jake Zeitlin to Ben Abramson, 24 June 1937, in *DHL's MSS*, 58.

"I liked her [...] he could": Lawrence Clark Powell, in *DHL's MSS*, 14.

207 "Why do [...] very stupid": unpublished letter, JMM to FL, 2 Oct. 1936, Turnbull.

208 "good milk": Angelo Ravagli to Jake Zeitlin, 19 Aug. 1936, in *DHL's MSS*, 44.

"being in another world": Craig Smith, *Sing My Whole Life Long: Jenny Vincent's Life in Folk Music and Activism* (Albuquerque: University of New Mexico Press, 2007), 21.

"I am thrilled": FL to Jake Zeitlin, in *DHL's MSS*, 69.

"being possessive": interview, Michael Squires with Jenny Wells Vincent, 16 July 1989, in *DHL's MSS*, 7.

"rather limited resources": letter of 27 Apr. 1937, in *DHL's MSS*, 87.

to Aldous Huxley: In the bookshop's reference copy of *The Manuscripts of D. H. Lawrence: A Descriptive Catalogue*, Jacob Zeitlin has annotated entry no. 14 (the holograph manuscript of *St. Mawr*) as follows: "destroyed in the fire at Huxley's home 1961." (Copy in the possession of the author.) The Huxleys lived in Beachwood Canyon, Los Angeles.

"book on Lawrence": Lawrence Clark Powell, *DHL's MSS*, 9.

24. THE CHALLENGE OF TEXAS

210 "to Harvard – ": FL to Jake Zeitlin, Sept. 1937, in *DHL's MSS*, 112.

211 "the outside world": telephone interview, Michael Squires with Matthew Huxley, July 1987, in *DHL's MSS*, 12.

"Frieda is [...] Aldous is working": Maria Huxley to Eddy Sackville-West, 23 June 1937, in Bedford, *Aldous Huxley*, 347.

212 "very much": unpublished letter, FL to Knud Merrild, 3 Mar. 1938, HRC.
"nice pottery": unpublished letter, FL to Knud and Else Merrild, 10 Oct. 1938, HRC.
213 "I would [...] on books": Jake Zeitlin, in *DHL's MSS*, 16.
"really cosmopolitan": FL to T. M. Pearce, 18 Mar. 1941, in Tedlock, *Memoirs and Correspondence*, 282.
214 "great deal": Grace Hubble, unpublished journal, 12 May 1938, Huntington Library, in *Living at the Edge*, 390.
"very aristocratic": *DHL Letters*, II:265, 28 Jan. 1915, to E. M. Forster.
"in America": unpublished letter, FL to Dudley Nichols, 25 Aug. 1944, Yale University.
"already an old [...] undramatic": Christopher Isherwood, in *Living at the Edge*, 396.
215 "publish it": unpublished letter, FL to Willard Hougland, [c. 2 Nov. 1944], UCLA.
"loved it best": unpublished letter, FL to Dudley Nichols, 2 Mar. 1944, Yale University.
"more economical [...] be discarded": Diana Trilling, *Nation*, 22 Apr. 1944.
"suffered tortures": unpublished letter, FL to Witter Bynner, 20 Mar. 1949, Harvard.
"must go on": unpublished letter, FL and Angelo Ravagli to Friedel Jaffé, 20 Dec. 1941, Roth Collection, New York City.
"so angry": FL to Richard Aldington, 8 Apr. 1941, in *Frieda Lawrence and Her Circle*, 80.
"rent to pay": FL to Witter Bynner, 3 Jan. 1943, in Tedlock, *Memoirs and Correspondence*, 287.
216 "very elemental": unpublished letter, FL to Friedel Jaffé, 24 July 1943, Roth Collection, New York City.
"in oneself": unpublished letter, FL to Dudley Nichols, 26 July 1945, Yale University.
217 "He will [...] is that": unpublished letter, FL to Friedel Jaffé, Sept. 1945, Roth Collection, New York City.
"chocolates": unpublished letter, FL to Dorothy Horgan, [c. 11 Aug. 1946], HRC.
"fun here": unpublished letter, FL to Brett, 14 Feb. 1947, University of New Mexico.
"We are [...] 'otherness'": unpublished letter, FL to JMM, 2 Mar. 1954, Turnbull.

25. LAST YEARS

220 "mountain streams": unpublished letter, FL to JMM, 26 Oct. 1946, Turnbull.
"for anything": DHL to FL, [28 Aug. 1923], "Further Letters of D. H. Lawrence," *Journal of D. H. Lawrence Studies* 3:1 (2012): 8.
"little Mexican beanie": telephone interview, Michael Squires with Miranda Masocco (Levy), 7 May 1999, in *Living at the Edge*, 413.
221 "At long last [...] to be myself": unpublished letter, FL to Richard Aldington, [c. 30 Apr. 1950], Southern Illinois University.
222 "keen language": Alfred Kazin, "Lady Chatterley in America," *Atlantic Monthly*, July 1959, 63.
"totaled 3,226,556 copies": Gerald J. Pollinger, "*Lady Chatterley's Lover:* A View from Lawrence's Literary Executor," in *D. H. Lawrence's "Lady": A New Look at "Lady Chatterley's Lover,"* ed. Michael Squires and Dennis Jackson (Athens: University of Georgia Press, 1985), 238.
223 "liked their adulation": telephone interview, Michael Squires with Amalia de Schulthess, 9 July 1989, in *DHL's MSS*, 22.

"all so vague": FL to Jake Zeitlin, 30 Jan. 1955, in *DHL's MSS*, 214.
"committed himself": Ronny Dugger, quoted in *Collecting the Imagination: The First Fifty Years of the Ransom Center*, ed. Megan Barnard (Austin: University of Texas Press, 2007), 25. Between 1958 and 1969 the university's regents designated seventeen million dollars for the purchase of research collections at the Ransom Center.

224 "very much longer": FL to Warren and Pat Roberts, 1 Jan. 1955, in *DHL's MSS*, 214.
"Angelino [. . .] and American": FL to Warren Roberts, 30 Nov. 1954, in *DHL's MSS*, 212.
"legally bind [. . .] the deal off": unpublished draft of letter, Angelo Ravagli to Harry Ransom, 24 Nov. 1954, quoted by permission of Barbara Horgan. Ravagli likely felt beholden to Frieda when he became a U.S. citizen in 1953, thereby losing his Italian army pension. "[A]nd we must," Frieda told Brett, "pay the wife another 50 dollars a month." Unpublished letter, FL to Dorothy Brett, 12 Jan. 1954, HRC.
"so quaint [. . .] flashing fire": Louis Gibbons, "The D. H. Lawrences," 139–42 (unpublished memoir [1960] in the possession of Michael Squires).

225 "Padre Island a lot": unpublished letter, FL to Louis Gibbons, 26 Dec. 1954, HRC.
"in the family [. . .] to get old": unpublished letter, FL to C. Montague Weekley, 5 Nov. 1955, University of Nottingham.
"and has [. . .] are lucky": unpublished letter, FL to Grace Hubble, 1 May 1955, Huntington Library.
"gift of life": *El Crepusculo* (Taos, NM), 16 Aug. 1956.

26. AT THE CLOSE

227 "each other": *DHL Letters*, IV:269, FL to Mabel Dodge Sterne, [21 June 1922].
"too quarrelsome": *DHL Letters*, IV:269, DHL to Mabel Dodge Sterne, [21 June 1922].
"valued at $200,000": inventory submitted to the district court in Taos, NM, 1957. Information courtesy of Professor Linda G. Lambert. Frieda owned shares in twenty-eight corporations, including General Motors and Standard Oil.

228 "staggered, overwhelmed": unpublished letter, FL to JMM, [Jan. 1931], Turnbull.
"purely through feel": unpublished letter, FL to JMM, [8 July 1930], Turnbull.
"an awful lot!": FL to JMM, 15 Apr. 1955, in Tedlock, *Memoirs and Correspondence*, 395.
"Aldous never him": unpublished letter, FL to JMM, [6 June 1930], Turnbull.

229 "Lawrence's and [. . .] relationship had": unpublished letter, FL to JMM, 26 Oct. 1946, Turnbull.
"man and woman": DHL, *A Propos of "Lady Chatterley's Lover,"* 318.

Index

Note: Italicized page numbers indicate illustrations.

Aaron's Rod (Lawrence), 68, 75, 77, 82–83, 94, 96
Ad Astra Sanatorium, 185–87, 191, 193
Adelphi (magazine), 115, 117
adultery, 2, 12, 16, 34, 68, 76–77, 119, 143, 152–54, 217, 222, 229
affair with Rosalind Baynes, 75–78, 85. *See also* adultery
Akins, Zoë, 214
Aldington, Richard, 42, 59, 68, 174–75, 221, 253n
Alires, Fred, 137
America, 45, 48–49, 60, 62, 66–68, 81, 83, 89–90, 96–97, 98–104, 108, 112, 120, 121, 147, 173–74, 183, 185, 188, 191, 192–94, 199–200, 203, 210–18, 220
American embassy in Mexico, 134
American literature, essays on, 60, 66–67, 101
American obscenity laws, 215, 222. *See also* British obscenity laws; Comstock Laws
American publishers. *See* Huebsch, Benjamin; Knopf, Alfred; Knopf, Blanche; Seltzer, Adele; Seltzer, Thomas
Amores (Lawrence), 51
anti-German fervor, 41–42, 49

Apocalypse (Lawrence), 184, 190
A Propos of "Lady Chatterley's Lover" (Lawrence), 182, 229
Aquitania, 120
Archuleta, Trinidad and Rufina, 135, 137
Asquith, Lady Cynthia, 42
Australia, 93–96
Austria, 15–17, 85, 163, 212, 220

Baden-Baden, Germany, 39, 82–85, 117, 119, 163, 173
Bandol, France, 175–80, 184–85, 219
Barnum & Bailey Circus, 112–13
Barr, Stuart, 203
Barrie, J. M., 74, 239n
Baynes, Godwin, 68
Baynes, Rosalind, 68, 70, 74–78, 85
Beckett, John, 214
"Bei Hennef" (Lawrence), 17
Bennett, Arnold, 23
Beresford, J. D., 50
Berry, Hedley (DHL's cousin), 63
Birds, Beasts and Flowers (Lawrence), 77, 109
Black Forest, 28, 83–85
Blake, Robert P., 208

Blas, Julie and Camilla, 28–29
"The Blind Man" (Lawrence), 61
Blue Review, 36
"The Border-Line" (Lawrence), 119–20
"Both Sides of the Medal" (Lawrence), 17
Bournemouth, England, 26
Braque, Georges, 37
Brett, Dorothy, *84,* 116, *116,* 117, 119, 120, 122–33, 137, 140, 146–47, 194, 203, 210, 213, 219–20, 227; memoir of DHL, 191–92
Brewster, Earl and Achsah, 83, *84,* 86–89, 91–92, 144–46, 161, 164, 165, 172–74
Brewster, Harwood, 83
British obscenity laws, 48, 222
British publishers. *See* Heinemann, William; Lane, Allen; Secker, Martin
Brooke, Rupert, 63
Brownsville, Texas, 216–17
Buckinghamshire cottage, 41, 47, 88
Buenos Aires, Argentina, 202
Burrows, Louisa, 11, 24–27
Bynner, Witter, 104, 105, 221

Campbell, Gordon and Beatrice, 39
Cannan, Gilbert, 42, 88
Cannan, Mary Ansell, 71, 74, 83, 85, 114, 239n
Capri, Italy, 68, 70–71, 82–83, 86, 144–46
"The Captain's Doll" (Lawrence), 85–86, 91–92
Carswell, Catherine, 114, 115, 117, 118, 141, 168, 191
Cearne cottage, England, 34
ceramic tile of D. H. Lawrence's phoenix (Ravagli), *212*
Ceylon, 86–87, 89, 91–93, 145
Chambers, Jessie, 23–24, 44, 207
Chambers, Maria Cristina, 173, 193–94
Chapala, Mexico, 106–9, 115
chapel and tomb for Lawrence, 54, 188, 192–93, 203, *204–5,* 225
Chapel Farm Cottage, 64–65
Chaplin, Charlie, 214
Chilchui Indians, Guadalajara, Mexico, 125–26

children, Frieda's, 3, 10, 12–13, 18, 19, 27, 29, 31–34, 36, 40, 41, 45, 111, 116–17, 140–43, 195, 219
Clarke, Ada (née Lawrence) (DHL's sister), 20, 34, 61–64, 111, 145, 195–97, 199, 207
Clarke, Eddie, 63, 142
class, 5, 10–11, 44, 143, 153–56, 159–60, 164–65, 167, 221
coal strike, England, 152–53
codes in writing, 5, 47, 75, 155
Colombo, Ceylon, 91–92
Comstock Laws, 171, 174
conflict between miners and mine owners, England, 152–53
Congregational chapel, Eastwood, 20
Contadini (Lawrence), 184
Conte di Savoia, 203
copyright(s), 168, 174, 183, 190, 197, 210, 222
Cornwall, England, 50–58, 79, 88, 101, 115, 137, 215
Crichton, Kyle, 139
Croydon, London, 24–25

Danes. *See* Götzsche, Kai; Merrild, Knud
David (Lawrence), 138, 195, 213–14
Davidson Road School, 24
Davies, Rhys, 178, *179,* 181–82
Dax, Alice, 27
Death of a Hero (Aldington), 174, 253n
Delavenay, Emile, 196
Del Monte Ranch, New Mexico, 100–103, 110, 123, 124, 128, 132, 134–35, 137, 201
Depression in America, 193–94, 206, 208–9
D. H. Lawrence, Son of Woman (Murry), 191–92
D. H. Lawrence Chapel. *See* chapel and tomb for Lawrence
D. H. Lawrence's Manuscripts (Squires), 7
Dial Press, 215
Dickens, Charles, 2
Dieterle, William, 214
"Difficult Death" (Lawrence), 186–87
disloyalty, 16, 26, 57, 109–10, 117, 146, 150, 151, 169, 175, 185, 196, 229

Dodge, Edwin, 98
Douglas, James, 48
Douglas, Norman, 69–70, 83, 104, 157, 197–98, 228
Duckworth (publisher), 20, 39

Eastwood, England, 11, 20–23, 27, 32, 34, 51, 61, 66, 111, 139, 196; remembered, 163
Eder, David, 42
Eliot, George, 19
El Paso, Texas, 129, 134
emotional disruptions, 1–3, 34, 45
"The Enkindled Spring" (Lawrence), 51
estate, of DHL, 193, 195–98, 199, 222
estate, of Frieda, 220, 225, 227
Etruscan Italy, 151, 161, 162
Ewart, Wilfred, 105
expatriate community, 69–70, 104

Fiascherino, Italy, 36–37, 66
fidelity, 6, 34, 57, 145, 146, 188, 217, 227, 229. *See also* loyalty
Fire-Dance (Lawrence), 178
Fitzgerald, F. Scott, 2
Florence, Italy, 69–70, 74–78, 86, 147–64, 168–73, 190, 197
Florence edition of *Lady Chatterley's Lover*, 183, 222
Fontana Vecchia, Taormina, 73–75, 78, 80, 82–83, 87, 128
Forster, E. M., 47
Forsyth, Anna, 112
Frere-Reeves, Alexander, 201, 221
Frohnknecht, Otto, 217

Gargnano, Italy, 17–18, 19–20, 33–34
Garnett, Bunny, 15–16
Garnett, Constance, 38–39
Garnett, Edward, 26, 34–35, 38–39, 160, 228
Garsington Manor, England, 43–44
gay expatriate community, 69–70, 104
Gerhardie, William, 141
Gertler, Mark, 42, 51, 117

Ghiselin, Brewster, 179–80, 192
Gibbons, Louis, 224–25, 227
Goddard, Paulette, 214
Goodwin, Walter, 201
Götzsche, Kai, 8, 101–2, 110, 112–14, 118, 122, 125, 146, 201
Goyen, William, 219, 225
Gray, Cecil, 55–56, 62
Greatham cottage, England, 47–48
Griffin, Johnie, 216, *216*
Gross, Dr. Otto, 16, 29–31, *30*, 39, 144, 165, 193, 221–22, 228
Grove Press edition of *Lady Chatterley's Lover*, 222
Gsteig bei Gstaad, Switzerland, 172–73
Guadalajara, Mexico, 104, 106, 113–14, 125

Hampstead, England, 114–15
Hanley, Thomas Edward "Ed," 210–11, 213, 227
Harvard University, 207–8, 210, 224
Hawk, Rachel and William, 100, 134
H.D. (Hilda Doolittle), 59
Heard, Gerald, 211
Heinemann, William, 24, 195, 201
Hermitage, England, 59–60, 64–65
Heseltine, Philip, 51–52, 88
Higher Tregerthen, Cornwall, 52–54, 57–58, 71, 128
Hilton, Enid Hopkin, 62, 174
Hobson, Harold, 15–16
Hocking, William Henry, 8, 55–57, *56*
Holderness, George, 22–23
Hollywood, 212–14, 217
homosexuality, 57, 104, 166, 226–27. *See also* gay expatriate community
Hopi Indians of Arizona, 127
Horgan, Dorothy, 217
Hotel Beau Rivage, France, 175–78, 184
Hotel Deutscher Hof, 12
Hotel de Versailles, 181
Hotel Francia, 130, 133
Hotel Imperial, 134
Hotel Palumbo, 146

Hotel Príncipe Alfonso, 183–84
Hougland, Willard, 215
Huayapa, Mexico, 130
Hubble, Grace and Edwin, 214, 225
Huebsch, Benjamin, 67, 79, 89
Huxley, Aldous, 158, *158*, 168, 184, 185–87, 190, 195, 211, 213–14, 225, 228; house fire, 257n
Huxley, Maria, 5, 158, *158*, 168, 180, 183, 185–87, 209, 211, 213–14, 225
Huxley, Matthew, *158*, 211

Ilkeston Training Center, 22–23
Indian Pueblo, 212
Indians, 87, 98–99, 103–4, 107–8, 123–27, 129–31, 212
infidelity. *See* adultery
Innsbruck, Austria, 83–85
"Insouciance" (Lawrence), 176–78
intuition, 6, 37, 46, 176, 179, 182, 183
Isherwood, Christopher, 214

Jaffé, Edgar, 32, 36, 40
Jaffé, Friedel, 137, 215–17, 249n
James, Rebecca, 221
Jenkins, Anna, 93
Johnson, Harry, 112
Johnson, Willard "Spud," 104, 105, 109, 138, 219
Journey with Genius (Bynner), 221
Joyce, James, 2, 5

Kandy Lake, Ceylon, 92–93
Kangaroo (Lawrence), 5, 94–96, 108, 109
Kent, England, 26, 34
Kingsley Hotel, 220–21
Kingsley Pictures v. Regents, 222
Kiowa Ranch, New Mexico, 100, 123–28, 134–41, 194–95, 200, 201–2
Klages, Ludwig, 29
Knopf, Alfred, 140, 160–61, 168
Knopf, Blanche, 140, 142
Koteliansky, S. S., 42, 68, 83, 114, 117–18, 185, 228
Krenkow, Hannah (DHL's cousin), 27

Krug, Johanna (née von Richthofen) (Frieda's sister), 12, 28, 85, 163, 220

Lady Chatterley's Lover (Lawrence), 4–6, 150, 171–80; Dial Press edition of, 215; distribution strategy, 171–74; entry into America, 170; film adaptation of, 222; film rights to, 214; first version of, 154–56; Florence edition of, 222; manuscript of, 160–61, 222–24; and Orioli, 157, 169, 172–73; Paris edition of, 182–83; piracy of, 168, 174, 180–82; press clippings of, 175; profits from, 176; second version of, 159–60; third version of, 162–70; and Titus, 182–83; typescript of, 213; typesetting of, 169
Lahr, Charles, 183
Lake Chapala. *See* Chapala
Lake Constance, 83
Lake Garda, 17, 66, 76, 219
Lambert, Cecily, 64–65
Lane, Allen, 221
Last Poems (Lawrence), 190
Lawrence, Ada. *See* Clarke, Ada (née Lawrence) (DHL's sister)
Lawrence, Arthur (father), 20
Lawrence, D. H. (David Herbert), life:
—birth of, 20; early years in Eastwood, 20–23; Lawrence family portrait, *21*
—prepares to teach, 23–24; as schoolteacher in Croydon, 10, 24–26
—death of Lydia Lawrence (mother), 11, 25
—contracts pneumonia, 26–27
—travels to Germany and Italy, 12–18, 33–39
—marries Frieda, 39–40
—in London, Buckinghamshire, and Greatham, 41–49
—in Cornwall, 50–59; with Murry and Catherine, 54–55; with Hocking family, 55–57, 59
—at Mountain Cottage, England, 61–64; illness, 63–64
—in Capri and Taormina, Italy, 66–81
—in Germany and Austria, 82–86

—visits Ceylon and Australia, 87–96; studies politics, 94–95
—in New Mexico, 97–104; at Del Monte Ranch, 100–103
—in Mexico, 105; and Chapala, 106–109
—visits Los Angeles and circus, 112–13
—in Guadalajara, Mexico, 114–17
—sails to London, 118–20
—returns to USA and Taos, 121–28
—in Oaxaca, Mexico, 129–34; illness (tuberculosis), 131–35
—recovers at the Kiowa Ranch, 136–40
—visits Spotorno, Italy, 142–45
—meets Brett in Capri, 145–47
—settles in Florence, 148–72; rents Villa Mirenda, 148–50; *vendemmia*, 151–53
—writes *Lady Chatterley's Lover* in three versions, 154–67; corrects typescripts and proofs, 168–72; distributes published novel, 172–74; fights pirates, 174, 181–83
—moves to Bandol, France, 175–85
—enters Ad Astra Sanatorium, Vence, France, 185–86
—death of, 186–88
—estate of, 190–91, 195–99
—chapel for ashes, 203–205
Lawrence, D. H. (David Herbert), works: *Aaron's Rod,* 68, 75, 77, 82–83, 94, 96; *Amores,* 51; *Apocalypse,* 184, 190; "Bei Hennef," 17; *Birds, Beasts and Flowers,* 77, 109; "The Blind Man," 61; "The Border-Line," 119–20; "Both Sides of the Medal," 17; "The Captain's Doll," 85–86, 91–92; *Contadini,* 184; *David,* 138, 195, 213–14; "Difficult Death," 186–87; "The Enkindled Spring," 51; *Fire-Dance,* 178; "Insouciance," 176–78; *Kangaroo,* 5, 94–96, 108, 109; *Last Poems,* 190; "The Lemon Gardens," 19; *Look! We Have Come Through!,* 17; *The Man Who Died,* 6; *Mastro-don Gesualdo* (Verga), 109; "Medlars and Sorb-Apples," 76–77; "Mr. Noon," 79, 82; *The Plumed Serpent,* 6, 131–32, 134, 136, 140, 200, 214;

A Propos of "Lady Chatterley's Lover," 182, 229; *Quetzalcoatl,* 106–10, 126, 131–33; *The Rainbow,* 4–5, 39, 45–48, 50–51, 52, 79, 89, 94, 107, 156, 160, 171, 206–7; "Reflections on the Death of a Porcupine," 138–39; "The Rocking-Horse Winner," 139–40, 150, 195; *Sea and Sardinia,* 78–79; "Snake," 74; *Sons and Lovers,* 13–15, 19–20, 46, 123, 160; *Studies in Classic American Literature,* 101; "Tickets Please," 60–61; *The Trespasser,* 4, 26, 31, 46; *Twilight in Italy,* 19; *The Villa Mirenda,* 159; *The Virgin and the Gipsy,* 143; *The White Peacock,* 10, 24; "The White Stocking," 23; "The Woman Who Rode Away," 5, 124, 140; *Women in Love,* 5, 45, 67, 96, 102; *Women in Love,* first version, 52–57. See also *Lady Chatterley's Lover* (Lawrence)
Lawrence, Emily (DHL's sister), 20, 63, 93, 111, 142, 153, 185, 197, 199
Lawrence, Ernest (DHL's brother), 22
Lawrence, Frieda (née von Richthofen)
—birth of, 27
—early life and education, 27–28
—marries Ernest Weekley, 29; disillusion, 31–32
—birth of children, 29
—and Dr. Otto Gross, 29–31, 39, 165
—in Gargnano, Italy, 33–34
—in Fiascherino, Italy, 36–38
—marries DHL, 39–40
—in London, Buckinghamshire, and Greatham, 41–49
—sees her children, 45; and in London, 140
—in Cornwall, 50–59
—at Mountain Cottage, England, 61–64
—in Italy and Germany, 66–86
—visits Ceylon and Australia, 87–96
—goes to New Mexico, 97–104, and Mexico, 105–109
—sails for England, 110–11
—in London with Murry and her children, 115–20

Lawrence, Frieda (*continued*)
—goes to USA, 121, Taos, 121–23, and her ranch, 123–28
—visits Oaxaca, Mexico, 129–34; nurses DHL, 133–34
—recovers at the Kiowa Ranch, 136–40
—visits Spotorno, Italy, 140; meets Ravagli, 143–45
—moves to Florence, 148–72; rents Villa Mirenda, 148–50; gap in FL letters, 151–52
—characterized in *Lady Chatterley's Lover*, 155
—and DHL's illnesses, 162–63, 169, 185
—on Port-Cros, France, 174–75
—moves to Bandol, France, 175–85
—and DHL's death, 186–88
—and DHL's will, 190–91, 195–98
—goes to America, 193–99, 200–201; writes memoir, 201; meets the Lucianis, 201–202
—and the chapel for DHL's ashes, 203–205
—and DHL's manuscripts, 206–13, 222–24
—and the Lower Ranch, El Prado, 212–16
—in Port Isabel, Texas, 217–20
—marries Ravagli, 220
—death of, 225
Lawrence, George (DHL's brother), 111, 190–91, 195–97, 199, 209
Lawrence, Lydia (DHL's mother), 11, 20, 25
"The Lemon Gardens" (Lawrence), 19
Les Diablerets, Switzerland, 168
Living at the Edge (Squires), 7
Lloyd George, David, 63
London, England, 8–9, 18, 20, 22, 33–34, 39–49, 59, 63, 116–19, 140–41, 183–84, 195, 206, 220–21
London Times (newspaper), 41
Look! We Have Come Through! (Lawrence), 17
Lorenzo in Taos (Luhan), 191
Los Angeles, California, 112–13, 206–7, 213
Los Angeles Times, 114
Love and Loyalty (Squires), 7
Lowell, Amy, 52
Lower Ranch, El Prado, New Mexico, 212–13, 216, 219, 223, 224

loyalty, 12, 15, 45, 60, 77, 85, 103, 110–11, 114, 118, 120, 135, 148, 203. *See also* disloyalty; fidelity
Luciani, Nicholas, 201–2
Luhan, Mabel Dodge, 4, 87–89, *88*, 97, 98–104, 121–25, 127, 144, 191–92, 194, 203, 213, 227
Luhan, Tony, 97, 98–99, 123, 194
Lusitania, 48, 58

Mackenzie, Compton, 68, 71
Magnus, Maurice, 69–70, 74–75, 83, 104, 228; death of, 89
male solidarity, 95, 108
Mallorca, Spain, 183
Malta, 89
Mansfield, Katherine, 2, *35*, 35–36, 39, 54–55, 63, 114, 117; death of, 103
manuscripts, 45, 79, 123, 160–61, 188, 190, 199–200, 206–7, 210, 213, 215, 222–24
The Man Who Died (Lawrence), 6
Margate, England, 35–36
Marina Piccola, Capri, 71, 146
marriage, 26, 28, 40, 77, 96, 101, 108, 111, 119, 122, 144, 169, 194, 228; balance in, 86; boundaries of, 151–52; in "The Captain's Doll," 85–86; as central relationship, 226–27; as compromise, 126; context, 1–6; exploration of, 229–30; foundation of, 148; fraying of, 62–65; and *Kangaroo*, 108; and *Lady Chatterley's Lover*, 154–55, 167; redefined by Frieda, 192; in "The Rocking-Horse Winner," 139; in *Sea and Sardinia*, 78–79; and travel, 91; and *Women in Love*, 45
Marsh, Edward, 42
Masocco, Miranda, 220
Mastro-don Gesualdo (Verga), 109
Mayrhofen, Austria, 15–17
McLeod, Arthur, 24, 45
Mediterranean Sea, 37, 70, 140, 141, 142. *See also* Bandol, France
"Medlars and Sorb-Apples" (Lawrence), 76–77

Medley, Charles D., 196–97
Melville, Herman, 60
Merrild, Else, 201
Merrild, Knud, 8, 101–2, 110, 112–13, 115, 118, 199–202, 212, 217
Merrivale, Lord, 198, 199
Methuen (publisher), 39, 45–48, 160
Metz, Germany, 11–12, 27–28
Mexico, 4, 103–4, 105–11, 113–15, 118, 127–28, 129–35, 214, 226. See also *Quetzalcoatl* (Lawrence)
Mexico City, Mexico, 105, 129, 133–34
Meynell, Viola, 47
Midlands, 11, 59, 61, 63, 117, 141, 142, 150, 152, 161, 163, 207. See also Eastwood, England
Miller, Donald, 131
Mirenda, Alessandro, 150
Mohr, Max, 142
money, 15, 22, 39, 47, 49, 59, 61, 80, 89, 91, 93–97, 103, 115, 120, 121, 151; advances, 20, 140–41; economic conditions in America, 207, 210–11; and Frieda's estate, 220, 225, 227; investments, 168; and Lawrence's estate, 193, 195–99; and manuscripts, 190, 206–7, 210–11, 213, 222–24; profits from *Lady Chatterley's Lover,* 176; royalty payments, 124, 210; security for Frieda, 191, 195, 206, 209, 220, 227; for travel, 146. See also Depression in America
Monk, Violet, 64
monogamy, 16, 30, 145, 229
Monroe, Harriet, 63
Monte Carlo, 145
Monte Carlo Hotel, 105
Morland, Dr. Andrew, 185
Morrell, Lady Ottoline, 42–45, *43,* 47, 53, 99
Morrell, Philip, 42–43, 195
Mountain Cottage, England, 61–64, 128
Mountsier, Robert, 79–80, 83–85, 88–89, 93, 102–3, 127
"Mr. Noon" (Lawrence), 79, 82
Munich, Germany, 16, 29, 184
Murray, Scott, 137

Murry, John Middleton "Jack," 8, *35,* 35–36, 39, 47, 54–55, 114–20, 125, 161, 166, 191–92, 196–98, 201, 207, 221, 228
"My Skirmish with Jolly Roger," manuscript, *182*

New Jersey, 109–11
New Mexico, 87, 98, 107–8, 118, 127–28, 134–35, 199–200, 202. See also Taos, New Mexico
New Orleans, 89, 202
New York City, 8, 89, 109, 120, 121, 140, 193–94, 195
New York Sun, 174
Nichols, Dudley, 214, 215–17
Nichols, Robert, 187, 191
Not I, But the Wind (Frieda Lawrence), 201
Nottingham, England, 3, 9, 22, 27–32, 42
Nottingham High School, 22
Nottingham University College, 23–24, 28

Oaxaca, Mexico, 126, 129–35, 137, 138, 151
Obregón, Álvaro, 114
obscenity, 48, 184, 215, 222. See also Comstock Laws
Occidental College, 213–14
Orbita, 110
Orient Line, 90. See also SS *Osterley*
Orioli, Giuseppe "Pino," 157, *157,* 160, 168–69, 172–73, 190, 197–98, 207

Padre Island, Texas, 224–25
paintings by Lawrence, 159, 178–79, 183–84, 224
Palermo, Italy, 82
Palmer, Cecil, 53
Paris, France, 28, 119, 181–83
Paris edition of *Lady Chatterley's Lover,* 182–83
Patmore, Brigit, 4, 174–75
Penguin Books, 221–22
Pensione Balestra, 69
Pensione Lucchesi, 148

Perahera pageant, 92–93
Perth, Australia, 93
Pfitscherjoch Pass, 15–16
photolithography, 180
piracy of *Lady Chatterley's Lover,* 168, 174, 180–82
The Plumed Serpent (Lawrence), 6, 131–32, 134, 136, 140, 200, 214
Poe, Edgar Allan, 60
poetry of Lawrence, 17, 51, 76–77, 109, 176–78, 229
Pollinger, Laurence, 195, 199, 202–3, 221
Pollinger Limited, 222
Ponte Vecchio, Florence, 70, 86
Port-Cros, France, 174–75
Porthcothan, England, 50, 58
Port Isabel, Texas, 217–21, 224
Portrait of a Genius, But . . . (Aldington), 221
Port Said, 92
Powell, Lawrence Clark, 206–8
Prince George Hotel, 193
publication of Lawrence's letters, 190, 195
Puebla, Mexico, 129
Purnell, Idella, 114, 118

Quetzalcoatl (Lawrence), 106–10, 126, 131–33

Radford, Dollie, 64
The Rainbow (Lawrence), 4–5, 39, 45–48, 50–51, 52, 79, 89, 94, 107, 156, 160, 171, 206–7
Rananim, 42, 45, 50
Random House, 210
Ransom, Harry, 223–24
Rauh, Ida, 138, 187
Ravagli, Angelo, 3, 143–46, 148, 150, 151, 169, 175, 193–96, 199–203, 206, 207–9, 211, 212–20, 216, 223–25, 229–30
Ravagli, Serafina, 144
Ravello, Italy, 146, 161
realism, 15, 19, 23–24

"Reflections on the Death of a Porcupine" (Lawrence), 138–39
Ritchie, Ward, 207
Roberts, Warren, 224
"The Rocking-Horse Winner" (Lawrence), 139–40, 150, 195
Rosalino, 130–32
Rosset, Barney, 222
royalty payments, 120, 124, 190, 210, 215, 222
Russell, Bertrand, 42, 44, 47–48, 207
Rydal Press, New Mexico, 201

San Domenico Hotel, 75
San Francisco, 96–97
San Gervasio fruit poems, 75–77, 94
Santa Fe, New Mexico, 134, 201, 215, 225
Sardinia, Italy, 78–79
Savona, Italy, 199
Scheyer, Galka, 206
Schloffer, Friedel, 29
Schulthess, Amalia de, 223
Schulthess, Hans de, 223, 224, 227
Scotland, 85, 152, 166
Scott, Evelyn, 85
Sea and Sardinia (Lawrence), 78–79
Secker, Martin, 67, 115, 117, 140–41, 142, 151, 168, 183, 206, 221
Secker, Rina, 141
Seligmann, Herbert J., 174
Seltzer, Adele, 102–3, 110, 115–16, 120, 140
Seltzer, Thomas, 67, 96, 102–3, 120, 121, 124, 134, 138, 140, 210, 228
sex and sexuality, 3, 5–6, 8, 14–15, 16, 23, 31, 38, 48, 53, 76, 95, 108, 125, 139, 146, 154–56, 160, 164–67, 174, 176–78, 183, 221, 228–29. *See also* homosexuality; obscenity
Sicily. *See* Taormina, Italy
Sierre, Switzerland, 117
"The Sisters" (Lawrence). *See The Rainbow* (Lawrence)
Skinner, Mollie, 176
"Snake" (Lawrence), 74

Sons and Lovers (Lawrence), 13–15, 19–20, 46, 123, 160
Sorbonne, 28
Southern California, 213–14
Spain, 183–84, 211
Spotorno, Italy, 141–43
Sri Lanka. *See* Ceylon
SS *Conte Grande,* 193
SS *Osterley,* 90, 91–93
Stephensen, P. R., 178–79, 183
Stern, Benjamin, 193
Sterne, Maurice, 98
St. John's Wood, 114
Strachey, Lytton, 44
Stroh, Earl, 221
Studies in Classic American Literature (Lawrence), 101
Suez Canal, 92
Sumner, John S., 215
Switzerland, 30, 117, 142, 168, 172–73
Sydney, Australia, 93–94
Sydney Bulletin, 94
Sydney Morning Herald, 93

Tahiti, 96
Talbot, Lynn K., 6
Taormina, Italy, 71–74, 78, 87
Taos, New Mexico, 87–88, 97, 98–104, 119–22, 193–95, 200–203, 207–9, 216–17, 220–21, 225
Taos Indians, 87, 98, 104, 107
Teotihuacán, Mexico, 105–6
Terry's Guide to Mexico, 104
Thirroul, Australia, 93–96
This Quarter, 182
Thrasher, Carlota, 80
Thrasher's Farm, Connecticut, 80
"Tickets Please" (Lawrence), 60–61
Tipografia Giuntina, 169
Titus, Edward W., 182–83, 187, 190, 192
Torgovnick, Marianna, 57
travel essays and sketches, 19, 151

The Trespasser (Lawrence), 4, 26, 31, 46
Trilling, Diana, 215
tuberculosis, 51, 103, 134–35, 162–63
Turner, Reginald, 70
Twilight in Italy (Lawrence), 19

Uffizi Gallery, Florence, 148
United States Customs, 170, 174
University of New Mexico, 225
University of Texas at Austin, 79, 223–24, 258n

van Pelt Bryan, Fred, 222
Van Vechten, Carl, 220
Vence, France, 185–87, 190, 200, 203
vendemmia, 151, 153, 164
Venice, 78
Veracruz, Mexico, 118
Verga, Giovanni, 109
Victorian prudery, 23, 31, 34, 47
Viking Press, 195, 201
Villa Beau Soleil, 184–85
Villa Belvedere, 75–76
Villa Bernarda, 142–48
Villa Canovaia, 75
Villa Cimbrone, 146
Villa Mirenda, Florence, *148–49,* 148–53, 157–64, 169
The Villa Mirenda (Lawrence), 159
Villa Robermond, 187
The Virgin and the Gipsy (Lawrence), 143
Virginia Quarterly Review, 214
von Maltzahn, Edward and Hanni, 211–12, 223
von Richthofen, Anna (Frieda's mother), 12, 28, 83, 141, 151–52
von Richthofen, Else (Frieda's sister), 12–13, 28–29, 31–32, 36–37, 40, 163, 207
von Richthofen, Frieda. *See* Lawrence, Frieda (née von Richthofen)
von Richthofen, Johanna. *See* Krug, Johanna (née von Richthofen) (Frieda's sister)
von Schreibershofen, Max, 85

Waldbröl, Germany, 12
Walpole, Hugh, 206
war, 50–52. *See also* World War I; World War II
Warren, Dorothy, 183–84, 195
Warren Gallery, 183–84
Washington Square, New York City, 140
Weber, Alfred, 28
Weekley, Barbara (Frieda's daughter), 29, 117, 144–45, 187–88, 191, 192, 203, 217
Weekley, Elsa (Frieda's daughter), 29, 117, 145
Weekley, Ernest (Frieda's first husband), 3, 10–11, 13, 27–29, 31–32, 33–34, 143, 155, 228
Weekley, Frieda. *See* Lawrence, Frieda (née von Richthofen)
Weekley, Maude, 40
Weekley, Montague (Frieda's son), 18, 29, 117, 161, 220–21, 225
Wells, Harry K. "Dan" and Jeanette "Jenny," 207–8
The White Peacock (Lawrence), 10, 24
"The White Stocking" (Lawrence), 23
Wicca Pool, Higher Tregerthen, Cornwall, 52, 59
Wilkinson, Arthur, 148, 153–54, 159, 161, 162, 164, 168–69, 201
Wilkinson, Lily, 153–54, 159, 162, 164, 168–69, 201

will, of Frieda, 225
will, of Lawrence, 2, 169, 185–86, 188, 190–91, 196–98
William Jackson (booksellers), 173
Wilson, Woodrow, 63
The Withered Root (Davies), 178
Witt, Nina, 140
"The Woman Who Rode Away" (Lawrence), 5, 124, 140
Women in Love (Lawrence), 5, 45, 67, 96, 102; first version, 52–57
Woolf, Virginia, 2, 5, 37, 44, 54
working class, 10–11, 13, 36, 159–60, 165, 180, 221
World War I, 41–45, 48–49, 61, 62–63, 66–67, 96, 144
World War II, 215–16
Wurlitzer, Helene, 221
Wyewurk, in Australia, 93–96

Yorke, Arabella, 174–75
Young, Thomas, 224

Zapotec Indians, 126, 129, 131
Zeitlin, Jacob "Jake," 206–9, 210, 213, 223
Zennor, Cornwall, England, 52, 59